Paul S.

Companion to the Revised Common Lectionary

9. Dramatic Dialogues

Two-Person Sketches for the
Three-Year Cycle

EPWORTH PRESS

British Library Cataloguing in Publication data

*A catalogue record for this book is available
from the British Library*

0 7162 0567 X

*First published 2003
by Epworth Press
4 John Wesley Road
Werrington
Peterborough, PE4 6ZP*

Second impression 2004

*Typeset by Regent Typesetting, London
and printed in Great Britain by
Biddles Ltd, King's Lynn, Norfolk*

Companion to the
Revised Common Lectionary

9. Dramatic Dialogues

Already published

Companion to the Revised Common Lectionary

1: Intercessions

2: All Age Worship Year A

3: All Age Worship Year B

4: All Age Worship Year C

5: Before We Worship

6: Mining the Meaning Year A

7: Mining the Meaning Year B

Forthcoming

8: Mining the Meaning Year C

To Dad.
For inspiring my love of drama.

Contents

Acknowledgements

I owe a huge debt of thanks to a number of people for the contents of this book. Firstly to my wife, Janet, for having the patience to read, listen to, and act in a number of these sketches. Thank you – it would not have happened without you. To the staff and students of Ashville College for more inspiration than they will ever know, and for road-testing a number of the dramas. To Gerald Burt for reading, offering encouragement and giving much needed guidance, and to the members of the Harrogate Methodist Circuit for unwittingly testing some of this material.

Foreword

Just a word about the contents of these pages. The dramas here are all dialogues. Why? Simply for ease of presentation in even the smallest of churches. They have largely been based on the set Gospel lesson for each Sunday only because that is the lesson most likely to be used each week.

I do not want to be too prescriptive about how the sketches are to be presented – creativity and imagination are to be encouraged. It might, however, be wise to give one or two words of advice. Costume, in most cases, would be best to be kept to a bare minimum. Prepare each dialogue carefully beforehand and always speak more slowly than you think is necessary – people need time to process ideas and thoughts. I have tried to keep stage directions to a minimum but feel free to add your own ideas. A number of characters appear in more than one sketch – some in consecutive weeks, others elsewhere in the book – wherever possible try to have the same actor play the part on each occasion.

Most importantly, have fun performing them!

Paul Glass

YEAR A

FIRST SUNDAY OF ADVENT

Matthew 24.36–44

READY AND WAITING 1

(One character – an old man – is sitting centrally.)

Gillian: *(Entering)* Are you still out here Grandpa?

Joe: Where else would I be?

Gillian: I don't know. I thought you might have decided to come in by now.

Joe: And watch some rubbish on the television? I don't think so.

Gillian: *(Sitting by him)* It's cold out here tonight.

Joe: Is it? I hardly noticed.

Gillian: Shall I go and get you a hot drink?

Joe: Maybe later.

Gillian: Grandpa, what's up?

Joe: I don't know what you mean.

Gillian: Sure you don't. You and Mum have hardly spoken all evening.

Joe: She doesn't understand.

Gillian: Understand what?

Joe: Why I have to wait. Be ready.

Gillian: Be ready for what? Grandpa, what are you waiting for?

Joe: Something wonderful.

Gillian: But what is it exactly?

Joe: Exactly, I can't tell you.

Gillian: What about vaguely then?

Joe: All I know Gillian is that something incredible is going to happen and I want to be ready for it when it does.

Gillian: And sitting here looking up at the night sky helps with that does it?

Joe: Now you're making fun of me.

Gillian: No Grandpa I'm not. You know me better than that. Remember when I was little and I used to come and stay at your house?

Joe: *(Smiling)* Those were good times.

Gillian: I'd be all ready for bed in my night-dress and dressing gown and you'd take me out onto the back porch and instead of reading me a bedtime story you'd point out the constellations of stars to me.

Joe: I enjoyed those times together.

Gillian: So did I. I just want you to know Grandpa that if you think this thing, whatever it is, is worth waiting for then I'm behind you all the way.

Joe: Thank you Gillian, that means a lot to me. You know we spend all of our time rushing around. We want everything to be here yesterday. Instant food, instant everything. But there are some things you just have to wait for, patiently, and be ready when they come.

Gillian: What do you mean, be ready?

Joe: I wish I knew. I'd love to know what I should have done. The kind of person that I should be. I think in the end it's about being open to possibilities, being spiritually prepared.

Gillian: Can I sit and wait with you?

Joe: Of course. I'm just taking some time to sit and think and look at the stars. Looking for answers.

Gillian: I'll go and get us a cup of hot chocolate. *(She exits.)*

SECOND SUNDAY OF ADVENT

Matthew 3.1–12

READY AND WAITING 2

(Joe is busying himself. His daughter Julie enters.)

Julie: Look, Dad, I'm sorry.

Joe: For what?

Julie: For not trusting you, for not understanding, for being a pain. I'm just finding all of this a little difficult to understand.

Joe: I know you are, love. But you mustn't worry.

Julie: I'm your daughter – it's my job to worry.

Joe: I'm all right.

Julie: Are you?

Joe: Yes, of course. But I must get ready now.

Julie: You see. There you go again, 'getting ready'. For what?

Joe: He's coming.

Julie: Who's coming? Is he going to stay here? Shall I get the guest bedroom ready?

Joe: No, it's God.

Julie: Who's God?

Joe: The person who's coming.

Julie: Oh well that makes complete sense.

Joe: Actually it does. At first I wasn't sure what I had to be ready for. What the waiting was in aid of, but now I know.

Julie: Dad, you're scaring me.

Joe: Now don't be scared. It's just becoming clearer. If someone or something as important as God is on his way then there'll be some preparations to be done. Some sorting out of life, some getting ready.

Julie: Some getting ready? What on earth do you mean?

Joe: Well if God's on his way then we need to be prepared don't we? Make sure our lives are in order. Clean up our acts a bit, ask for forgiveness.

Julie: But I've not done anything to be ashamed of.

Joe: Nobody ever thinks they have. That's the plague of twenty-first century life. Everybody thinks they're a good person. It comes from all those self-help programmes you're so keen on. The fact is that all of us are in need of being forgiven. Especially if we're to be ready when he gets here.

Julie: There you go again with that 'being ready' thing.

Joe: Well, it's important.

Julie: So you say.

Joe: Look Julie. I don't want to argue with you. I love you too much for that.

Julie: Oh Dad, I'm just so worried.

Joe: I know you are. But there's honestly no need. The voice is coming to prepare the way, and I'm just thinking about my life. Taking stock if you will, so that when he comes I'll not be wanting.

Julie: Dad, if there's anyone who'll be ready when God comes, it'll be you.

Joe: Well, you never can tell. The problem with most people is they live their lives as though he doesn't care about what they do – but he does.

Julie: Well Dad, say a prayer for me, will you?

Joe: Julie – you can say one for yourself.

THIRD SUNDAY OF ADVENT

Matthew 11.2–11

READY AND WAITING 3

(Julie and her husband, Peter, are sitting centrally.)

Peter: Look Julie, I know you're worried about your Dad. But what I'm trying to say is what if he's right?

Julie: I can't believe you'd say that Peter, that you'd side with him against me.

Peter: It's not a matter of taking sides.

Julie: Oh isn't it? Easy enough for you to say. You're not the one who's watching their father having a mental breakdown.

Peter: That's a bit harsh.

Julie: Is it? All this nonsense he's talking about. Being ready and waiting for the coming of God. Sitting out on the back steps night after night just watching the stars. He's even got Gillian believing in him.

Peter: Gillian's eighteen years old. She's not a little girl any more. She can believe what she wants. You know how close she's always been to him.

Julie: But she's our daughter.

Peter: And she shouldn't feel like she's got to choose between you and your Dad.

Julie: Oh Peter, I don't know what to think any more.

Peter: I know that. And it's all right. He's your father and you're worried. It's a matter of expectation.

Julie: What do you mean?

Peter: Well, we expect our fathers to be a certain way don't we? To act, to speak, to behave like fathers. Your Dad's doing a whole bunch of things you didn't expect him to do. It comes as quite a shock.

Julie: I suppose you're right. I just can't see where all this is going. It's so out of character for him.

Peter: I know you're finding all of this difficult. But is what your Dad is doing really that bad?

Julie: Well, it's hardly normal is it?

Peter: Who cares if it's normal or not? He keeps on talking about the importance of being ready, he's talking a lot about sorting his life out, waiting for the coming of God. What if he's right?

Julie: Oh Peter, I can't even contemplate that.

Peter: Why not? What would be so terrible? That's our problem isn't it? We expect God to come in certain ways, to be seen in certain things. What if we're looking in all the wrong places? I mean we go to church every Sunday, we listen to services that are more or less interesting, sometimes we even take part in worship.

Julie: I like going to church.

Peter: I'm not saying that I don't. But that can't be all that God's about. What if we've been so busy looking in one direction we've completely missed the fact God's been busy somewhere else? What if God's completely different from what we've been waiting for and your Dad's spotted that?

Julie: I don't like this Peter. I don't feel safe.

Peter: I don't think following God's about safety – I think it's about faithfulness. And I can't help wondering if your Dad hasn't spotted something that *we* should have seen as well.

FOURTH SUNDAY OF ADVENT

Matthew 1.18–25

READY AND WAITING 4

(Joe and Gillian are sitting centrally.)

Gillian: You know Grandpa, I'm really proud of you.

Joe: Proud? Of an old fool like me? Don't be.

Gillian: Now don't put yourself down. You've been through a lot the past few weeks.

Joe: Well, it hasn't always been easy. I'll give you that.

Gillian: Exactly. All this stuff about waiting, being ready for God. Preparing your life. It must have been really hard. Especially with Mum breathing down your neck all the time.

Joe: Ah, now Gillian, you mustn't be too hard on your mother. It's been tough on her too. You expect your parents to be the same as they've always been, never to change. She's found it . . . difficult.

Gillian: You're telling me. You haven't had to live with her!

Joe: Oh Gillian, I'm sorry.

Gillian: Don't be. I've enjoyed being part of all of this. It's made me do a lot of thinking and I don't often get time for that.

Joe: Gillian – you must always make time to think. To be with God. I can't think of anything more important.

Gillian: I'm beginning to see that. So tell me . . .

Joe: Tell you what?

Gillian: When is it all going to be over? The waiting and being ready?

Joe: Oh very soon now. He's almost here.

Gillian: Excellent. I'm so excited!

Joe: You know what Gillian? I'm pretty excited too!

Gillian: What's been the hardest part?

Joe: What do you mean?

Gillian: Well – of the waiting – I mean it can't always have been easy.

Joe: No it hasn't. I think the thing that surprised me most was the amount of courage I needed.

Gillian: I can see how that might be.

Joe: It hasn't been easy. Especially when everybody else thinks you've gone a little bit nuts.

Gillian: Not everybody.

Joe: No – I'm sorry. But your mother, and a lot of my friends. I'm not blind, or deaf. I can see the looks of disbelief, hear the words of mockery. It's very hard to stand up for something that sounds so strange, so different from everyday life, from what people expect. I must admit sometimes I even questioned things myself.

Gillian: Sticking up for what you know to be right isn't easy.

Joe: And it sometimes brings all kinds of attacks.

Gillian: You see Grandpa – that's why I'm proud of you.

Joe: And I want to thank you Gillian, for sticking by me through everything.

Gillian: It's been . . . great.

Joe: It has hasn't it? And you know what? Now I feel ready for God to arrive.

Gillian: You know what Grandpa . . . so do I.

6

CHRISTMAS EVE

Luke 2.1–14

ROBERT AND KATY ON CHRISTMAS EVE

(Robert and Katy are seven-year-olds played by adults.)

Robert: Can't wait, can't wait, can't wait!

Katy: Neither can I.

Robert: Is everything ready then?

Katy: Absolutely everything. The stockings are hanging up.

Robert: Cool. Are they bigger than last year's ones? 'Cos I thought they were a bit mingy size-wise.

Katy: Yep, I got two old potato sacks. They should be difficult to fill up to the brim with presents.

Robert: Brilliant!

Katy: What about the stuff for Santa?

Robert: It's all ready. I've got six of Auntie Jane's stupendously delicious mince pies on a plate together with three glasses of brandy and some aniseed balls for the reindeer.

Katy: How'd you know that reindeer like aniseed balls?

Robert: It's in Buster's book of little-known Christmas facts.

Katy: Oh, okay then.

Robert: I've turned on the security light in the back garden so that he can see where we are.

Katy: Right. I've wrapped all my presents up, have you done yours?

Robert: Yeah. What you got for Dad this year?

Katy: Socks.

Robert: Hey, wait a minute, it's my turn to buy him socks.

Katy: No it isn't. You bought him socks last year.

Robert: No I . . . oh maybe I did. Oh well, he won't mind two pairs will he?

Katy: Oh Robert! I thought we were going to get organized this year.

Robert: We were . . . I just forgot.

Katy: Boys – useless. I bet you don't even know where Mum and Dad hide the presents.

Robert: I do too – they're at the back of the wardrobe.

Katy: Well that shows how much you know 'cos they're not this year. They've moved them to the garden shed.

Robert: Cor, that's a bit sneaky of them.

Katy: Well it's after you found them and poked holes in all of the gift wrap last year.

Robert: Ah, great. It'll soon be time to go to bed.

Katy: I'm going to stay up all night this year.

Robert: So am I.

Katy: Bet you won't.

Robert: Bet you I will.

Katy: Ah, I just love Christmas, it's so exciting.

Robert: And we're all ready.

Katy: As ready as we'll ever be. Presents wrapped.

Robert: Cards sent.

Katy: Food bought.

Robert: Decorations put up.

Katy: You know I keep on feeling we've missed something out.

Robert: Nah . . . you'll be wanting to bring Jesus into it next. Come on. *(They exit talking excitedly.)*

7

FIRST SUNDAY OF CHRISTMAS

Matthew 2.13–23

LAYING WASTE

(Two actors are standing centrally.)

One: There are some stories that are too terrible to believe.
Two: Some actions that chill us to the bone.
One: There are some events which sadly remind us . . .
Two: Exactly what humanity is capable of.
One: Take a small town.
Two: And the surrounding countryside.
One: Full of life.
Two: A normal day.
One: People going about their business.
Two: Children playing in the streets.
One: And then in the distance.
Two: A sound is heard.
One: It gets closer and closer.
Two: Soldiers are approaching the village.
One: Their horses' hooves pound the earth.
Two: Their image shimmers in the heat.
One: They enter this peaceful community.
Two: And bring chaos in their wake.
One: Sights and sounds tell their own story.
Two: The glint of swords.
One: The screams of children.
Two: The crying of parents.
One: And when the soldiers leave . . .
Two: Every boy two years old and under is dead.
One: Murdered.
Two: Their tiny lifeless bodies lying useless on the ground.
One: And why has this happened?
Two: Who has ordered this massacre?
One: This carnage has happened because a paranoid ruler . . .
Two: Knows that what little power he has is trickling away.
One: A small frightened little man.
Two: In a world that doesn't need him.
One: Hears of one more threat to his power.
Two: But this one is different.
One: This is a threat he can do something about.
Two: And so Herod acts decisively.
One: He orders the wholesale murder of the children of his own people.
Two: All because he's afraid of a baby.
One: A tiny, vulnerable, harmless baby.
Two: In the interests of protecting power that he doesn't have.
One: And a throne that he thinks is under threat.
Two: The saddest thing of all is that the baby . . .
One: And God who is his father.
Two: Has no interest in Herod's throne.

SECOND SUNDAY OF CHRISTMAS

John 1.10–18

RALPH AND JIM ON SEEING GOD

(Ralph and Jim are sitting centrally on stools.)

Ralph: So then Jim mate.

Jim: So then Ralph.

Ralph: You're, ah, you're looking a bit pensive today Jim.

Jim: What's that then?

Ralph: Pensive mate, thoughtful, introspective, absorbed, reflective.

Jim: Oh, oh yeah, I am a bit yeah. Just thinking you know.

Ralph: So what are you thinking about then Jim? Where are you letting your massive mind wander in this vast universe of thought? What great, all encompassing problem have you set your mind to sorting out?

Jim: Wind, Ralph.

Ralph: I say, steady on a bit Jim mate, that's a trifle rude isn't it?

Jim: No, not that kind of wind.

Ralph: Oh good, it's just that I could sense the conversation drifting in a very unhelpful direction.

Jim: No, I was just thinking about wind. I mean you can't see it can you?

Ralph: That is true Jim, you can't see it.

Jim: To that extent it's a bit like God, innit?

Ralph: It is?

Jim: Absolutely, 'cos we're told we can't see God aren't we? God is remote, far away, up in heaven somewhere, leaning on a cloud.

Ralph: I guess so Jim.

Jim: Well, that's just the thing. God is beyond us. Can't be touched, smelt, seen – anything really. As the hymn says – immortal, invisible and only wise.

Ralph: I s'pose so Jim.

Jim: You seem a little doubtful Ralph.

Ralph: Well I am, Jim. I am.

Jim: Why's that then?

Ralph: Well, it seems to me Jim mate, not to put too fine a point on it, that you have left Jesus out of your thinking entirely.

Jim: Jesus?

Ralph: Yes mate, Jesus. Son of God, the eternal word, God made flesh.

Jim: What's he got to do with all of this then?

Ralph: Everything! The whole point of Jesus is that God has come to earth. Has lived like us. Has got his hands dirty, and his face bruised. God isn't up on a cloud somewhere is he? God's been here an' he knows what it's like to be us.

Jim: So God ain't remote or far away at all?

Ralph: No.

Jim: God's walked the earth.

Ralph: Full of grace an' truth – exactly.

Jim: That's a pretty big thought Ralph mate.

Ralph: The biggest, mate, the biggest.

Jim: Well – it's made me more pensive than ever, mate.
(Ralph sighs and exits.)

SUNDAY BETWEEN 7 AND 13 JANUARY INCLUSIVE

Matthew 3.13–17

GETTING WASHED

(Ben – a teenager – crosses the stage, followed by his mother.)

Rachael: Ben, Ben, where are you going?

Ben: I'm . . . ah, I'm just going to get washed Mum.

Rachael: Washed – will wonders never cease? My son – a mealtime approaching and words about washing on his lips. I can hardly believe it.

Ben: Well, there you go Mum, quite a turn up for the book, eh?

Rachael: Indeed, quite a turn up. So why are you heading out of the house then?

Ben: Pardon?

Rachael: I'm sorry, have you gone deaf as well? Why are you heading out of the house to get washed when we have a perfectly good wash basin here?

Ben: It's warm.

Rachael: I beg your pardon?

Ben: The water in our bowl, it's got warm and I wanted to wash in nice cold water from the well down the street.

Rachael: Nice cold water from the well down the street? Ben, I am your mother – I have been your mother for the last eighteen years, God help me, and I have never known you go down the street to get cold water before. So why don't you tell me exactly what it is you're going to do?

Ben: I never could hide the truth from you.

Rachael: No you couldn't.

Ben: And I shouldn't now – particularly now. When I said I was going to get washed, Mother, I was telling the truth.

Rachael: Not John the Baptist Ben! He's so wild and smelly and hairy. Anna from next door says he eats locusts and honey. Think what his teeth must be like.

Ben: Oh but Mother you haven't heard him. The force of what he says – it's incredible. It's kind of uncomfortable but hypnotic all at the same time.

Rachael: I don't have to hear him to know that he's trouble.

Ben: But what he says is right Mum. About our lives needing to be clean, about our sins being washed away. And what if he's right?

Rachael: I can't imagine he could be right about anything.

Ben: But what if there is somebody coming – somebody even greater than John? Mum, I need some hope.

Rachael: Look, I know things have been difficult for you Ben. But is this really the way?

Ben: Mum, I have never been more certain about anything in my entire life. He's down at the river this evening. I want to go and get washed.

Rachael: Well . . . if you're going then I'm going too.

Ben: *(Overjoyed)* Really Mum – that'd be brilliant!

Rachael: An important event like this in my son's life and his mother not there to witness the happy occasion. What kind of parent would that make me? People would start to talk.

Ben: Thanks Mum, you're wonderful.

Rachael: Yes, yes I know. Now let's just get going before I change my mind. And does it really have to be in the river? What about a nice clean pond? *(Exit.)*

SUNDAY BETWEEN 14 AND 20 JANUARY INCLUSIVE

John 1.29–42

FOLLOWING

(Two characters are sitting in chairs – one has a Minute Book and pen.)

Jeremy: Okay, I'd like to start off by welcoming you all here tonight to this Church Leaders' Meeting. If we could start off by looking at the minutes of the last meeting.

Pat: Uh, Jeremy, I hate to be the one to burst your bubble, but look around you.

Jeremy: Yes, Pat, what is it?

Pat: Well, in case you hadn't noticed there isn't anybody else here. We're the only ones who have turned up.

Jeremy: Your point being?

Pat: My point being, why on earth are we having this meeting if nobody could be bothered to come?

Jeremy: I think that's a very negative point of view, Pat.

Pat: Oh yes, and how do you figure that one out?

Jeremy: Well, there could be any number of reasons why people aren't here, other commitments, home problems . . .

Pat: Some kind of life.

Jeremy: Exactly, some kind of life . . . no, wait a minute, look Pat these meetings were called to discuss the leadership of our church.

Pat: And what does tonight's turn out tell you?

Jeremy: That people are very busy.

Pat: No, Jeremy. No. It tells you that people are fed up with discussing things in aimless circles month in and month out. It tells you that people don't care about this meeting. It tells you that they'd rather stay at home with a cup of tea, a chocolate digestive biscuit and a good book.

Jeremy: But the leadership of our church is important.

Pat: Yes Jeremy it is. And people want to follow – really they do. But they want leadership that's going to be imaginative, exciting, creative, inspiring. They want to feel like they're going somewhere. That they're actually doing something brave and radical for God.

Jeremy: But we've always done things this way at St Oswald's.

Pat: Yes Jeremy and if we continue doing things this way in six years' time there won't be a church anymore. Even Bertie Paxton in the choir can see that.

Jeremy: But I thought . . .

Pat: That's the trouble Jeremy, you think too much. You weigh up in your mind what everybody might want and then to upset as few people as possible, you pick a middle way that's so bland nobody wants it.

Jeremy: Oh.

Pat: I'm sorry, but what we need, what we want, is to feel something of the living Christ calling us to do something that we'd never believe or expect that we'd have to do. Something that scares us silly – but we'll do it because we want to follow him.

Jeremy: But following like that has a tremendous cost.

Pat: Yes. Yes it does. But in the end it's the only kind of following that's worthwhile. So pack up that Minute Book and let's get going. *(Exit.)*

SUNDAY BETWEEN 21 AND 27 JANUARY INCLUSIVE

Matthew 4.12–23

FOLLOW ME!

(Two pirates enter.)

Pete: So then Cut-throat Reg, are ye ready?

Reg: Absolutely Cap'n – I'd follow you anywhere, so I would.

Pete: Especially if it's in aid of sunken treasure eh?

Reg: For sunken treasure I'd follow you anywhere Cap'n.

Pete: But shiver me timbers Reg me boy, what if it wasn't for golden doubloons an' pieces of eight, would ye follow me then?

Reg: But it is for golden doubloons an' pieces of eight, ain't it Cap'n?

Pete: Well, yes it is. But what if it wasn't?

Reg: But it is.

Pete: I know that, ye daft landlubber. But suppose, just suppose, it wasn't.

Reg: I don't quite understand – you're the greatest pirate ever to sail the Spanish Main, you've got chests of gold in every port from here to Jamaica. Of course there's sunken treasure.

Pete: Yes, I know there is, of course there is, loads of it. But what if there wasn't – would you follow me then?

Reg: Are you sure you're all right Cap'n?

Pete: Look, ye scurvy bilge rat, it's a simple enough question. Would ye follow me through thick an' thin just because I asked ye to?

Reg: Well, I don't rightly know Cap'n. That's a very difficult question.

Pete: No, I don't think it's very difficult at all. You're one of me pirate crew right?

Reg: Right.

Pete: One of me jolly mates, always ready to join a pirate jape or two.

Reg: Absolutely.

Pete: Ready to risk life an' limb to bring back the gold.

Reg: Lead on Cap'n!

Pete: Well the question I'm asking ye is this. Would ye be prepared to follow me if ye didn't know where we was goin', and there was no guarantee that ye were going to get rich by doing it?

Reg: Well to do that Cap'n I'd have to be really sure that you was a person I wanted to follow through thick an' thin.

Pete: Precisely.

Reg: There'd have to be something really special about ye, something that would make me follow ye anywhere.

Pete: Indeed.

Reg: You'd have to touch something deep inside of me that'd make me think, wherever this man goes I've got to be there just to listen to what he says.

Pete: True, very true.

Reg: And I'm sorry Cap'n, I just don't think you've got it.

Pete: What, ye lily livered swab!

Reg: Well ye asked for me opinion an' I've given it. I'm quite happy to follow ye for gold Cap'n, but ask me to give me life to you – that's an entirely different matter. But I have got one question for ye.

Pete: Oh yes, an' what's that?

Reg: Who would you give your life to Cap'n? *(Exit.)*

SUNDAY BETWEEN 28 JANUARY AND 3 FEBRUARY INCLUSIVE

Matthew 5.1–12

HOW HAPPY!

(Two actors are standing centrally.)

Voice 1: How well liked are you?

Voice 2: Well actually now that you come to mention it I am rather popular.

Voice 1: You are? How is that then?

Voice 2: Well, I'm cheerful, I make friends easily, Mrs Rodley offered me a chocolate biscuit the other day and let me tell you she doesn't do that to just anybody.

Voice 1: So I've heard.

Voice 2: Indeed, it's the ultimate sign of approval. So I'd have to say that broadly speaking, I am pretty well thought of.

Voice 1: That's what I was afraid of.

Voice 2: Come again?

Voice 1: That's what I was afraid of. We're not meant to be well liked.

Voice 2: We aren't?

Voice 1: No, we're meant to be faithful.

Voice 2: So everybody's meant to hate us?

Voice 1: Well I'm not sure about that either. It's all very confusing.

Voice 2: It sounds it. Try and explain.

Voice 1: Okay – Matthew Chapter 5 . . .

Voice 2: Ah, the beatitudes.

Voice 1: Yes, the beatitudes. Jesus says that if we're properly following him then we're not going to be very popular.

Voice 2: We're not?

Voice 1: No, in fact people are going to insult us, persecute us and tell lies about us.

Voice 2: Why is that then?

Voice 1: Well I assume it's because our lives are going to be so radical, our words so difficult to hear, that it's going to be a bit uncomfortable living with us.

Voice 2: *(Pause)* Oh.

Voice 1: Exactly, oh. When was the last time we said something that was so radical people were upset by it?

Voice 2: When was the last time we did something that shocked others?

Voice 1: I'm afraid to say that it's beginning to look like we've lost the plot a little.

Voice 2: But I don't want people to hate me.

Voice 1: That's the problem – we all want to be liked and loved.

Voice 2: And given chocolates and pressies sometimes.

Voice 1: But it would be better if people didn't like us.

Voice 2: Found it uncomfortable to have us around.

Voice 1: Signed petitions against us.

Voice 2: Held rallies to get rid of us.

Voice 1: We're rather a long way from that happening aren't we?

Voice 2: Yes we are. But it makes you think doesn't it?

Voice 1: What does it make you think?

Voice 2: Well does all of this mean we're a long way from following Jesus?

Voice 1: It could well do.

Voice 2: Then some changes need to be made. Don't they? *(Freeze.)*

SUNDAY BETWEEN 4 AND 10 FEBRUARY INCLUSIVE

Matthew 5.13–20

TURN OUT THE LIGHT

(Two lighthouse keepers are standing centrally.)

Keeper 1: Now No. 2, lets get this absolutely straight.

Keeper 2: Right *ho*, No. 1! I love getting things straight.

Keeper 1: I'm sure you do.

Keeper 2: The straighter the better, that's me.

Keeper 1: Quite.

Keeper 2: Straight as straight can be.

Keeper 1: Yes. And last night was your first night on duty as lighthouse keeper in charge of Duxford lighthouse wasn't it No. 2?

Keeper 2: Oh and I was so excited, No. 1.

Keeper 1: I'm sure you were. So let's be very clear about what happened. You climbed up the stairs to the light.

Keeper 2: That's right.

Keeper 1: You turned on the light.

Keeper 2: Indeed.

Keeper 1: And then you draped a huge great tarpaulin sheet all over it.

Keeper 2: Affirmative.

Keeper 1: This may seem a rather odd question to you No. 2, but why did you do that?

Keeper 2: Well it was so bright No.1; it hurt my eyes so I just had to cover it up.

Keeper 1: Let's go back over this again No. 2. The whole purpose of a lighthouse is that it has a great big light on the top of it . . . correct?

Keeper 2: Yes boss.

Keeper 1: That, strangely enough, is why we call it a *light*house. And why does it have that great big light?

Keeper 2: So that people can see it and be safe No. 1.

Keeper 1: Correct. It's almost as if you know what you're doing No. 2.

Keeper 2: I like to think so.

Keeper 1: That still brings us back to the point that because you covered the light with a sheet of tarpaulin there was no light was there, No. 2?

Keeper 2: Ah, technically no.

Keeper 1: And what is the point of having a lighthouse without a light, No. 2?

Keeper 2: Not a lot No. 1.

Keeper 1: Quite right. In fact I would go so far as to say that the very reason for it's being had been taken away from it – wouldn't you say so, No. 2?

Keeper 2: I suppose so, No. 1.

Keeper 1: What is the point No. 2 of going to all the expense of having a lighthouse out here if the light in it is going to be covered up?

Keeper 2: None, No. 1.

Keeper 1: People could be in all sorts of danger and there would be no light to guide them safely home would there?

Keeper 2: Not as such.

Keeper 1: So I'm going home now No. 2, and what are you going to do?

Keeper 2: Keep my light shining, No. 1!

Keeper 1: Very good, No. 2. Carry on. *(Exits.)*

SUNDAY BETWEEN 11 AND 17 FEBRUARY INCLUSIVE

Matthew 5.21–37

SETTLING DEBTS

(Two guests at a wedding reception are sitting centrally – one is a minister, the other an elderly lady. The conversation is stilted.)

Minister: Hello.

Lady: Hello.

Minister: *(Pause)* Nice wedding isn't it?

Lady: Oh yes, it was such a lovely service.

Minister: Oh, thank you very much . . . I gather the food here is very good.

Lady: Good.

Minister: *(Pause)* So what relation are you to the bride?

Lady: I'm her grandmother.

Minister: That's wonderful – you must be very proud.

Lady: Oh I am, Susan's a wonderful girl.

Minister: I think I've met her other grandmother here as well haven't I?

Lady: *(Suddenly very frosty)* You might have.

Minister: Isn't she that lady right down at the far end of the next table?

Lady: She might be. I wouldn't know.

Minister: I'm sorry, have I said anything wrong? Only I seem to have upset you in some way.

Lady: I'm sorry, it's just that there's been trouble.

Minister: Trouble. Oh dear. Sounds serious.

Lady: Serious enough. Violet and I don't speak – not after what she did to me.

Minister: Oh. So you two are not on speaking terms at all then?

Lady: Certainly not.

Minister: How long has this been going on?

Lady: Since 1972.

Minister: But that's over thirty years!

Lady: It's her fault – talk to her about it, not me.

Minister: But I'm sitting next to you.

Lady: Yes, and I don't want to talk about it.

Minister: But this is a day of celebration – a wedding. Surely you and Violet could bury your differences for Susan's sake?

Lady: As I've said – the argument was none of my doing – it's all her fault. If there's 'sorry' to be said, it's her that's got to say it not me.

Minister: And this makes you happy does it?

Lady: What do you mean?

Minister: This stubbornness, this anger and hatred. It makes you feel good?

Lady: That's nothing to do with it.

Minister: And you go to church do you?

Lady: There every Sunday – wouldn't miss it.

Minister: And you say the peace at communion services?

Lady: Absolutely – vital part of the worship of God.

Minister: And you do all of this knowing that you've got this feud going on?

Lady: Yes Vicar, but as I've said and you don't seem to have heard me, the argument is . . .

Minister: . . . all her fault, none of yours. I get the picture. *(Freeze.)*

SUNDAY BETWEEN 18 AND 24 FEBRUARY INCLUSIVE

Matthew 5.38–48

AN EYE FOR AN EYE

(A police officer and a member of the public are standing centrally.)

Police: *(Writing notes on a pad)* Now let me just get this straight sir.

Man: Oh absolutely officer. Anything to assist an agent of the law.

Police: Yes, quite. Now, as I understand it, you were the victim of an incident of violence today.

Man: Indeed I was.

Police: So could you tell me what happened, sir?

Man: Certainly officer – I was walking along like this *(Walks)*, or was it like this? *(Walks in a different way)* Anyway, I was definitely walking.

Police: And?

Man: Oh, sorry yes. I was walking along and this man came up and slapped me.

Police: Was there any particular reason for this altercation sir?

Man: I don't think so. I'd never met the man before.

Police: I see. And where did he slap you?

Man: On the cheek, officer.

Police: Must have been painful.

Man: Yes it still is, actually. Look, it's all red and swollen.

Police: Yes I can see that sir. Now I won't beat around the bush with you. Suffice it to say that we have a number of eyewitnesses to this cheek-slapping scenario who claim that you then went on to do something very odd. Can you tell me what that was sir?

Man: Odd, constable?

Police: Yes sir, very odd.

Man: I don't quite know what you mean.

Police: Sir did you or did you not then offer your other cheek to this man for him slap that one also?

Man: Oh yes, that.

Police: What do you mean, 'Oh, yes, that'? A complete stranger comes out of the blue, slaps you on the cheek and you immediately offer him the other cheek to hit as well. That strikes me as unusual behaviour.

Man: Does it officer, why's that?

Police: Well, sir, most people would have retaliated – hit back.

Man: What good would that have done? Then you'd be talking to two people with swollen cheeks not one.

Police: Well that is true sir. But what if he'd taken up your offer to slap the other cheek?

Man: But he didn't. In fact he looked a little bit sheepish actually. Rather embarrassed by the whole thing. Like somebody had just knocked all the wind out of his sails.

Police: Well I suppose, sir, he wasn't expecting that response.

Man: No – and that's a shame in itself.

Police: Sir?

Man: We just seem to expect violent responses – lack of restraint.

Police: I don't suppose you even want to press charges sir?

Man: Heavens no – but I would like some cream for this cheek.

SUNDAY BETWEEN 25 AND 29 FEBRUARY INCLUSIVE

Matthew 6.24–34

ANXIETY ATTACK

(Two actors are standing centrally.)

Voice 1: I am a worrier. I worry about everything. All the time.

Voice 2: She's right, you know, she is a worrier.

Voice 1: I lie in bed at night working my way through a list of all the things I have to worry about.

Voice 2: Will it rain tomorrow? How will this event go? Did I get enough food in? What are people saying about me when I'm not there?

Voice 1: Even when there is nothing to worry about, I worry.

Voice 2: Things are going far too well – there must be something terrible about to happen very soon. You know the kind of thing.

Voice 1: It's awful. My stomach is tied up in knots. I feel ill, I check everything six or seven times to make sure that it's all right and I still worry.

Voice 2: I am her friend.

Voice 1: She's right. She is my friend. And she doesn't worry at all.

Voice 2: That's right – happy go lucky, that's me.

Voice 1: Have you any idea how frustrating that can be to a worrier? Here I am working up a nice level of steam about something – and she's not worried at all. 'Leave it,' she says, 'it'll be all right.'

Voice 2: I'm really annoying sometimes.

Voice 1: You really are.

Voice 2: And then of course I make things even worse by saying those two words guaranteed to get up the nose of any serious worrier.

Voice 1: 'Don't worry.' She says, 'Don't worry.' As though that's meant to make everything all right. Have you any idea how frustrating it is to a natural worrier like me to be told not to worry? It's like saying, 'Don't breathe.' I have to worry – it's what I do best.

Voice 2: I mustn't be unkind. Because I know how guilty she feels about it.

Voice 1: She's right. I do feel terribly guilty.

Voice 2: She's a Christian you see. And Jesus said not to worry.

Voice 1: Which is just bound to make me feel so much better isn't it?

Voice 2: You see you could claim that the worry was about a lack of faith. If you believed everything was in God's hands you wouldn't worry so much.

Voice 1: Yes, thank you. I know what the argument is.

Voice 2: I'm sorry, I mustn't tease.

Voice 1: No, you mustn't.

Voice 2: Well it does give you one more thing to worry about.

Voice 1: I hadn't thought about that. Thank you very much.

Voice 2: You're welcome.

Voice 1: And you know, it's not that I don't believe in God – I just can't stop myself getting worried.

Voice 2: Even though God's got it all under control and loves us hugely.

Voice 1: Poor God, so many people to love. It's all a bit worrying isn't it?

Voice 2: I think that's quite enough.

Voice 1: I'm worried – do you think it's time to go?

Voice 2: Long past. *(Exit.)*

SUNDAY BEFORE LENT

Matthew 17.1–9

TRANSFIGURING LIGHT

(Two people are standing centrally.)

James: Hi, the name is James. I've got a brother called John – and over the last few months my life has been completely turned upside down. You wouldn't believe it. We were fishermen – John and I. And if I do say so myself, we were very good at it. I'm not saying we didn't have our occasional ups and downs – we haven't been named the 'Sons of Thunder' for nothing. But generally we were doing well. And then suddenly Jesus turned up. Believe me – you have never met anybody quite like Jesus. With the smile and the stories and the words that cut straight through you. Just an amazing guy. We dropped everything – left everything, and followed him. Dad said we must be mad. And perhaps we were, just a little bit. But everything he said made such sense – all that he did was so full of power and truth. We couldn't let him go around without us. We needed to be there to hear what he said – to help in whatever way we could. The strange thing is I'm not like that – I don't follow people easily – I've got too strong a sense of my own place. Anyway we have been trailing round after Jesus for months now and everything was fine until a few days ago. Something's happened – changed. Jesus flat out asked us the other day who we thought he was – and Peter (it's always got to be Peter) said he thought Jesus was the Messiah. I'm not saying it hasn't occurred to some of us – but it's not the kind of thing you say out loud. Anyway Jesus seemed happy – pleased that Peter had said what he'd said. It seemed to open up a floodgate of some sort and he started talking about how he was going to die soon. I don't like to even think about where this is heading but I get the feeling I'm about to find out, because Jesus has invited John and Peter and me to go with him on a trip up the mountain today.

(Matthew 17.1–9 is read.)

John: *(Rather withdrawn)* I don't know what to say. I . . . ah . . . I can't find the right words. Which is a bit unusual for me because usually I've got no problem saying what I think. But what we've just experienced – I can't express it. I can hardly even think about it without getting a bit giddy. But the others are going to want to know – so how do you say it? There was light – everywhere. And we didn't just see it – it was a light you felt, deep in the pit of your stomach. You closed your eyes but it was still there, you held your hand up to shield your face – it was still there. And there was sound – huge sound – all around us. We were terrified. And I mean really frightened. I was just never aware that there was power like that. Power that sweeps over you and drowns you in its wake. And then there was the most incredible, eerie silence and then the next thing I was aware of was the hand of Jesus gently touching my shoulder. He was really calm – as if nothing had happened. He told us to get up and not be frightened. And you know I'm not – not frightened. I just have no idea how to talk about what we three have felt and seen. Somehow I feel that if I try and put the experience into words it will destroy it. It's too precious. But what do I say to the others? What do I say?

FIRST SUNDAY IN LENT

Matthew 4.1–11

THE LENTEN INTERVIEWS 1

(Two characters are sitting as in a television interview.)

Digweed: Good morning everybody – I'm Maria Digweed and welcome to the show that asks the questions others shy away from – *Digging the Dirt with Digweed*. We have a fascinating guest on this morning's programme. As you all know, rumours about the Messiah are everywhere at the moment. What kind of person is he going to be? What will he do? When is he coming and will he use my favourite brand of mouthwash? Well I have here today someone who claims to know the answers to at least some of those questions – Professor Theodore Didimus.

Didimus: Hello.

Digweed: Let's get straight down to it Professor. War hero or freedom fighter – which is the Messiah going to be?

Didimus: Well Maria, I think he's going to be a little bit of both. Obviously his first order of business is going to be getting rid of the Romans.

Digweed: Well, obviously.

Didimus: I think that he will then concentrate on ruling the whole of the world in a wonderful era of justice and peace. I guess that he will set up his palace and centre of operations here in Jerusalem.

Digweed: Good for employment.

Didimus: Oh, absolutely.

Digweed: So what about the ordinary everyday man or woman in the street – what can they expect to happen?

Didimus: Well I'm sure that the first thing that will happen is that poverty and hunger will be ended immediately.

Digweed: That's a pretty tall order, Professor.

Didimus: To any of us, yes. But you forget, Maria, we're dealing here with the Messiah – the Chosen One. He has tremendous power and it's unthinkable that he wouldn't use that power to turn poverty into a thing of the past.

Digweed: Wonderful – so stones turned into bread, that kind of thing?

Didimus: Of course.

Digweed: Great – so tell me Professor – a worldwide kingdom and the end of hunger – what else can we expect to see?

Didimus: Well, I expect that we're going to be able to see some pretty spectacular demonstrations of the wonders of God.

Digweed: So, flaming chariots, angels flying up and down from heaven – that kind of thing?

Didimus: Indeed. The Romans think they're so clever with their chariot races and gladiator combats. I think that I can safely say that they will pale into insignificance against the spectacular acts of the Messiah.

Digweed: It sounds wonderful.

Didimus: I'm sure it will be. I don't think anybody will be disappointed. A massive kingdom, all your material needs met, great spectacles to enjoy. It's going to be wonderful.

Digweed: Professor, thank you. And remember folks – you heard it here first. Bye!

SECOND SUNDAY IN LENT

John 3.1–17

THE LENTEN INTERVIEWS 2

(Digweed and a male interviewee are sitting centrally.)

Digweed: Good morning and welcome once again to the show that gets to the truth – *Digging the Dirt with Digweed.* I'm your host Maria Digweed and this morning we have a man who has a strange and fascinating tale to tell. He's a Pharisee and his name is Nicodemus. Tell us, if you would, about the events of a couple of nights ago.

Nicodemus: Of course. I am a member of the Council.

Digweed: A man of some importance then.

Nicodemus: Oh, I wouldn't go as far as that. Anyway recently I've been keeping a fairly careful eye on a travelling teacher called Jesus.

Digweed: The man from Nazareth?

Nicodemus: Ah, you've heard of him.

Digweed: On this show we make it our business to know everything, Nicodemus.

Nicodemus: Quite. Anyway, a couple of nights ago I went to see him.

Digweed: Tell us Nicodemus, why see him by night? Why the cloak and dagger secrecy?

Nicodemus: I'd hardly call it cloak and dagger. The truth is I'd been fairly impressed by some of the things that this young man has said, but confused by others. I wanted an opportunity to talk with him without prying eyes and ears being present.

Digweed: I see. Rather a risky business even so. Tell me – what did this charismatic young man have to say for himself?

Nicodemus: Well, that's the rather strange thing. He told me that no one can see the kingdom of God unless they are born again.

Digweed: Did you say 'born again'?

Nicodemus: Indeed.

Digweed: Forgive me if I seem a little dense Nicodemus, obviously you are a great theologian and I am but a humble, though massively wealthy, TV chat show host. A rather basic question comes to my mind, and it's this – haven't I been born already?

Nicodemus: I would hope you have, yes.

Digweed: I mean I can't go back into the womb situation can I? I mean I think my mother would be rather shocked – she's eighty-two years old.

Nicodemus: I think your mother need not worry too much. But that is the question I asked this Jesus fellow – surely I can't go back into the womb?

Digweed: And his response?

Nicodemus: He just repeated himself really and talked about the birth being of water and the spirit.

Digweed: It sounds like he was missing from class the day they taught biology in school. So Nicodemus – you've met this Jesus and you must know of the gossip his actions are generating. Does he have a future?

Nicodemus: I really don't know, Maria. Unless he stops talking such nonsense I'm not sure that we'll be hearing very much more of him.

Digweed: Well – we'll be watching his progress with interest. Nicodemus, thank you. I'm off to re-read some biology textbooks. Goodbye.

THIRD SUNDAY IN LENT

John 4.5–42

THE LENTEN INTERVIEWS 3

(Digweed and a female interviewee are sitting centrally.)

Digweed: Good morning. This is *Digging the Dirt with Digweed* – the show that goes beyond to get to the truth. And this morning we really have gone beyond because love them or hate them, I have with me a Samaritan. Now I know I shouldn't really even be talking with you, but you've had a fascinating encounter recently with a young man who this show has been following with interest – Jesus of Nazareth. Tell us more.

Samaritan: Well, it was about noon and I'd gone to get water from the well as usual.

Digweed: Hold it just one minute.

Samaritan: Yes?

Digweed: It's noon – the hottest time of the day and you're carrying water. Dish the dirt – why can't you collect water with everybody else? What's wrong with you?

Samaritan: I'm, ah . . . I'm not very popular in my town.

Digweed: The reason being?

Samaritan: I've been married five times.

Digweed: Scandalous!

Samaritan: And I'm not married to the man I'm currently living with.

Digweed: Outrageous! Even for a Samaritan community that's pretty bad.

Samaritan: *(Becoming angry)* Stop it! I'm sick of being judged.

Digweed: I bet you are, dearie. Won't stop anybody from doing it though.

Samaritan: But Jesus was different.

Digweed: In what way?

Samaritan: Somehow he knew all about me. He knew who I was . . . what I was, and it made no difference. He talked to me. Cared about me. Made me feel that new beginnings and a new life were possible.

Digweed: So Jesus is now talking to women in broad daylight, and not just any women – loose-living Samaritan women – how wonderfully tacky.

Samaritan: It wasn't like that. For once in my life I found someone who cared about me – who was concerned about me.

Digweed: What else did he talk about?

Samaritan: Well I'm still not sure I understand this – but he asked me for a drink and then started talking about living water.

Digweed: And you have no idea of what he meant by that?

Samaritan: None at all. He just said whoever drinks the water that he gives will never be thirsty again.

Digweed: And he didn't tell you where to get this 'living water'?

Samaritan: No, I wish he had. Then I wouldn't have to go to the well again.

Digweed: Indeed – all that gossip, all those pointing fingers.

Samaritan: But he's helped me to see through that, to look forward with hope. He was wonderful with me.

Digweed: Yes I'm sure he was. So there you have it, very curious. Just when we think we've seen the most scandalous thing Jesus can do, he goes off and does something even more shocking. And what is this 'living water', and where will you be able to buy it? This is Maria Digweed. Goodbye.

FOURTH SUNDAY IN LENT

John 9.1–41

THE LENTEN INTERVIEWS 4

(Digweed and a male interviewee are sitting centrally.)

Digweed: Welcome to *Digging the Dirt with Digweed* – I'm Maria Digweed and if there's dirt to be dug up – I'm the one to do it. As our loyal viewers will know over the past few weeks we've been tracing the actions of a strange but fascinating young man, Jesus of Nazareth. Who is he and why does he do such outrageous things? The answer to that may come from our guest this morning who, until recently, was completely blind. I suppose the one question that everybody at home wants to know is – how do you feel?

Man: I feel good – very good. Great actually. But it's all a bit strange.

Digweed: How do you mean?

Man: Well I was born blind so this is the first time I've seen anything at all. Of course I've imagined how things would look, but some things are very different from how I pictured them.

Digweed: For instance?

Man: Well . . . noses are really long and prominent aren't they?

Digweed: Is that a personal comment?

Man: No, no, just a general observation.

Digweed: Good. So . . . who sinned?

Man: What do you mean?

Digweed: Well everybody knows that if you have a child who is disabled in any way either the parents have sinned or the child has. It stands to reason.

Man: You know that's just the question the disciples asked Jesus when they saw me.

Digweed: And what was the answer?

Man: Nobody. It was no one's fault. Then he said, 'I am the light of the world.' And he spat on the ground and rubbed the earth onto my eyes.

Digweed: Euughh! How unhygienic.

Man: Ah yes – but if it's going to give me my sight back, I don't mind at all.

Digweed: And then the Pharisees got involved.

Man: Ah yes, the Pharisees – they couldn't believe it, or they didn't want to believe it. Either way, they called my parents in to testify to the fact that I had been born blind.

Digweed: A frightening experience for them.

Man: Absolutely – they know how much the Pharisees hate Jesus – they were terrified of saying something wrong. So they let me speak for myself.

Digweed: And?

Man: I just said what was in my heart – all I know is that I was blind and now I see – how bad, how evil can Jesus be?

Digweed: Were they satisfied with the answer?

Man: Who can tell? Probably not.

Digweed: Well, ladies and gentlemen – there we have it. Again Jesus challenges the authorities, good taste and the status quo all in one afternoon. How much longer can this kind of thing go on before action is taken? I don't know, but we'll be there to cover the story. This is Maria Digweed. Goodbye.

FIFTH SUNDAY IN LENT

John 11.1–45

THE LENTEN INTERVIEWS 5

(Digweed is sitting with a female interviewee.)

Digweed: Welcome to *Digging the Dirt with Digweed* – I'm Maria Digweed. Well ladies and gentlemen we've bought you some strange and unbelievable stories in our time. Do you remember the man who ate a diet made up entirely of olives? Yes, some strange stories, but the story we're about to tell you is, frankly, so weird that I'm not sure that I believe it myself. You know that we've been following the actions and the encounters of the wandering preacher Jesus of Nazareth. We just thought it was a nice way to fill in some time on the show. But now we're getting reports of something incredible that has recently taken place. Please welcome Martha to the show. Now Martha – you have some relations.

Martha: Yes indeed Maria. There's my sister Mary, and our brother Lazarus.

Digweed: And you're good friends of this Jesus of Nazareth?

Martha: Oh, yes. Very good friends. He's eaten at our house, and it was Jesus our thoughts first turned to when it happened.

Digweed: When what happened?

Martha: Well, very sadly, a few days ago now, my brother Lazarus died. He'd suddenly fallen ill and very quickly afterwards passed away.

Digweed: It must have been a difficult time for you.

Martha: It was – incredibly difficult. When he'd first fallen ill we'd sent a message to Jesus but by the time he was able to come to Bethany, Lazarus had already been dead four days.

Digweed: Viewers will understand in a moment why I'm going to ask what might seem an insensitive question. Are you sure he was dead?

Martha: Absolutely. We'd anointed the body and he'd been in the tomb four days.

Digweed: So Jesus turned up late.

Martha: Yes. Mary and I immediately rushed to see him. I have to admit I was really quite angry.

Digweed: Understandably – if Jesus had been there, as far as you were concerned, none of this would have happened.

Martha: Exactly. And I told Jesus so. I'm afraid I was a little rude. But then Jesus said the strangest thing – 'I am the resurrection and the life', he said. 'No one who lives and believes in me shall ever die.' And then he looked straight at me with those piercing, kindly eyes of his and said 'Do you believe this?' And I said I did.

Digweed: And?

Martha: He went to the tomb and asked for the stone to be rolled away. I was worried about the stench, but we did as he said. Then Jesus called out in a loud voice 'Lazarus – come out.' There was the longest silence and then in the tomb entrance there stood Lazarus, alive. Almost as in a dream.

Digweed: Martha – thank you for coming in today. For once this hardened TV journalist doesn't feel like digging the dirt. This family obviously believes what they are saying – and who are we to try and destroy that? But it does leave even more questions about Jesus. Hoax or genuine article? Exactly who is this man, and what is he going to do next?

23

SIXTH SUNDAY IN LENT

Matthew 21.1–11

THE LENTEN INTERVIEWS 6

(Digweed and Didimus are sitting centrally.)

Digweed: Welcome ladies and gentlemen to this special edition of *Digging the Dirt with Digweed* with me, Maria Digweed. Well, it's finally happened – the preacher Jesus of Nazareth has, at last, made his move. And we're here in Jerusalem to bring you all the latest. We welcome back an old friend of our show Professor Theodore Didimus to give his expert opinion about the extraordinary events of the past few minutes.

Didimus: It is quite incredible Maria. Just a short while ago Jesus made the most public and high profile of entrances into Jerusalem. And with the city being full to capacity for the Passover festival this week this move must have been calculated to draw as much publicity as possible.

Digweed: It was a quite extraordinary sight Professor – what did you make of it?

Didimus: Well Maria it seems to me that Jesus judged things to perfection. Sat on the back of a donkey with crowds of people lining the way into the city cheering and shouting and waving palm leaves all over the place. It really was quite festive.

Digweed: I know, Professor, that you've been combing Scripture for us. Have you come up with anything interesting?

Didimus: Well Maria, there is a prophecy in Zechariah which talks of the King coming on a donkey. This is very exciting – it seems that Jesus is making a direct bid to be the Messiah.

Digweed: That is very exciting Professor. For weeks we've been watching this Jesus do and say the most amazing things but he always seemed to be a bit too quirky, a tad too radical for good taste to endure. But now – well it seems he's decided to make a definite move towards the main stream.

Didimus: Indeed. And with the level of support we've seen today, I would expect that we will see a military or political move very soon now. He's got the whole city in the palm of his hand. To wait would be disastrous.

Digweed: What sort of military strategy do you think he's got planned Professor, and how on earth do you think he's going to take on the might of Rome?

Didimus: You must remember Maria that if we really are dealing with the Messiah here then we're talking about the Chosen One of God. I'm sure he's got all kinds of tricks and mighty wonders up his sleeve for dealing with the Romans or anybody else.

Digweed: Just one thing's got me a little worried, Professor, I hope that I know my Scriptures as well as anybody else. Doesn't that prophecy in Zechariah talk about peace and the destroying of war chariots?

Didimus: Well technically yes. But I don't think we need to worry our heads about that. A Messiah without massive military victories is not an option. He will fight and he will win, and we shall see the downfall of Rome, and the beginning of the glorious reign of the kingdom of God.

Digweed: Professor, it sounds very exciting indeed. Stick with us ladies and gentlemen because I hear that Jesus has just entered the precincts of the temple. What wonders will he perform there I wonder? We'll be right back after this advertising break.

EASTER DAY

John 20.1–18

EASTER INTERVIEW

(Digweed and Caiaphas are sitting centrally.)

Digweed: Well ladies and gentlemen, welcome to this special Passover edition of *Digging the Dirt with Digweed* with me, Maria Digweed. And what an incredible week it's been. To talk us through some of the events we're privileged to have with us our own High Priest, Caiaphas.

Caiaphas: Good evening Maria, I've always thought what a charming presenter you were.

Digweed: You old smoothy. But as you well know Caiaphas, we here on this programme have been closely following the exploits of Jesus of Nazareth. Viewers of this show were tremendously excited by his entry into the city on the back of a donkey just a few short days ago. And now he's dead. What happened?

Caiaphas: Well Maria, I realize that Jesus was popular with a number of your viewers but I am afraid you have all been very seriously misled by a very believable confidence trickster. The fact is that Jesus was a very dangerous young man and action had to be taken.

Digweed: That action had to be taken rather quickly didn't it Caiaphas?

Caiaphas: I'm not quite sure I follow you.

Digweed: Well see if you follow this. We have inside information that the trial of Jesus in front of our own religious court was illegal on several counts.

Caiaphas: That's a very serious accusation to make. You'd better have some evidence to back it up.

Digweed: Oh, we do. For example we have a source who claims that several of the key witnesses at Jesus' trial disagreed with each other – meaning the case should have been abandoned immediately. Am I right?

Caiaphas: I really don't recall.

Digweed: It was only on Friday night Caiaphas, your memory really isn't very good is it? And what about the fact that the trial and the verdict were both given on the same day – that too is illegal isn't it?

Caiaphas: Really – I didn't come on this show to be harangued.

Digweed: All right. If you won't answer those simple questions – what about this? Just before we came on air today we received a report which claims that something has happened at the tomb of Jesus.

Caiaphas: *(Increasingly nervous)* I can assure you that there is no truth to that story at all.

Digweed: So it is not the case that the stone has been rolled away from the tomb entrance? There is also a rumour spreading that grave robbers have stolen the body.

Caiaphas: None of that wicked rumour-mongering is true.

Digweed: Jesus was reported as saying to his followers that he would rise from death – so it wouldn't be in your interests for the grave to be empty – would it, Caiaphas?

Caiaphas: *(Very angry)* The tomb is sealed, the body is still there!

Digweed: Well, after your record on the trial you'll forgive us if we don't take your word too seriously – won't you? It seems, viewers, this case is still open.

SECOND SUNDAY OF EASTER

John 20.19–31

I HAVE MY DOUBTS

(Two actors are sitting centrally. One of them is writing.)

Voice 1: Wotcha doing?

Voice 2: Writing.

Voice 1: I can see that. *(Pause)* Wotcha writing?

Voice 2: None of your business.

Voice 1: Oh now don't be like that.

Voice 2: It's private.

Voice 1: Let's have a look *(Grabs the piece of paper)*.

Voice 2: Give me that . . .

Voice 1: It's a letter. *(Reads)* 'Dear God . . .' You're writing a letter to God?

Voice 2: Yes.

Voice 1: Why on earth are you doing that? I mean, you're hardly going to get a reply are you?

Voice 2: It helps me put my thoughts in order.

Voice 1: What thoughts are those then?

Voice 2: Oh, very funny.

Voice 1: Sorry. Can I read it? Please, please, please!

Voice 2: Oh all right.

Voice 1: *(Reads)* 'Why is it that you seem so far away, so distant sometimes? I cry and scream out for help and you're never there.'

Voice 2: See, I told you it was private.

Voice 1: So, what are you trying to do with this?

Voice 2: I'm trying to express something of the doubts that I have.

Voice 1: Is that a good thing?

Voice 2: Oh you're not going to be one of those, are you?

Voice 1: One of what?

Voice 2: One of those people who say that having doubts is wicked, terrible. It shows a weakness of faith and a questioning attitude that can only get you into trouble.

Voice 1: Well does it really help?

Voice 2: Absolutely. Talking about my doubts, being honest about them is vital for me. If I can't face up to the things that I find difficult, what hope have I got?

Voice 1: But shouldn't we believe?

Voice 2: I do believe. But I can't ignore my questions. They're not going to go away just because I pretend they're not there – they're just going to get bigger and worse.

Voice 1: And writing them down helps?

Voice 2: It helps. I can see them. I have to put them into words.

Voice 1: And do you get answers?

Voice 2: Sometimes yes, sometimes no.

Voice 1: What happens when you don't find an answer?

Voice 2: I go on asking the question, I go on looking, and I go on believing.

Voice 1: It all sounds very unsettling.

Voice 2: Nobody ever said having faith was going to be easy.

THIRD SUNDAY OF EASTER

Luke 24.13–35

YOU DON'T SAY!

(Hannah and Anna are standing leaning over a garden wall.)

Hannah: Morning, Anna.

Anna: Morning, Hannah.

Hannah: You're looking very nice today.

Anna: Well, I do try my best. But him down at No. 4 isn't making it very easy.

Hannah: Oooh, not that Cleopas again.

Anna: In and out at all hours of the day and night, chattering and carrying on.

Hannah: I don't like the company he's keeping. Bunch of weirdos, if you ask me.

Anna: They're all mixed up in something very nasty – you take my word for it. Take last night for example.

Hannah: Oooh, is there some juicy gossip? Something scandalous that I ought to know about?

Anna: Well, you know they've been in the city for a few days?

Hannah: What they wanted to be going to Jerusalem for at this time of year is beyond me. Hot, grimy, packed for Passover. You can't move for tourists getting under your feet everywhere you go.

Anna: I know, I know. Anyway he and the wife get back last night and they've got a man with them.

Hannah: Oh yes, who's that then? Do we know him?

Anna: Well that's the thing – even though I had a good view through my kitchen window, I didn't get a very good look at him. Tall, dark and mysterious I reckon.

Hannah: Oooh, how exciting.

Anna: It gets better.

Hannah: No!

Anna: Yes. No sooner have they gone in for a meal then old Cleopas an' his wife are zipping out through the front door as quick as you like. They're off back down the Jerusalem road looking like they've seen a ghost or something.

Hannah: And what about Mr Tall, Dark and Mysterious?

Anna: Well that's the strange thing. I've been keeping a very close watch on the place and I've not seen him leave.

Hannah: You mean he's still in there?

Anna: Well he's got to be hasn't he?

Hannah: What do you think is going on then?

Anna: Your guess is as good as mine. But I did hear Cleopas going on about having to get back with the news.

Hannah: News about what? About who?

Anna: I don't know.

Hannah: Oh this is awful – we can't have Cleopas knowing something we don't.

Anna: You don't think the news could be about Jesus do you?

Hannah: What, that crazy preacher they were following? How could it be? They crucified him on Friday. He's dead.

Anna: You're right. It can't be anything to do with him. What kind of exciting news could there be about a dead man?

FOURTH SUNDAY OF EASTER

John 10.1–10

A TEMPTING OFFER

(One actor is standing centrally. A second enters from the back.)

Chatsworth: *(While walking)* Excuse me sir, excuse me – a minute of your time?

Jones: I'm sorry?

Chatsworth: A minute of your time sir if I may. Please? I know you must be a very busy man but trust me, this will only take a moment.

Jones: Okay, what is it?

Chatsworth: Do you believe world peace is possible in our time, sir?

Jones: Well, I don't think about it very often.

Chatsworth: Well, think about it now sir.

Jones: Well then, no, I don't think it is.

Chatsworth: Does that depress you?

Jones: Well, it hardly has me skipping up and down for joy.

Chatsworth: So it makes you feel anxious, worried, forlorn, depressed.

Jones: I suppose.

Chatsworth: What if I was to tell you that I could make all those depressed feelings go away sir?

Jones: Feelings that *you've* created.

Chatsworth: Just think of it sir. A feeling of joy and peace like nothing you've ever known before, a sense of relaxation and total fulfilment.

Jones: It sounds very nice.

Chatsworth: And where is this heaven on earth sir?

Jones: I give up. Where?

Chatsworth: Biggleswade!

Jones: Biggleswade?

Chatsworth: Yes sir. For a very modest amount of money indeed the group I represent could send you away on a week of relaxation, meditation and pampering at our five star life centre and health spa.

Jones: So this is a sales pitch.

Chatsworth: Not at all sir. It's an offer of a better, more fulfilling, stress-free life. Of course if you want to buy the study guide that is essential to your future well-being it will only cost you £8.99.

Jones: And how much for the week at the health spa?

Chatsworth: It's more than just a health spa – it's a total life transformation centre.

Jones: So it costs more then?

Chatsworth: Perhaps a little.

Jones: How much?

Chatsworth: £800 for the week – but that is all-inclusive. And we throw in a complimentary bath mat and foot warmer.

Jones: No, thank you.

Chatsworth: Oh please, sir. I've had no takers all morning.

Jones: I'm not surprised. The world's full of people like you offering spiritual answers for cash. And anyway, I've found my way.

Chatsworth: Oh yes – and where's that then?

Jones: It's in that church over there.

Chatsworth: Oh come off it sir. Nobody goes to church anymore . . . Do they?

FIFTH SUNDAY OF EASTER

John 14.1–14

LOSING THE WAY

(A man and woman are sitting in a car. The man is driving.)

Sally: I just don't believe it.

Graham: What?

Sally: We're lost aren't we?

Graham: No we're not, I know exactly where we are.

Sally: Oh yeah? Well that's the second time we've passed that Post Office.

Graham: I'm pretty sure it's this way.

Sally: 'Pretty sure'? What kind of answer is that?

Graham: A good one. Now stop complaining.

Sally: If you'd listened to me, we wouldn't be in this mess.

Graham: This is not a mess.

Sally: We've been driving around in circles for the last forty minutes.

Graham: Your point being?

Sally: It looks pretty much like a mess to me.

Graham: Oh and if we'd followed your advice everything would be all right.

Sally: I've no idea because we never follow my advice.

Graham: That is not true.

Sally: It is so. We go out for these drives in the country and will you let me bring a map? No, it's always 'Don't worry Sally, I know what I'm doing, I'll just follow my nose.' And we end up miles from anywhere up some dirt track that obviously goes nowhere.

Graham: You're a fine one to talk. We don't bring a map because you can't read one.

Sally: You liar! I got grade B GCSE Geography. I can read a map.

Graham: Look, all of this arguing is getting us nowhere.

Sally: You're right, let's just pull in and ask for directions.

Graham: No, I'm sure we're almost there.

Sally: You are so pig-headed. Why don't you just admit that you don't know the way?

Graham: I do. I'm just going the scenic route.

Sally: That would be the route that takes us thirty miles out of our way and ends up with us going nowhere.

Graham: Look, I don't want any advice, I don't want any help, and I don't want any directions. I know the way and I can get there by myself without any interference from anybody else, thank you very much.

Sally: Oh Graham you could make life so much easier and more enjoyable if you just asked for help once in a while.

Graham: Perhaps I like doing things my way.

Sally: I'm sure you do – and meanwhile we achieve nothing, we go nowhere because you have no idea of what you're doing. You do not know the way!

Graham: YES I DO!

Sally: Well, o mighty finder of the way, if you know the directions so well how come we've just passed that Post Office for the third time?

Graham: Euurgghh! *(Buries head in hands.)*

SIXTH SUNDAY OF EASTER

John 14.15–21

NEVER ALONE

(Two actors are standing centrally.)

One: There is something within us.
Two: That comes to us.
One: All shapes and sizes of us.
Two: Young.
One: Old.
Two: Annoying.
One: Lonely.
Two: Attractive.
One: There is something within us.
Two: That realizes our need.
One: That reaches out to God.
Two: That touches the heavens.
One: That is the spirit of truth.
Two: And we know that no matter where we go.
One: Or who we meet.
Two: That spirit of truth.
One: That counsellor.
Two: Will be right by our side.
One: There is something within us.
Two: Gently guiding.
One: Speaking words of love.
Two: And mercy.
One: And challenge.
Two: So we will never be alone.
One: Nor friendless.
Two: Nor without help.
One: Because that spirit will be there.
Two: Cradling and protecting us.
One: There is something within us.
Two: And there are those who cannot understand.
One: Who pour on ridicule and scorn.
Two: Because they do not see.
One: Or will not open their eyes to see . . .
Two: The God of love and power.
One: Who is everywhere they look.
Two: They may well think we are stupid.
One: Or dangerous.
Two: Or just plain weird.
One: They will attempt to make our lives difficult.
Two: But we know that we have not been left alone.
One: And so we continue to show the love.
Two: That we ourselves have been shown.
One: The love of the God of creation.
Two: And we do it by the power of his Spirit.

SEVENTH SUNDAY OF EASTER

John 17.1–11

SHARON AND MICHELLE ON PRAYER

(Sharon and Michelle are sitting on stools.)

Michelle: Get me a pint willya Sharon, it's been one of them weeks.

Sharon: Oh yeah Michelle, why's that then?

Michelle: Well I've just been thinking, that's all.

Sharon: Thinking? Why'd you want to do that?

Michelle: I dunno. I was watching some really brainy programme the other day.

Sharon: What was that then? *Panorama*? *Everyman*?

Michelle: No, *Blue Peter*.

Sharon: Oh I love that show. All them lovely cuddly pets they've got.

Michelle: Yeah an' the presenters are pretty fit too.

Sharon: Oooh yeah. Anyway – it set you thinking did it?

Michelle: It certainly did Sharon. They were talking about all them poor people where there's been torrential rains and winds. Where was it?

Sharon: Clacton?

Michelle: No. Somewhere overseas.

Sharon: Oh I was never very good at geography. Back at St Olave's Institute of Chronic Neglect, Brother Rupert said I couldn't tell my scree slopes from my convectional rainfall.

Michelle: Yeah well I'm sure this country was a long way away. Somewhere near Europe. An' these people had had a terrible time, homes washed away. An' I just thought to myself what a sad world we live in.

Sharon: I s'pose so.

Michelle: There doesn't seem much we can do about it does there?

Sharon: Well we could give money.

Michelle: Yeah, well we could do that.

Sharon: An' Rodney says we should pray about it.

Michelle: Not Rodney Simpkins the Christian, from down in Packing? You really have got to stop talking to him Sharon. He's putting ideas into your head.

Sharon: Yeah, well Rodney says prayer is really important. He says Jesus prayed for himself and other people.

Michelle: Yeah well Jesus would wouldn't he, 'cos he was like dead holy an' close to God. That doesn't mean we have to do it.

Sharon: But Rodney says all kinds of things can be changed by prayer – that it really helps to put things straight in your mind like. In fact he said that he prays for us.

Michelle: He does what?

Sharon: Rodney said he remembers us in his prayers sometimes an' just keeps us in his thoughts.

Michelle: You an' I don't need nobody's prayers Sharon.

Sharon: Don't we?

Michelle: No we don't. What does that Rodney Simpkins think he's doing?

Sharon: He said he was bringing us before the glorious throne of God's grace.

Michelle: Yeah well I don't need any throne of grace.

Sharon: No – all you need is your pint of shandy, ain't that right Michelle?

Michelle: You're an answer to my prayers, Sharon!

PENTECOST

Acts 2.1–21

H. J. HACKSTER IN THE CASE OF THE CHANGED LIFE

(H. J. is a private investigator.)

H.J.: *(Walking on from the back of the building)* It had been a hot and humid night that was turning into an even hotter, more humid day. The air-conditioning was on the fritz again, and I had no money for the repair. Suddenly, into my office walked a strange small man who smelled of aniseed balls and wore a baseball cap.

Ron: *(Entering from the side)* Are you H. J. Hackster the Private Eye?

H.J.: That's the name that's on the door. Don't wear it out.

Ron: I need your help, Mr Hackster.

H.J.: You an' every other no-hope, two-timing, back-stabbing, glory-seeking little man on the block. Pull up a seat – what's the problem, Mr . . .?

Ron: Griswald, Ron Griswald.

H.J.: How did I know it was going to be a name like that? Okay Ron, normally I only deal with beautiful damsels in distress, but you're lucky. I need air-conditioning and for that I need money. So what's your problem?

Ron: It's my wife.

H.J.: It always is, little man, it always is.

Ron: Over the last few weeks she's completely changed.

H.J.: In what way?

Ron: Well, she's become kind, loving, considerate. She's always smiling at me. It's driving me nuts.

H.J.: I can see how a loving, kind, considerate wife could be a real problem.

Ron: No, you don't understand. She didn't used to be like that at all. She was cruel, ruthless, horrible. Now she's just the opposite. It's really weird.

H.J.: Look, Ron, I hate to say this, but it seems to me like there's no case here to investigate. Your wife was horrible – now she's wonderful. Deal with it. It sounds pretty good to me.

Ron: If only she hadn't gone to that church.

H.J.: What do you mean – church?

Ron: Well – just before the change she started going to St Hilda's down on 44th and Main.

H.J.: I think we've found the answer to your problem then Ron.

Ron: We have? How's that?

H.J.: Seems to me like your wife's met the big G, the man with the plan, the big boss.

Ron: She's found religion?

H.J.: Oh yeah. She's got the Spirit all right.

Ron: The Spirit?

H.J.: Oh yeah – the Holy Spirit – it can turn your life round just like that. Horrible one minute, sainthood the next – seen it happen a million times. Total life transformation.

Ron: Ain't there nothing I can do?

H.J.: 'Fraid not Ron. You're going to have to get used to the fact that your wife has become a beautiful person full of the power of God.

Ron: Well thanks a lot Mr Hackster. I guess I'll have to get used to it. *(Ron exits.)*

H.J.: And with that the strange little man left to go home to his transformed wife an' I got to thinkin' about the power of the Big G and the heat of another day.

TRINITY SUNDAY

Matthew 28.16–20

H. J. HACKSTER IN THE CASE OF THE THREE-IN-ONE GOD

(H. J. is sitting centrally.)

H.J.: It had been a slow week. I was behind on the rent and I had a brain that was just itchin' for some action. There was two-week-old bread in the kitchen and three-month-old dust on my note book. Then suddenly in walked Lenny.

Lenny: *(Entering)* Hi there, H. J.

H.J.: *(Still addressing audience)* Lenny and I went way back. He was my best friend at 4th Street Elementary School. We went separate ways but we kept in touch. If there was anything happening out on the streets Lenny knew about it. *(To Lenny)* So, what's up?

Lenny: Ah nothing much H. J. Things have been quiet all round.

H.J.: Quiet isn't good for business, Lenny.

Lenny: I know – but what you gonna' do? Tell you what though – I did find this screwed up piece of paper in your mailbox.

H.J.: Let me see that. *(Takes paper and reads)* What's three in one and one in three?

Lenny: I dunno. Is that what it says?

H.J.: That's what it says.

Lenny: It isn't much to go on.

H.J.: Except for the fact that there's a small cross printed on the corner of the note.

Lenny: What . . . like a Christian cross?

H.J.: Yeah – like a Christian cross. What other kind of cross is there?

Lenny: So what do you think it is, H. J.?

H.J.: Lenny, I think it's a message from the big guy upstairs.

Lenny: What, Mr Krapowski? Why would he be sending you notes like that? He doesn't even like you.

H.J.: Not *that* guy upstairs. I mean the Big G, the main man with the plan, I think he's trying to tell me something.

Lenny: Like that he's three in one and one in three?

H.J.: Could be.

Lenny: How can that be H. J.?

H.J.: Simple enough Lenny. You see that ice-box over there?

Lenny: Yep.

H.J.: What do you think is in it?

Lenny: Ice?

H.J.: Correct. But what if I took the ice out of the ice-box?

Lenny: It would turn back into water.

H.J.: And then if I put it onto the stove to boil to make a cup of my favourite Java?

Lenny: Some of it would turn into steam.

H.J.: Very good Lenny – you're not as dumb as you look. Ice, water, steam, all different, all same. Perhaps the Big G is telling us something.

Lenny: Like there's no one way to describe him? That he's so great an' powerful he works in different ways?

H.J.: Could be. That's the thing about the Big G – you can spend a lifetime trying to figure him out.

Lenny: That'd be a lifetime well spent, huh?

H.J.: None better Lenny, none better.

SUNDAY BETWEEN 24 AND 28 MAY INCLUSIVE

Matthew 6.24–34

THE FIRST DAY

(Jane and Richard stand centrally looking out of a window.)

Jane:	Ahhh, look at him, there he goes.
Richard:	His first day.
Jane:	He looks so worried. I want to go and bring him back.
Richard:	You can't do that. He'll be fine.
Jane:	I want to check his lunch box again.
Richard:	You've done that three times already.
Jane:	But he looks so lost.
Richard:	He's eleven years old, he can look after himself.
Jane:	But on the open day all of the other children looked so much bigger.
Richard:	We've not moved into the land of the giants or something.
Jane:	What if he falls in with the wrong crowd? What if he doesn't like his teachers? What if the work's too difficult for him? What if he gets lost? It was a very big building.
Richard:	What if they all sprout three heads and start breathing fire as soon as he walks into the playground? Nothing is going to happen. He will be fine. You will be fine.
Jane:	But he doesn't know anybody else.
Richard:	He soon will do. Look I know the move here hasn't been easy but Christopher is going to be okay.
Jane:	It's all right for you, you don't worry about anything.
Richard:	That's not true, but in this case worrying isn't actually going to get us anywhere is it?
Jane:	Well no. But that doesn't stop me having sleepless nights.
Richard:	We've met the teachers, we got on well with the Head, Christopher really liked it when he looked round. Don't imagine problems when there aren't any.
Jane:	I'm trying to be brave, honest.
Richard:	I know, and you're doing a very good job of it.
Jane:	I hate worrying this much. I mean I've got faith. I believe. I'm meant to be stronger than this.
Richard:	You're allowed to be human you know.
Jane:	But I'm sure it says somewhere in the Bible you're not meant to worry.
Richard:	Yeah but I'm not sure that means you never will.
Jane:	It's just I worry all the time.
Richard:	I think some people just come that way.
Jane:	So am I allowed to pace the floor today?
Richard:	Just a little bit. As long as you tell people at work why you're doing it.
Jane:	Oh, I'd forgotten about work entirely.
Richard:	Oh that's good, the Chief Executive Officer of the company forgetting work.
Jane:	I'd better get going.
Richard:	Yep, see you later.
Jane:	Remember he'll be home about 4 p.m.
Richard:	Go. And don't worry. He'll be fine. *(She exits reluctantly.)*

SUNDAY BETWEEN 29 MAY AND 4 JUNE INCLUSIVE

Matthew 7.21–29

DIGGING A HOLE

(Rodney is on stage. Steve enters.)

Rodney: Ah, thank goodness you've come.

Steve: Well it sounded very urgent on the phone.

Rodney: It is, oh it is. And you've come very highly recommended.

Steve: I like to think that my work's good quality.

Rodney: So you handle repairs then?

Steve: Oh absolutely, it's one of my specialities.

Rodney: Well then you're just the person. Here it is. *(Points to the floor.)*

Steve: What do you mean, 'Here it is'?

Rodney: This is it. This is my house. Now I admit it's not very much to look at.

Steve: It's a pile of planks of wood.

Rodney: Yes, well I had a rather unfortunate accident.

Steve: It looks like a tornado's hit it.

Rodney: Well you're not far off actually.

Steve: And what's it doing down here on the beach?

Rodney: Well that's where I built it.

Steve: You what?

Rodney: Lovely sea views, none of the hassle of foundations and digging.

Steve: Sound of the sea lapping at the door.

Rodney: Well if you're going to be like that.

Steve: Look, this is madness. You see that house on the cliff over there? That's where you should have built.

Rodney: Well it just seemed so much simpler down here. Sand is a lot easier to build on than rock you know.

Steve: Now why do you think nobody else has thought of that?

Rodney: I don't know. Guess I'm just a bit of a genius.

Steve: It's because they've got more sense, you idiot!

Rodney: Look are you going to help me repair my house or not?

Steve: What caused this flat-pack look in the first place?

Rodney: Well there was a bit of a storm you see.

Steve: And when we've finished doing all these repairs, what's to stop the house getting blown down again?

Rodney: Well I thought I might use an extra tube of glue this time.

Steve: You glued the planks together?

Rodney: Just another example of my genius.

Steve: You are beginning to do my head in.

Rodney: Oh go on – do help me. Please?

Steve: Only if you build your house with a better foundation.

Rodney: But the rock looks so much like hard work.

Steve: If you want to be safe from the storms – that's where you've got to be.

Rodney: I suppose you're right.

Steve: I know I am.

Rodney: So where's all your workers then?

Steve: I'm looking at them.

Rodney: What me? Oh no!! *(Stomps off.)*

SUNDAY BETWEEN 5 AND 11 JUNE INCLUSIVE

Matthew 9.9–13, 18–26

PROFESSIONALS

(Flora and Dora walk on deep in conversation.)

Flora: Well I think it's the height of rudeness myself.

Dora: Absolutely, it shows no manners at all.

Flora: After all, we're professionals.

Dora: Years of training.

Flora: Sensitive and compassionate.

Dora: Caring and sharing.

Flora: And then he comes in and ruins it all.

Dora: It makes us look like idiots.

Flora: Like we don't know what we're doing.

Dora: I mean the girl had been ill for ages.

Flora: Everybody knew that.

Dora: So we went round right away when we heard she'd died.

Flora: Well, when you want a proper job done you go to the best.

Dora: Flora and Dora the professional mourners.

Flora: Loud weeping and wailing our speciality.

Dora: We'll leave some business cards at the back if you like.

Flora: No funeral is complete without our special brand of grieving.

Dora: We offer all kinds of services.

Flora: From a little sensitive sniffling and dabbing of the eyes.

Dora: To full-on hysterics.

Flora: We're very good.

Dora: We'll even bring musicians for a little mood-creating flute music.

Flora: So we'd heard the girl had died and were outside the house.

Dora: Doing a little bit of tasteful mourning.

Flora: Wailing, weeping, a nice bit of flute music in the background.

Dora: Sharing in the family's grief.

Flora: Creating an atmosphere.

Dora: When that long-haired hippie comes in.

Flora: Jesus.

Dora: That's right, Jesus. Complete with hangers-on.

Flora: And he throws us out.

Dora: Tells us to pipe down.

Flora: She's not dead he says, just sleeping.

Dora: Well did you ever hear of anything so ridiculous in your life?

Flora: But of course then she goes and gets up.

Dora: Right as rain.

Flora: No consideration some people.

Dora: No consideration at all.

Flora: Healing people. Raising the dead.

Dora: It's going to put people like us out of a job.

Flora: Jesus wants to think about that the next time he plans on helping people.

Dora: Anyway we do hope you'll consider using our services in the future.

Flora: We're thinking of moving into karaoke.

Dora: We hear there's a lot of call for it.

SUNDAY BETWEEN 12 AND 18 JUNE INCLUSIVE

Matthew 9.35—10.8

UP TO YOU

(Jed and Billy are standing centrally.)

Jed: Now this here's the most important moment for you Billy – here's the badge *(Produces Sheriff's badge from pocket)* – wear it with pride, son.

Billy: Aw, Jed – do I have to go? I ain't ready yet.

Jed: Course you're ready Billy. This land's just full o' nasty critters which need your attention. I can look after the law in these here parts. But you need to get out there an' show you've got what it takes.

Billy: But what if I get scared? What if I can't cope? What if the robbers an' varmints is stronger than me?

Jed: They ain't as strong as you an' you know that.

Billy: I'm not sure I can do this without you.

Jed: You'll be fine.

Billy: But I'll be all alone.

Jed: No you won't. I'll be with you.

Billy: Great – you mean you're coming with me after all?

Jed: No, I'm stayin' right here. I've got to.

Billy: But you said you'd be with me.

Jed: I will Billy. I will. Look down at your badge, son. What does it say?

Billy: Billy Watson – Sheriff with the full authority of the Senior Marshal.

Jed: That's right Billy. I called you. I equipped you. I love you like my own son. You are mine. I'll always be with you. But sometimes you've got to stand on your own two feet and show what you're made of.

Billy: What if I don't have what it takes Jed?

Jed: Trust me Billy, you've got what it takes. An' I'll be there to help you every step of the way.

Billy: But what if people won't listen to me?

Jed: Did people always listen to me?

Billy: No.

Jed: Then why should you be any different? Listen Billy, the world is a dangerous place. It needs people like you an' me standin' up for what's right.

Billy: I just wish I didn't feel so nervous.

Jed: I'd be worried if you didn't Billy. But you put your trust in me, an' all I taught you, an' you're gonna see some pretty amazing things take place. This world needs people like you.

Billy: It needs you more Jed.

Jed: Billy, I'm sending you out with my authority. Your words are mine. What you say I'll back up.

Billy: Okay Jed, if you say so.

Jed: I do say so. You'll be back before you know it.

Billy: Okay then Jed. You take care of yourself y'hear?

Jed: Oh I will Billy. An' don't you worry. Think about my words an' put them into action an' you can't go far wrong.

Billy: I just wish you could come with me.

Jed: I know. I do too. But you've got to do this on your own Billy. An' you take my authority with you. Wear the badge with pride son, adios. *(Billy exits slowly.)*

SUNDAY BETWEEN 19 AND 25 JUNE INCLUSIVE

Matthew 10.24–39

FEAR AND FREEDOM

(Julie is standing forward. The Voice needs to be standing to one side.)

Julie: Hi there. I'm Julie – I'm sixteen years old and I have all the usual problems that a sixteen-year-old has. Where to start? My parents don't really understand me. I'm not sure that I always understand myself. I feel really insecure most of the time. Do I look all right? What do boys think of me? Am I too tall? Too short? Why is life so difficult? But then I've got another problem.

Voice: She certainly has.

Julie: Now there, you see? Did you hear that? That is the *Voice*. The *Voice* is forever talking inside my head.

Voice: Well somebody needs to help you.

Julie: You see – there it goes again, giving me advice. It won't leave me alone. I'll be walking down the street minding my own business, looking in shop windows and suddenly the *Voice* will be there too, asking me uncomfortable questions, making me think about things.

Voice: Julie – you were going to tell them about your problem.

Julie: Oh yeah – sorry. Look – this is really embarrassing.

Voice: Only if you make it so.

Julie: Okay, okay. Look, I go to church. I'm a Christian.

Voice: There, now was that so difficult?

Julie: No, but it's different when you're in front of your friends at school.

Voice: How so?

Julie: Well they're my friends for a start.

Voice: Yes . . .

Julie: And I don't know whether you've noticed this or not but being sixteen years old and a Christian in this country is hardly a 'normal' thing to be.

Voice: So you're worried about what people will say.

Julie: Just a little bit.

Voice: Why don't you tell them and then you'll find out.

Julie: Easy for you to say – you're a voice inside my head. I'm afraid – can't you see that?

Voice: Yes, I can see that Julie. But there is no need to be afraid, honestly.

Julie: Again – easy enough for you to say.

Voice: Julie you're living your life by fear anyway. Fear that your friends will find out. Do you want to be free?

Julie: Of course I do.

Voice: Then cast out the fear. Talk to them, tell them. You can only be free when you are not allowing fear to rule your life.

Julie: But what if they all think it's just a bit weird?

Voice: They won't – not if they're real friends.

Julie: I would like to be free.

Voice: Of course you would. Free to become the person God wants you to be.

Julie: Free to stop hiding and worrying.

Voice: Free to grow.

Julie: I'm glad we had this little chat – thanks *Voice*.

Voice: You're very welcome Julie. Take care of yourself. *(Exit.)*

SUNDAY BETWEEN 26 JUNE AND 2 JULY INCLUSIVE

Matthew 10.40–42

'RECEIVE'

(Brimstone – a devil – is standing by a flip-chart. Scabbers is sitting.)

Brimstone:	All right Scabbers, let us try this one more time.
Scabbers:	I'm sorry Brimstone; I don't think I'm ever going to be a senior tempter like you.
Brimstone:	Nonsense, of course you will. Although your progress has been remarkably slow, and being incredibly evil I have very little patience.
Scabbers:	I just can't seem to get the hang of this.
Brimstone:	Look, you fool, it really is quite straightforward. The key word here is 'receives'. Do you understand that? RECEIVES. *(He writes it on the flip-chart.)*
Scabbers:	But what does it mean, o hideous one?
Brimstone:	Let me give you a pathetically simple example. Say you are sent up to the tempting zone to keep one of those wonderfully weak human beings from falling into the enemy's hands.
Scabbers:	I have always dreamt of such a task.
Brimstone:	You dream on a very low level don't you Scabbers? Anyway, to get back to this human. One day a Christian calls on him and asks whether he can come inside for coffee and a chat.
Scabbers:	Oh, that's very nice of him.
Brimstone:	Yes it is, very nice – therefore do we let it happen?
Scabbers:	Uh . . .
Brimstone:	The answer, you blithering idiot, is 'No'. No we do not let it happen. Not in a thousand lifetimes do we let it happen.
Scabbers:	Oh, okay. But why?
Brimstone:	You really haven't learned anything have you? Because of the word 'receives'.
Scabbers:	One little word?
Brimstone:	And all that it stands for, yes. The enemy has said that anyone who receives one of his followers is also receiving him.
Scabbers:	I'm still not sure I understand.
Brimstone:	It's as if Jesus himself is walking in through that door. If your target welcomes in the Christian, he welcomes in Jesus.
Scabbers:	But we don't want him to welcome in Jesus.
Brimstone:	*(Losing patience)* Which is exactly why we don't want him to receive the Christian into his home. That would be a bad thing.
Scabbers:	There's more to being a devil than meets the eye.
Brimstone:	No, there's less to your brain than meets the eye. Look Scabbers, it's quite simple. The enemy wants people to welcome him into their lives. So it's made easy for them. What we have to do is to stop that from happening. And we will do it by any means possible.
Scabbers:	By fair means or foul?
Brimstone:	We hardly ever use fair means Scabbers, you should know that by now. It's so demeaning. So what is the word of the day Scabbers?
Scabbers:	'Receive'.
Brimstone:	Very good – we may make a tempter of you yet.

SUNDAY BETWEEN 3 AND 9 JULY INCLUSIVE

Matthew 11.16–19, 25–30

EXPECTATIONS

(Matilda and Regina are middle-aged ladies.)

Matilda: We'd have expected better.

Regina: Oh we certainly would, much better.

Matilda: We here at Upper Middling in the Marsh don't ask for much.

Regina: We usually don't get it either.

Matilda: But there are certain things we expect of our minister.

Regina: So when the Revd Nick Samuel arrived last month we were a little surprised.

Matilda: Indeed shocked to find that we had been sent a man of the cloth who had . . . I can hardly bring myself to say it.

Regina: Courage Matilda, fortitude.

Matilda: An ear-ring *(Slight gasp)* and . . .

Regina: Great big bean bags you had to sit in rather than a nice three-piece suite at the Manse.

Matilda: But that's not all.

Regina: Not a bit of it.

Matilda: Because no sooner had our new minister arrived than very unsettling tales began to reach our ears. Very unsettling indeed.

Regina: It appears that every week.

Matilda: Regular as clockwork.

Regina: The Revd Nick Samuel has been going down to the local pub.

Matilda: Wearing his clerical collar.

Regina: And there in the Stag and Ferret he's been talking to all and sundry about religion over a pint.

Matilda: What's more, the locals seem to like it.

Regina: Well they would, wouldn't they? Uncouth rabble.

Matilda: The next thing you know he'll be inviting them to church.

Regina: They're not sitting in my pew.

Matilda: Mine neither.

Regina: Matilda and I are very upset.

Matilda: Very upset indeed. Regina and I are members of committees.

Regina: We wield considerable power in Upper Middling.

Matilda: And we are not going to stand idly by and watch our church destroyed by this upstart.

Regina: He's going to parties.

Matilda: Hanging around with undesirables.

Regina: This is not the way we expect our ministers to behave.

Matilda: Not at all. And why would he want any of these awful people to come to church anyway?

Regina: They wouldn't know what to do.

Matilda: They'd end up getting in the way and being a dreadful nuisance.

Regina: And we don't want that.

Matilda: So our minister can take his radical ideas somewhere else.

Regina: I'm sure Jesus would never approve.

Matilda: He'd have socialized with respectable people. Like us.

SUNDAY BETWEEN 10 AND 16 JULY INCLUSIVE

Matthew 13.1–9, 18–23

STONY GROUND

(A 1930s school – there is a knock on the door of Bulstrode, the Head.)

Bulstrode: Come. *(Jenkins enters rather sheepishly.)*

Jenkins: You asked to see me, sir?

Bulstrode: When I require you to speak, Jenkins, I will make it quite clear, understood? *(There is silence.)* I said understood?

Jenkins: Oh sorry sir, yes sir. It just wasn't quite as clear as you said it was going to be sir. Very sorry, sir.

Bulstrode: It would have been clear Jenkins if you had listened to my original question carefully enough. But that's just your problem isn't it Jenkins?

Jenkins: Problem, Mr Bulstrode sir?

Bulstrode: Yes, problem Jenkins – issue, bone of contention, cause of head scratching and worrying looks all round.

Jenkins: I didn't realize I had a problem sir.

Bulstrode: That, my boy, is because you never listen to what anybody ever says to you. Your head is the original stony ground.

Jenkins: Stony ground, sir?

Bulstrode: Rocky terrain Jenkins. The pearls of wisdom that fall from the mouths of the masters and mistresses here at St Olave's Institute of Chronic Neglect seem to come into contact with your eardrums and bounce right off them, boy.

Jenkins: What a wonderful set of images sir.

Bulstrode: Yes, I was quite pleased with them myself actually. But that's not the point. What is at issue is what happened during period 3's French lesson yesterday.

Jenkins: Ah yes.

Bulstrode: Exactly. Caught looking out of the window day-dreaming when declining verbs was the order of the day.

Jenkins: Yes sir.

Bulstrode: A mind is an incredible thing, Jenkins.

Jenkins: It is Mr Bulstrode?

Bulstrode: Absolutely boy. You could be hearing the most important information that you will ever receive but if your mind has decided it's not going to take any notice then the message will fall on deaf ears.

Jenkins: I see sir.

Bulstrode: I wish I could be more confident that you did see, Jenkins.

Jenkins: I will try sir.

Bulstrode: I would like to be even more confident of that statement.

Jenkins: Sir, you sound as though you're not sure that a person can change from being stony ground to something else. In which case I have no chance at all – do I sir?

Bulstrode: Not at all Jenkins. I am sure that people can change in the most dramatic of ways, and I hope that will be true of you.

Jenkins: Then I can change sir. And I will try, honest.

Bulstrode: We shall see. Now off you go Jenkins, and send in van de Graff on the way out would you? Run along. *(Jenkins exits.)*

SUNDAY BETWEEN 17 AND 23 JULY INCLUSIVE

Matthew 13.24–30, 36–43

GARDEN TIME

(Derek and Trudy are gardeners and are standing centrally.)

Derek: Well good morning everybody and welcome to *Garden Time*. It's me, Derek Composter, here again to answer all your little gardening queries and worries. Everything from drooping dahlias to greenfly on your gardenias. I'm here with everybody's favourite garden goddess, Trudy Groundwater.

Trudy: Hello everybody. Derek, I'm not sure I like the look of your lilac today.

Derek: No, it is looking a bit sorry for itself isn't it?

Trudy: I've got a chemical that'll deal with that. Anyway, enough of this chit-chat, we've got plenty of problems and paradoxes to buzz around this week.

Derek: We certainly have. Ruth from Rochester writes in to say that she's found that the fur she combs out of her cat makes an excellent bonding agent in her compost heap.

Trudy: That's lovely Ruth. We do love it when you share your little secrets for success with all of the other gardeners across the nation. So keep those postcards coming.

Derek: Yes indeed.

Trudy: And we've got another letter, this time from Tony of Tadcaster. He writes, 'What should I do about the weeds that are coming up all over my garden?'

Derek: Well, Tony, my simple advice to you is, don't do anything with them. Just let them grow up alongside everything else that's in your flower bed.

Trudy: Have you gone mad?

Derek: Ah, no Trudy, I don't think so.

Trudy: This is a gardening show you know.

Derek: Yes, I realize that.

Trudy: And the whole aim of this programme is to help people to have beautiful looking gardens. Not weed infested scrap heaps.

Derek: But I like a garden that reflects life. You know, the good and the bad rubbing along together.

Trudy: Yes well I think that the sponsors of our show, 'Kill it Quick' garden fertilizer, will have something to say about that.

Derek: I suppose so.

Trudy: You'll advise Tony to pull up his weeds then?

Derek: I didn't say that.

Trudy: But our sponsors!

Derek: Ah, I wouldn't worry about them. *(Speaking to audience)* The thing is folks, life isn't pretty as a picture. Not all of the time. Sometimes it's important to recognize that. Things just grow up together and they're pretty hard to separate. Perhaps it's better that we don't even try. Perhaps we ought to leave that to somebody who's got a wiser head on their shoulders. *The* wisest head actually.

Trudy: Well we've had quite enough of that for one week. It's time to go.

Derek: From Trudy and me, goodbye. And Tony, don't pull up those weeds!

SUNDAY BETWEEN 24 AND 30 JULY INCLUSIVE

Matthew 13.31–33, 44–52

SELL, SELL, SELL!!

(Deirdre is on stage. Roger enters excitedly.)

Roger: Deirdre, come quick!

Deirdre: Evening, you sound excited.

Roger: I am. Start packing everything.

Deirdre: What do you mean, 'Start packing'?

Roger: *(Looking around and calculating)* About a hundred for the TV, two hundred for the three-piece suite, fifty for the dresser. How much do you think the dining room table and chairs would go for?

Deirdre: I don't know, about sixty, why?

Roger: Because we're selling them.

Deirdre: What on earth do you mean, 'We're selling them'? We've only had that set a couple of years. It took ages to pick it out. Why on earth would we want to get a new set?

Roger: Uh . . . I didn't say we were getting a new set. I just said we were selling the one we've got.

Deirdre: What?

Roger: About fifty for the bed. You don't mind sleeping on a camp bed do you? Two thousand for the car.

Deirdre: Roger, you're beginning to scare me. What is this all about?

Roger: We've got to sell it. All of it, or we'll never have enough.

Deirdre: Never have enough for what?

Roger: Oh Deirdre, it's wonderful. If only you could have seen it.

Deirdre: Seen what?

Roger: I was just browsing – looking for something else entirely – and there it was. Looking at me.

Deirdre: Roger, I'm beginning to lose my patience. What in heaven's name are you talking about?

Roger: A pearl, Deirdre. The most beautiful, stunning pearl you have ever seen. To have something of that beauty in your life . . . incredible.

Deirdre: A pearl?

Roger: Yes.

Deirdre: You're talking about selling everything we own to get enough money to buy a pearl.

Roger: Not just any pearl. *The* pearl. It's the most wonderful thing I've ever seen. I've got to have it.

Deirdre: Is this some kind of joke?

Roger: Deirdre, I've never been more serious in my life. But it's going to take a lot to get it. Probably everything.

Deirdre: Everything?

Roger: Well, I'll leave us clothes to stand up in.

Deirdre: *(Heavy with sarcasm)* Wonderful.

Roger: Oh and perhaps a couple of plates. We'll need something to eat off. *(Moves to exit excitedly)* How much do you think we'll get for the guinea pig?

Deirdre: *(Running after him)* Roger!

SUNDAY BETWEEN 31 JULY AND 6 AUGUST INCLUSIVE

Matthew 14.13–21

THE INTERVIEW

(Interviewer and Sir Anthony are sitting centrally.)

Interviewer: I'm here tonight with Sir Anthony St John Smythe, head of Condescending Overseas Planning for the present Government.

Sir Anthony: Good evening.

Interviewer: Now Sir Anthony, latest predictions tell us that we are on the brink of a global catastrophe the like of which we've never seen before.

Sir Anthony: They do?

Interviewer: Yes. A million close to starvation in Ethiopia, endemic AIDS throughout Southern Africa, civil conflict, lack of clean water. The list goes on and on.

Sir Anthony: Ah yes. And the Government are doing all they can to help in these terrible situations.

Interviewer: They are?

Sir Anthony: Oh indeed. Volunteer programmes, aid workers, initiatives in education and health care. We've been very busy supporting charities on the ground.

Interviewer: So, getting somebody else to do the work for you?

Sir Anthony: I wouldn't say that exactly.

Interviewer: What would you say . . . exactly?

Sir Anthony: Well there's problems you see, lots of problems. Just as we're trying to fund educational programmes or health initiatives some pesky flood or famine or something will happen and we have to divert the money to that instead.

Interviewer: Heaven forbid you should actually come up with more money.

Sir Anthony: Yes exactly *(Realizing what he's said)* . . . No, it's just that the money is limited.

Interviewer: What about transforming people's lives minister?

Sir Anthony: Transforming their what?

Interviewer: Encouraging giving.

Sir Anthony: I think we do that already. I myself gave 50p to Oxfam just the other day.

Interviewer: Big deal.

Sir Anthony: I beg your pardon?

Interviewer: You heard what I said, big deal. How many corporate boards and trusts are you on Sir Anthony?

Sir Anthony: Well I'm er . . . I'm not sure.

Interviewer: Well let me tell you . . . it's eleven. And how much did you earn after tax last year Sir Anthony?

Sir Anthony: I . . . I . . .

Interviewer: It was £350,000. And you gave 50p to somebody rattling a tin for Oxfam. So, as I said before, big deal.

Sir Anthony: Look, you unpleasant little person, we can't feed the population of the whole world just like that. It would mean too much of a change for people. They'd never accept the sacrifices needed.

Interviewer: I would say generosity has a transforming power wouldn't you, Sir Anthony? A power to transform real generosity, real giving into something that will change lives. Or is that not worldly enough for you?

44

SUNDAY BETWEEN 7 AND 13 AUGUST INCLUSIVE

Matthew 14.22–33

RISING TIDE

(Two actors enter from the back – speaking as they walk.)

Voice 1: Drowning.

Voice 2: Feeling the waters of life gently closing in around you.

Voice 1: A rising tide of panic wells up in your throat.

Voice 2: You cry out.

Voice 1: But no one seems to hear.

Voice 2: Life comes at you from all sides.

Voice 1: Do this.

Voice 2: Go there.

Voice 1: Be the kind of person . . .

Voice 2: Who is never overwhelmed.

Voice 1: Never out of their depth.

Voice 2: Entirely comfortable at all times.

Voice 1: Except those kinds of people . . .

Voice 2: Don't exist.

Voice 1: And still the waters rise.

Voice 2: So many demands of energy and time.

Voice 1: Frantically you look for an escape.

Voice 2: But see none.

Voice 1: Do you have enough faith to break out?

Voice 2: To see things entirely differently?

Voice 1: To look at the world in a whole new light?

Voice 2: Do you have enough belief to grab the hand that reaches down?

Voice 1: A strong, welcoming hand ready to pull you out?

Voice 2: A hand that reaches down through the chaos of your life.

Voice 1: And invites you to take hold.

Voice 2: And be pulled to safety.

Voice 1: But taking the hand means letting go.

Voice 2: Letting go of all your preconceptions.

Voice 1: Of the things that you think are important.

Voice 2: Of the world as you know it.

Voice 1: Taking hold of that hand means giving up.

Voice 2: And letting go.

Voice 1: It's a hard thing to do.

Voice 2: To hand your life over to somebody else.

Voice 1: And say, 'I give up.'

Voice 2: I'm fed up with going wrong.

Voice 1: Of doing things my way.

Voice 2: Especially when my way doesn't work.

Voice 1: You need to believe and let go.

Voice 2: Have faith and trust.

Voice 1: Reach out and take the hand that is offered.

Voice 2: Knowing that life will change.

Voice 1: And having faith that it will be wonderful.

Voice 2: For you have been rescued from drowning.

SUNDAY BETWEEN 14 AND 20 AUGUST INCLUSIVE

Matthew 15. (10–20) 21–28

PERSISTENCE

(Joel and Ruth are standing centrally.)

Joel: I still can't believe you did it.

Ruth: What else was I to do Joel? Nothing else has worked.

Joel: But to be so blatant about it. So open.

Ruth: Joel, it's our daughter. Do you understand that? Our daughter. And how long has she been sick? Five months? Six?

Joel: So that makes it okay to talk to a man in broad daylight? A man we know nothing about? Some wandering teacher.

Ruth: He has a name, Joel, as you well know.

Joel: Yes, yes, Jesus. And so you nag and pester him until you get what you want – is that it?

Ruth: What is your problem Joel? Is it that I did it without asking you? Is it that I argued with him? Arguing with a man in front of everybody, in broad daylight. That would never do.

Joel: You should have known better.

Ruth: She's cured isn't she?

Joel: Well I can't deny that. But that might have happened anyway.

Ruth: You don't believe that.

Joel: It just makes us look so desperate.

Ruth: Joel, we are desperate, or at least we were. Now, praise God, everything seems to be all right.

Joel: I still don't like it.

Ruth: Well Joel, you can sulk all you want, but what's done is done.

Joel: You argued with him.

Ruth: Yes, I argued with him, and I think he enjoyed it.

Joel: What do you mean, 'enjoyed it'?

Ruth: Well think about it. Perhaps he wanted me to fight back. Perhaps he wanted to see how far I was prepared to go, how much I felt it.

Joel: He got more than he bargained for with you.

Ruth: Joel, you know me. I speak my mind. Always have, always will. And when he made that comment about dogs, well I just saw red. I couldn't help it.

Joel: I guess he deserved what he got.

Ruth: Once I get the bit between my teeth, I'm off.

Joel: To be honest you scare me sometimes.

Ruth: Not half as much as I scare myself. I think he really wanted to see how much this mattered to me. How much I believed that he could do something about it. And once he saw that, things changed.

Joel: He's certainly a strange one.

Ruth: But the funny thing is, I never felt he was being cruel to me. In fact I'm pretty sure he wanted to help.

Joel: Look, Ruth, about what I said earlier. I didn't mean to be unkind. The truth is I'm proud of you. Scared, but proud.

Ruth: I'm just glad we've got our daughter back.

Joel: How is she?

Ruth: Sitting up in bed, demanding something to drink – just like always.

SUNDAY BETWEEN 21 AND 27 AUGUST INCLUSIVE

Matthew 16.13–20

SAYING IT

(John enters.)

John: The first thing you need to know, I suppose, is that I am not one of the twelve. I'm not one of the inside group who go around with Jesus all the time. There's all sorts of reasons for that – some of them are even good ones – and it's okay. Really. I don't mind not being there every second of every day. I do go as often as I can. If Jesus' travels are bringing him in this direction I normally get to hear about it. Somebody will come into my shop, usually very excited, and say, 'John, guess who's coming our way?' And I'll shut up the shop and go and listen. Somebody asked me the other day who I thought Jesus was. I guess they were asking what I think his significance is. Is he a prophet? Elijah back from the dead or something? I said I thought that was nonsense. Well, it is isn't it? But then I got to thinking. Who is Jesus? What do I make of him? Why do I feel this need to go and listen to him every time he's within ten miles of my village? They're important questions. I just wish I had an answer to them. It feels like I should have an answer to them. After all, I spend a good part of my life chasing after the man – you'd have thought by now I'd have formed some opinion about who he is. But I haven't. Not really. And I wonder, sometimes, whether that's because I'm afraid of what the answer might be. We've all done it haven't we? Not asked some really important question because we know deep down what the answer is. The problem is it would change our lives too much if we admitted it. Who is Jesus? That's the all-important question. I think I know, but I can't bring myself to say it – I just can't.

(Reading of Matthew 16.13–20 – after the reading Peter enters.)

Peter: Well, I've said it. The words just came out. I couldn't believe I'd said it. The others just looked at me – I think not because they didn't agree, they were just amazed that I'd said the words. 'Who do you say I am?' he said. And I just blurted it out. The words hung there in the air with nobody saying anything much, their impact settling into people's minds. He seemed quite pleased. He smiled at me. It was a smile tinged with relief. Almost as if he was glad somebody had cottoned on, had figured out some huge secret. 'At last someone understands!' When you think about it, it is pretty massive. I mean, if what I've said is right, and I think it is, then everything changes. Absolutely everything. I mean life will literally never be the same again. If Messiah has come – and we are seeing God in human form . . . the mind almost bursts with the importance of it. And I believe it. I suppose I wouldn't have said it if I didn't. But even now the significance of that statement is only just beginning to sink in. Mother always said I was a bit slow. She was probably right. But this means that Jesus is worthy of everything I can give. Every ounce of energy and loyalty and commitment that I can muster. Even then it can't be enough. What could be enough for the living God? I will follow him. I will tell others about him. I will tell everybody about him, absolutely everybody.

SUNDAY BETWEEN 28 AUGUST AND 3 SEPTEMBER INCLUSIVE

Matthew 16. 21–28

TOO DIFFICULT

(Joyce and Maureen are on stage drinking tea.)

Joyce:	So Maureen, I guess you're wondering why I came round today.
Maureen:	It had crossed my mind, yes.
Joyce:	I don't know quite how to say this – it's just that you haven't been to church recently and I was wondering whether there was anything wrong? We miss you.
Maureen:	Ah . . . that. Well Joyce it's difficult to explain.
Joyce:	Try me.
Maureen:	It's all just . . . it's too difficult, that's what it is.
Joyce:	Too difficult? What do you mean?
Maureen:	Well, you know, Robbie has football on Sunday mornings and Jenny has rehearsals for her school play, and Dave always has a million and one things he wants to do around the house.
Joyce:	And you're not allowed to have a life because of that?
Maureen:	It's not that. Going to church just got in the way.
Joyce:	Oh well heaven forbid it should get in the way of anything.
Maureen:	Joyce, you know what I mean.
Joyce:	Actually, Maureen, I'm not sure that I do.
Maureen:	It was all too demanding. I just wanted to go from time to time – perhaps once a month or so. So I walk into church and the first thing I realize is that they expect me to go every week.
Joyce:	Terrible.
Maureen:	Then they want me to join a house group, to give to charity, who knows what else?
Joyce:	How upsetting.
Maureen:	But you know what the final straw was?
Joyce:	No, Maureen, what?
Maureen:	It was all that talk about Jesus, and following him, and your life changing, and being prepared to suffer.
Joyce:	And what's so awful about that?
Maureen:	It's so religious. It wants too much from me. It expects me to give everything.
Joyce:	But that's what Christianity's about.
Maureen:	I just want to sing some well-known hymns, feel all nice and warm inside, put a little bit of money in the collection plate, and go home.
Joyce:	So as soon as it gets demanding you pack up your bags?
Maureen:	Well you've got to admit it is time consuming.
Joyce:	Look Maureen, I love you, I really do, but it sounds to me like you want Church Lite. No demands, no challenges, just cosy, comforting words from time to time. It's not like that.
Maureen:	Well it should be if that's what people want.
Joyce:	It's not about what people want. It's about what God wants.
Maureen:	There you go, bringing God into it again.
Joyce:	Yeah, pesky isn't it? You see the issue is – God has given everything to us. The question is, what are we prepared to give back?

SUNDAY BETWEEN 4 AND 10 SEPTEMBER INCLUSIVE

Matthew 18.15–20

ESCALATING CONFLICT

(Two people enter carrying a board game.)

Voice 1: Good morning everybody.

Voice 2: Good morning indeed.

Voice 1: We are in sales.

Voice 2: Now before you throw us out the door.

Voice 1: We want to show you our brand new product.

Voice 2: It's a board game.

Voice 1: An exciting evening of fun for all the family.

Voice 2: It's called 'Hit Back'.

Voice 1: Let us show you how it works.

Voice 2: You're given a situation.

Voice 1: For example *(Pulls out card and reads)* 'You have had a huge row with your best friend: do you (a) . . .

Voice 2: *(Also reading from card)* Calmly talk it through and realize you both could have handled things differently?

Voice 1: (b) . . .

Voice 2: Go off in a huff and take a couple of days to calm down?

Voice 1: Or (c) Go round to their house and dig up all the rose bushes in their front garden?'

Voice 2: Every time you answer a question you get points.

Voice 1: And points mean rungs up the ladder.

Voice 2: There are three ladders on the board.

Voice 1: The calming ladder of sensitive tranquillity.

Voice 2: The eye for an eye, tooth for a tooth ladder of equal retribution.

Voice 1: Or the thermonuclear response ladder of violent viciousness.

Voice 2: Which ladder would you choose?

Voice 1: The ladder of sensitive tranquillity leads to a world of harmony, peace and love.

Voice 2: The eye for an eye ladder eventually leads to the whole world being blind and toothless.

Voice 1: The thermonuclear response ladder leads to the destruction of life as we know it in four moves.

Voice 2: It sounds a lot of fun doesn't it?

Voice 1: Are you capable of keeping a cool head?

Voice 2: Especially when everybody around you is losing theirs?

Voice 1: Or are you the kind of person who over-reacts?

Voice 2: Who has a vicious temper?

Voice 1: Whose response to everything is to crank up the tension?

Voice 2: How do you react when someone does you wrong?

Voice 1: Are you a bomb waiting to go off?

Voice 2: Or is your way the way of peace and love?

Voice 1: Either way we know you'll want to play our new game.

Voice 2: It's in the shops now.

Voice 1: And the name is . . .

Voices 1 and 2: Hit Back!

SUNDAY BETWEEN 11 AND 17 SEPTEMBER INCLUSIVE

Matthew 18.21–35

'CAN YOU FORGIVE?'

(Enthusiastic game show presenter enters with shy contestant.)

Presenter: Hi there folks and welcome to *Can You Forgive?*, the game show where we really find out what our contestants are made of. We all know the Bible tells us to be forgiving, but is it really as easy as that? Let's welcome today's contestant, Sharon from Sheffield.

Sharon: Hello everybody.

Presenter: Now then Sharon, you work in a bank, is that correct?

Sharon: That's correct Jerry, yes.

Presenter: And we happen to know that one of your co-workers is really giving you some grief at the moment isn't she?

Sharon: Snotty Sheila.

Presenter: So what's she been doing?

Sharon: Oooh everything. She's always going on about how much better she is than everybody else. She's always smarming up to the boss, and she's borrowed money from me and never given it back.

Presenter: Well Sharon, that's a pretty impressive list of wrongdoing – but we can do better than that.

Sharon: What do you mean?

Presenter: We placed secret cameras all around your workplace and we caught Sheila talking about you behind your back. And last Tuesday lunchtime we filmed her opening your bag and rifling through the contents.

Sharon: No!

Presenter: Yes, I'm afraid so.

Sharon: I'll . . . I'll . . .

Presenter: Listen Sharon, before you say something you may very well regret, let me tell you a couple of things. We talked to Sheila yesterday, confronted her with all the evidence and told her how upset you were.

Sharon: Well that won't have done any good.

Presenter: Actually it did.

Sharon: What do you mean?

Presenter: Well Sharon, I have to tell you, Sheila had no idea you felt this way and she is incredibly sorry for any hurt that she's caused you.

Sharon: She is?

Presenter: So what I have to ask you now, Sharon from Sheffield, is this, can you forgive Sheila?

Sharon: Oooh, I don't know Jerry, it's all so difficult.

Presenter: Isn't it just? Let me give you this one piece of information that may help you make your choice.

Sharon: What's that?

Presenter: God is incredibly loving. Extravagant love given every day, forgiving us time and time again. God needs us to show that love and forgiveness to others. We're not even going to ask you to make that choice Sharon because we're going to get our audience to do it for you. So then folks, the choice is yours. You know what God wants, you know what Sheila's done. The question is, 'Can you forgive?'

SUNDAY BETWEEN 18 AND 24 SEPTEMBER INCLUSIVE

Matthew 20.1–16

THE MEETING

(A man and a woman enter and sit down.)

Ron: Greetings brothers.

Marge: I'm your sister, Ron.

Ron: Oh, sorry Marge. Greetings brothers and sisters.

Marge: There's only the two of us here.

Ron: Marge will you stop putting me off my stride?

Marge: Sorry. Just trying to point out the obvious.

Ron: We are here today to convene a special meeting of the Associated Vineyard and Amalgamated Wine-pressing Workers' Union to discuss the unwise and divisive actions of our employer with regard to his payment of casual labour.

Marge: And some of them are very casual indeed.

Ron: Here, here Marge.

Marge: But I want you to know Ron that I'm not entirely in favour of the action you're taking.

Ron: What do you mean Marge?

Marge: Well you want to take immediate strike action don't you?

Ron: I do indeed sister Marge, that's very true.

Marge: So you plan on sitting around that market place all day doing nothing then?

Ron: I'd hardly call it doing nothing Marge.

Marge: Oh yeah, well what would you call it then?

Ron: I'd call it taking a stand against the capitalist aggressor, standing up for our rights, making a point.

Marge: With no pay.

Ron: If that's what it takes, so be it.

Marge: Well I'm afraid I can't afford principles Ron, I've got four kids to feed.

Ron: So you'll just let the landlord pay whatever he wants then?

Marge: Ron, did you feel hard done by when you were hired?

Ron: That's hardly the point Marge.

Marge: Oh I think it's very much the point. Did you feel oppressed, unfairly treated?

Ron: Well . . . no.

Marge: So you'd been promised the going rate?

Ron: A little over actually.

Marge: So all this really boils down to the fact that Sid Temple got the same amount as you for working half as long?

Ron: Quite right – and it shall not stand.

Marge: Ron, stop being such a windbag.

Ron: Well, I've never been spoken to . . .

Marge: Oh you're full of hot air. You just can't cope with somebody else being lucky, can you? With generosity being shown? It's the landlord's money. He's got a perfect right to do what he wants with it. And if your heart isn't big enough to accept that then that's your problem. Not Sid Temple's, not the landlord's, but yours. Good night Ron.

SUNDAY BETWEEN 25 SEPTEMBER AND 1 OCTOBER INCLUSIVE

Matthew 21.23–32

WHOSE AUTHORITY?

(Two actors enter together.)

Voice 1: We like authority.

Voice 2: To have authority over others.

Voice 1: To have the knowledge that when we ask for something to be done . . .

Voice 2: That it will, in fact, be done.

Voice 1: To have the confidence that when we speak . . .

Voice 2: Others will listen.

Voice 1: We like to exercise authority.

Voice 2: We want to know that we are important.

Voice 1: That we have power over some small part of creation.

Voice 2: To feel that in some tiny . . .

Voice 1: Though vital way . . .

Voices 1 and 2: We matter.

Voice 1: Some people enjoy authority more than others.

Voice 2: There are some people who like power.

Voice 1: Who are impressed by the sound of their own voices.

Voice 2: Who know beyond a shadow of doubt that they are always right.

Voice 1: And they want other people to know that too.

Voice 2: They think they're pretty important.

Voice 1: Most of the time they're just pompous.

Voice 2: And the thing that annoys them most.

Voice 1: That they really can't abide.

Voice 2: Is someone who actually has real authority.

Voice 1: Genuine power.

Voice 2: Because they realize suddenly how small and weak they are.

Voice 1: Imagine, then, the discomfort.

Voice 2: The embarrassment.

Voice 1: The anger.

Voice 2: Of the chief priests and the elders.

Voice 1: When they met up with Jesus.

Voice 2: After all, these were people of power.

Voice 1: Of importance and note.

Voice 2: They wielded authority.

Voice 1: And were a little bit self-important.

Voice 2: But in Jesus they met somebody who was different.

Voice 1: Someone who had real power.

Voice 2: Genuine authority.

Voice 1: Someone who spoke and even the wind and the waves obeyed.

Voice 2: And his authority was not based on playing games of power.

Voice 1: Or having the best seat in the synagogue.

Voice 2: Or telling people what they should do.

Voice 1: His power was based on vulnerability.

Voice 2: And humility and gentleness.

Voice 1: But most of all on love.

Voice 2: And that they couldn't understand at all.

SUNDAY BETWEEN 2 AND 8 OCTOBER INCLUSIVE

Matthew 21.33–46

NEWS REPORT

(A news reporter and tenant farmer are standing centrally.)

Reporter: It's shocking, it's sordid. It's a tale of brutal, ruthless murder coldly planned and executed. Welcome to *Acts of Crime*. I'm Cynthia Hardhitter and tonight we have with us a farm worker who admits to killing two people, brutally beating others and hurling rocks at yet more.

Tenant: That's right and I'm not ashamed of any of it.

Reporter: You can see folks that this cold-blooded killer has no feelings of remorse for the terrible things he's done. Tell us the story in your own words.

Tenant: Well I'm a tenant farmer see.

Reporter: And relationships between you and your landlord have steadily got worse?

Tenant: I'm afraid they have, yes.

Reporter: So what was the problem? Did he grossly neglect your land?

Tenant: Oh no – he was very good about it. He planted the vineyard in the first place, then he built a wall around it – well you can't be too careful.

Reporter: Indeed.

Tenant: Then he dug a winepress and built a watchtower.

Reporter: He sounds like he provided for all your needs.

Tenant: Well he did really, yes.

Reporter: But then he abandoned you?

Tenant: Well I wouldn't say abandoned but he did go off on a journey.

Reporter: Forgive me, but I fail to see why all of this should lead to the terrible violence my audience are so desperate to hear about.

Tenant: Well harvest time came round and he sent some servants to collect his fruit.

Reporter: That seems reasonable enough. After all it is his vineyard.

Tenant: Yeah but we didn't want to give him any of it, and that's really when the violence started.

Reporter: Tell us everything – don't hold back on any gory details.

Tenant: Well at first he sent a bunch of servants and we got into an argument, see. Well one thing led to another and we beat one of them up, stoned another and killed a third.

Reporter: I believe the landlord then sent another group of servants.

Tenant: Yep, and we did the same to them too.

Reporter: Terrible. Tell me about the final horrendous act.

Tenant: Well the landlord sent his son to sort things out. We killed him.

Reporter: I'm still a little unclear. Why did you do it?

Tenant: Well we don't like being told what to do, do we?

Reporter: But it's not as if the land belongs to you.

Tenant: Well, no.

Reporter: And it's not as if the landlord dealt with you badly – in fact he treated you well. So basically you're just selfish, disloyal and violent.

Tenant: Just like the rest of humanity.

Reporter: I do hope there's more hope for us than that. Well folks – I've heard it all, a group of people who resorted to violence and murder simply because they didn't like the idea that somebody else was in control. Good night.

SUNDAY BETWEEN 9 AND 15 OCTOBER INCLUSIVE

Matthew 22.1–14

FREE

(Enter a servant frantically searching – a guest is sitting in a corner.)

Servant: There's got to be someone. There's got to be someone. I can't go back empty-handed, I just can't, I . . . *(Sees guest)*. Ah ha. Madam, excuse me, madam.

Guest: Who me?

Servant: Indeed you. This is your lucky day.

Guest: I haven't had too many of those recently.

Servant: I can see that. Well your life's about to change.

Guest: Change? Change how?

Servant: Oh, for the better. I have here, just for you, an invitation.

Guest: *(Not impressed)* Oh.

Servant: What do you mean, 'Oh'?

Guest: Don't you think I know what this is about? This is an invitation for me to apply for a credit card, or to buy insurance, or to say 'Look Mrs Jones, this lucky invitation to get our catalogue entitles you to an exciting free gift!'

Servant: But it's none of those things.

Guest: Oh yeah, so what is this an invitation to?

Servant: There's going to be a wedding banquet and you're invited.

Guest: I don't know anybody who's getting married.

Servant: You do now. The king invites you to the wedding banquet of his son, the prince.

Guest: Look, this isn't funny anymore.

Servant: It's not meant to be funny, I'm deadly serious.

Guest: A wedding banquet for the prince.

Servant: Indeed.

Guest: To be held at the palace.

Servant: You got it in one.

Guest: And I'm invited.

Servant: That's the general idea.

Guest: So how much do I have to pay?

Servant: Nothing, it's free.

Guest: No, really – how much are they asking for?

Servant: Nothing, nada, zip. No payment necessary.

Guest: So how much does it cost to get in?

Servant: You're not very good with this whole 'free' idea are you?

Guest: You don't get anything for free in this world.

Servant: Yes you do. Look, I'm begging you. I'll go down on my knees if you want. The king really, really wants you to come to the wedding banquet of the prince. It is free. Completely and utterly free. There are no strings attached, no forms to be filled in, no hidden extras. The king just wants you to come along and have a brilliant time. Will you come?

Guest: It's just that nobody's ever been this kind to me before. But if what you say is true then . . . *(Pause)* okay, I'll come.

Servant: YES!! Come on, it's time to join the party! *(Pulls out party blower and toots it – pulls Guest off excitedly.)*

SUNDAY BETWEEN 16 AND 22 OCTOBER INCLUSIVE

Matthew 22.15–22

CATCH ALL

(The two sections of this script are to be presented immediately before and after the Gospel reading. Two characters enter deep in conversation.)

Simon: Okay, okay, I've got it. What if we ask him about support for the Zealots. He'll never get out of that one.

Thomas: No, no, it's too obvious. It's been done before. If we're going to catch Jesus out we've got to be subtle, unexpected. I want something that's going to turn the people against him.

Simon: Just a minor question – why are we doing this?

Thomas: What do you mean?

Simon: What's our motivation? I mean here we are, spending all this energy on trying to catch Jesus out. Surely there are better ways to spend our time and resources?

Thomas: *(Suddenly ruthless)* You obviously haven't quite got this yet, which I can forgive you for. You're obviously not very intelligent. This Jesus is dangerous, incredibly dangerous, and we will stop at absolutely nothing to bring him down. Do I make myself clear?

Simon: *(Stunned)* Y . . . yes, of course. We need a trap. Something he'll never get out of. Something like power or money or . . .

Thomas: Money! That's it. What is it that the people hate doing more than anything else?

Simon: Paying taxes to Rome.

Thomas: But if Jesus says we shouldn't pay our taxes . . .

Simon: We've got him both ways – excellent!

(Reading of Matthew 22.15–22)

Thomas: I don't believe it! I thought you said it would work?

Simon: Hey, don't start blaming this on me. You're the one who came up with the idea.

Thomas: Tell me exactly what just happened?

Simon: I have no idea. I'm not even sure what he meant.

Thomas: Was it a clever get-out or a statement of belief?

Simon: Don't ask me. But the crowd seemed to like it.

Thomas: Yeah, why is that? They seemed to enjoy watching us being made to look stupid. It's almost as if they don't like us.

Simon: Well that's probably because they don't. I still can't believe how small he managed to make us look.

Thomas: Oh he's clever all right. More devious than I gave him credit for.

Simon: Why has it got to be deviousness?

Thomas: What do you mean?

Simon: Well what if he believed the things he said? That we should give God his due – worship and devotion, and give to Caesar the taxes that are due?

Thomas: Oh, so suddenly Jesus becomes a misunderstood hero.

Simon: His answer just seemed so sincere.

Thomas: Of course it did – he actually believes all this Son of Man nonsense and the people love him which makes it even more important that we crush him completely. We won't underestimate him again.

SUNDAY BETWEEN 23 AND 29 OCTOBER INCLUSIVE

Matthew 22.34–46

RALPH AND JIM ON COMMANDMENTS

(Ralph and Jim are sitting centrally.)

Ralph: Wotcha doin' Jim?

Jim: *(Distracted)* Oh, hello there Ralph.

Ralph: You seem to be in a pensive frame of mind Jim mate.

Jim: What's that then?

Ralph: Pensive Jim mate, thoughtful, pondering, considering great ideas.

Jim: Oh well, yeah I s'pose I am really.

Ralph: So, what great thought is zooming around in that massive and fertile brain of yours then?

Jim: Well, Ralphy boy, I was thinkin' about life.

Ralph: That's a pretty wide canvas to be spreadin' your thoughts on mate.

Jim: But more particular . . .

Ralph: Oh, we have particular thoughts, that's good.

Jim: More particularly on how we ought to live.

Ralph: Like what we ought to do?

Jim: Yeah, commandments an' all that. How should we live?

Ralph: Those are big thoughts Jim mate.

Jim: Big thoughts indeed Ralph.

Ralph: Y'know Jim mate, my old mother was a fount of knowledge when it came to wise words on how to live.

Jim: As was mine Ralphy boy.

Ralph: She'd say to me, 'Ralph', she'd say, 'eat the crusts on the toast boy, it'll make your hair nice an' curly.'

Jim: Wise words indeed Ralph mate.

Ralph: I like to think so Jim.

Jim: My old mum would often take me on her knee an' after she'd stubbed out her cigar she'd say, 'Jim, me little treasure, always look out for No. 1.'

Ralph: Yeah . . . I, ah, I hate to speak cruelly of your mother Jim mate, but are those actually words of wisdom or a really selfish way to live your life?

Jim: I could never figure that out either Ralph.

Ralph: The whole area is a bit confusing though, innit Jim?

Jim: Very confusing indeed Ralph.

Ralph: I mean, are we just grains of sand caught up in the great sandstorm of life, chaotically blown this way an' that?

Jim: Or are we masters of our own destiny – fully in control of our fate – accountable for our actions?

Ralph: Heavy stuff.

Jim: Heavy stuff indeed.

Ralph: 'Ere Jim – do you think God wants us to live our lives in particular ways?

Jim: My guess . . . and this is only a guess Ralph, is that God probably cares a great deal about how we live our lives.

Ralph: So what do you think God wants us to do then?

Jim: I think the word you're looking for, Ralph mate, is love. I think we need to love God an' love each other.

Ralph: You know Jim, that's so simple it might just catch on.

SUNDAY BETWEEN 30 OCTOBER AND 5 NOVEMBER INCLUSIVE

Matthew 22.34–46

BISHOP JOE

(Two actors – one dressed as a bishop – are standing centrally.)

Narrator: This is the story of Bishop Joe.

Bishop: Greetings and hello.

Narrator: Said Bishop Joe.

Bishop: I'm a wonderful person as you will see.

Narrator: Just as warm and as generous as can be.

Bishop: We all should be loving, generous and kind.

Narrator: The Bishop's words were good but the truth we must find.

Bishop: Look after the poor.

Narrator: Was the Bishop's law. But if you looked a little closer – something else you saw. For the Bishop said one thing and then did another.

Bishop: Everywhere and always you should love your brother.

Narrator: The Bishop was rather fond of saying, but in his deeds another truth was laying. The Bishop was only seen with folk who were rich.

Bishop: If you're poor you should just stay in the ditch.

Narrator: Were the unkind words which the Bishop thought. Then he went to his wealthy friends and passed the port. In public the Bishop said all the right stuff.

Bishop: Love the poor, the orphan – you can never give enough.

Narrator: He encouraged people to donate as much as they could.

Bishop: Give lots, give often, you know that you should.

Narrator: But his own personal giving to the plight of the poor was rather more akin to a locked tight door.

Bishop: I'm only a bishop, don't make a fuss.

Narrator: He said very loudly while riding the bus. But the Bishop was seen in all the best places.

Bishop: It helps to be photographed with all the right faces.

Narrator: He courted the rich, the powerful and greedy.

Bishop: I just don't have the time to think of the needy.

Narrator: Now don't get me wrong, he put on a good show.

Bishop: I pray long and loud for the sick and the low.

Narrator: But the words were just words – an expression of tact.

Bishop: If I really said what I thought I'm sure I'd be sacked.

Narrator: So he got all dressed up in his bishop's best.

Bishop: You know I even possess a purple vest.

Narrator: He had a very fetching bishop's hat.

Bishop: But I'm afraid my cassock makes me look fat.

Narrator: Yes, he loved all the fancy gold trimmings and braid.

Bishop: I'm sure that my glory will never ever fade.

Narrator: But God, I'm afraid, remained unimpressed.

Bishop: Does he not even like my purple vest?

Narrator: No, I'm afraid he doesn't give it much store. He really wants someone who lives by his law.

Bishop: That's easy, I've always pointed above.

Narrator: Yes, but what he's wanting are acts of mercy and love.

SUNDAY BETWEEN 6 AND 12 NOVEMBER INCLUSIVE

Matthew 25.1–13

BE PREPARED

(A lady is standing behind a desk. A man enters.)

Wendy: Can I help you sir?

Phil: Just show me where to board the plane and I'll be fine.

Wendy: Where to board what plane sir?

Phil: The flight to Hamburg.

Wendy: It left twenty minutes ago sir.

Phil: What? I don't believe it.

Wendy: You wouldn't happen to be Mr Griggs would you?

Phil: The very same.

Wendy: Well sir, we've been paging you for the last hour. Where have you been?

Phil: Well I ah . . .

Wendy: We held an entire planeload of people for you for twenty minutes.

Phil: Well that's very kind but it doesn't help me now does it?

Wendy: What happened?

Phil: Well there were some things that I'd forgotten to pack that I had to go and buy.

Wendy: Like what sir?

Phil: Well it's a bit embarrassing.

Wendy: Oh go on sir, I could do with a good laugh.

Phil: Socks, pants, deodorant, shampoo, a toothbrush, shirts, a jacket, a pair of trousers and a towel.

Wendy: Sounds like a complete wardrobe.

Phil: Pretty much. You see I wasn't ready when the taxi arrived this morning and I had to come out in a bit of a rush.

Wendy: Story of your life isn't it sir?

Phil: What is?

Wendy: Not being ready.

Phil: It is a bit, yes.

Wendy: But surely that wouldn't have made you an hour late.

Phil: Well no – then there was the quick forty winks.

Wendy: Forty winks?

Phil: Yes – I think it must have turned into eighty. And when I'm asleep, I'm *really* asleep.

Wendy: It would seem almost comatose.

Phil: I suppose so. And that pretty much brings us up to the present moment in time.

Wendy: Where you find out the flight you should have been on forty minutes ago left without you.

Phil: And the vitally important meeting I have to be at in Hamburg will now be missed. Which probably means I'll lose my job, and then my wife will leave me and my kids will end up hating me and I'll become a depressive recluse and . . .

Wendy: Perhaps a little dramatic sir. But it does underline one important point.

Phil: Oh yes – and what's that?

Wendy: Always, but always, be prepared.

SUNDAY BETWEEN 13 AND 19 NOVEMBER INCLUSIVE

Matthew 25.14–30

MAKE THE MOST OF IT

(An interviewer is sitting at a desk. A young woman enters.)

Interviewer: Welcome to Bridgetown College for the incredibly, wonderfully gifted, talented and blessed, Miss ah . . .

Rachael: Jennings. Rachael Jennings.

Interviewer: Yes of course. Now Rachael, which one of our incredibly sought after yet surprisingly cheap courses can we sign you up for?

Rachael: Well I don't know really. What have you got on offer?

Interviewer: What about our lessons in contemporary dance? They're very popular.

Rachael: Oh, I used to love dance. I was good at it too. Ballet, tap, jazz.

Interviewer: Great. I'll sign you up for it right away then.

Rachael: Oh no, I couldn't possibly. That was all ages ago – I haven't danced in years.

Interviewer: Okay. Well what about one of our advanced courses for gifted painters? You'll be the envy of all your friends.

Rachael: I was great at painting – my teacher said I had a real eye for colour.

Interviewer: Excellent.

Rachael: But I didn't do anything with it. I haven't painted since I was twelve years old.

Interviewer: What a shame. What about a master class in music then?

Rachael: You know I once did a test which showed I had the greatest musical ability in my class at school.

Interviewer: Wonderful.

Rachael: But I never had any lessons. It always seemed like I had better things to do.

Interviewer: Languages?

Rachael: Oh I had a real knack but . . .

Interviewer: Don't tell me – everybody spoke English so there didn't seem any point.

Rachael: Wow – how did you guess that? That's really spooky. Are you psychic or something?

Interviewer: Hardly – it just seems to be the story of your life doesn't it?

Rachael: What do you mean?

Interviewer: Well, think about it. Dance, painting, music, languages. Brilliant talents, wonderful skills and you've done nothing with any of them. You've squandered the lot.

Rachael: I think that's rather harsh. What I do with my life is my business.

Interviewer: Actually, Miss Jennings, no it's not, it's God's business. After all it was God who gave your gifts in the first place.

Rachael: Oh dear. Do you think he'll mind?

Interviewer: Well Miss Jennings – you've wasted an incredibly rich and varied set of wonderful gifts. What do you think?

Rachael: But I never had the time. There always seemed to be better things to do.

Interviewer: That's what they all say.

Rachael: So what can I do?

Interviewer: It's never too late to start making the best of yourself Miss Jennings, and it just so happens we have a course on making the most of things: sign here.

SUNDAY BETWEEN 20 AND 26 NOVEMBER INCLUSIVE

Matthew 25.31–46

IT'S DISTURBING!

(Two actors are sitting centrally.)

Voice 1: I've stopped reading the papers.
Voice 2: He has you know. Really he has.
Voice 1: Stopped watching the news on telly too.
Voice 2: Watches nothing but soap operas now.
Voice 1: Well it was all getting too much for me.
Voice 2: All far too much.
Voice 1: All that pain and suffering.
Voice 2: Starvation and death.
Voice 1: All those sunken, despairing eyes.
Voice 2: All those wasted, disease-ridden bodies.
Voice 1: Vast amounts of need traipsing into my living room every night.
Voice 2: Disturbing his ham, egg and chips.
Voice 1: Don't get me wrong.
Voice 2: No we wouldn't want you to get him wrong.
Voice 1: I'd like to do more.
Voice 2: More than nothing – which is what he does at the moment.
Voice 1: I just don't know where to start.
Voice 2: Making a start can be tough.
Voice 1: It all seems so huge.
Voice 2: So out of control.
Voice 1: What could one person possibly do to help?
Voice 2: What change could be made?
Voice 1: It's all just a drop in the ocean.
Voice 2: A vast, endless, ocean of need.
Voice 1: So I go to church.
Voice 2: Oh, he's very religious.
Voice 1: And I think about life.
Voice 2: Down on his knees.
Voice 1: And I ask Jesus to show himself to me.
Voice 2: 'Give me a sign!'
Voice 1: But nothing happens.
Voice 2: Nothing at all.
Voice 1: So I go back home and there are the eyes again. Staring out of the TV.
Voice 2: Searing through you. Pleading for help.
Voice 1: So where is Jesus in all of that?
Voice 2: After all – surely if there is a God he wouldn't allow all this pain to happen.
Voice 1: I mean, he can't need my help. Can he?
Voice 2: Perhaps he does.
Voice 1: But it's all so disturbing.
Voice 2: You might have to get your hands dirty.
Voice 1: And that would never do.
Voice 2: No, that would never do.
Voice 1: So I sit and wait because it's all so disturbing – and I do nothing.
Voice 2: And God weeps.

YEAR B

FIRST SUNDAY OF ADVENT

Mark 13.24–37

ADVENT SOAP – SUNSHINE BEACH 1

(In the style of an American soap opera – overacted.)

Jane: Jack, have you had the letter?

Jack: Not only the letter Jane, I've also had the phone call, the fax, the e-mail and the express package.

Jane: Oh no Jack. But . . . what does it all mean?

Jack: Well, I'll tell you Jane, I'm not sure. But I am sure of one thing, nothing is quite what it seems here on *Sunshine Beach*.

Jane: I'm just worried that something terrible is going to happen.

Jack: And you have every right to be concerned Jane. Mysterious events have been taking place for some time now.

Jane: Like when Dr Blake Jennings discovered his long-lost son living in a shack at the bottom of his garden and working in the local diner as a fast order chef?

Jack: That was kind of mysterious.

Jane: Or when Mrs Oppenheimer was abducted by Cuban terrorists and held to ransom and it was only then that we realized she was a secret operative for the CIA?

Jack: That too was pretty strange. But what I'm talking about Jane are the messages.

Jane: Messages Jack? What messages?

Jack: The messages you mentioned just a moment ago.

Jane: What? Oh yes, the letters.

Jack: Each one in its own way indicating that something important is going to happen.

Jane: What, like this one? *(She takes out a letter and reads.)* 'Something important is going to happen.'

Jack: There you go.

Jane: Or this one *(Takes out another)*, 'He is on his way.'

Jack: But who is on his way, and what does he want?

Jane: Oh Jack, I just feel like the end of the world is coming.

Jack: Well I don't know about that Jane. And anyway it would be foolish for us to speculate about when or how that dreaded day will come.

Jane: It would Jack?

Jack: Yes Jane I'm afraid it would. Worrying though our current crisis might be, it would be useless, useless I tell you, to try and predict when the end of the world will come.

Jane: So we just sit around and wait?

Jack: I didn't say that Jane. I think there are a number of things we could do.

Jane: Wonderful Jack. That makes me feel so much better. Tell me what I have to do and I'll do it.

Jack: Well Jane, we must prepare ourselves.

Jane: Prepare ourselves?

Jack: Yes, we must be ready when this stranger comes. Ready to welcome him into our homes, our very lives. We must be watchful Jane and full of hope, for who knows what might happen next on . . . *Sunshine Beach?*

SECOND SUNDAY OF ADVENT

Mark 1.1–8

ADVENT SOAP – SUNSHINE BEACH 2

(Jack and Lucille are standing centrally.)

Jack: You're going to have to calm down Lucille.

Lucille: I'm trying Jack, really I am, but it was madness, I tell you, madness.

Jack: Well, as ruggedly handsome odd-job man Jack Bannon, I've got used to the kind of madness that we see daily down here on *Sunshine Beach*.

Lucille: I realize that Jack. I also know that as Lucille DuPrez, resident oddball, I have to roll my eyes and look crazy every episode. But believe me, nothing's ever been as strange as this.

Jack: Tell me everything Lucille. I may be able to help.

Lucille: Well you know that the town's been all shook up about these messages that have been arriving?

Jack: Messages like, 'Something important is going to happen'.

Lucille: And 'He is on his way'.

Jack: What about the messages Lucille?

Lucille: Well, three days ago, a man came into town. A preacher man. His eyes were wilder than mine, and he had an interesting taste in clothes.

Jack: Sounds strange.

Lucille: There's more Jack. He started talking and his words just made me go goose bumpy all over.

Jack: Just a minute Lucille, wild eyes, odd clothes, strange but intoxicating words . . . you don't think he could be the one do you? The one the messages are talking about?

Lucille: He says not.

Jack: You don't mean he's talking about all of this?

Lucille: Yes I do Jack, I do indeed.

Jack: Stranger and stranger. What could this mystery man want?

Lucille: And what is he doing here on *Sunshine Beach*?

Jack: Did he say nothing Lucille? Nothing at all that would help us to discover what's going on?

Lucille: Oh I don't know Jack, it's all so hazy in my mind.

Jack: Think Lucille, think. You could be the key to this whole mystery.

Lucille: Don't pile the pressure on too much will you?

Jack: I'm sorry Lucille, but we have to know.

Lucille: Wait a minute, something's coming back to me.

Jack: Yes? YES!? Oh the tension, I can hardly stand it.

Lucille: He said something about another.

Jack: 'Another'? What did he mean?

Lucille: I think somebody else is on his way. I think this preacher man, whoever he is, is just preparing the way, getting things ready for someone far bigger, far more important.

Jack: So the real mystery man is on his way then?

Lucille: It seems so Jack.

Jack: Well Lucille, my manly bottom lip is quivering in anticipation. What will the coming of this mystery man mean for all of us here? We only know that drama and change are constant here on . . . *Sunshine Beach*.

THIRD SUNDAY OF ADVENT

John 1.6–8, 19–28

ADVENT SOAP – SUNSHINE BEACH 3

(Doc Jennings is on stage. Jane enters.)

Doc: Well hello there Jane.

Jane: Hi Doc Jennings.

Doc: What can I do for you?

Jane: Well Doc, you're so old and wise I thought you might be able to help me.

Doc: Well Jane, it's true I've been your family doctor for as long as I can remember. My wise words and twinkle in the eye are a way of life here on . . . *Sunshine Beach.*

Jane: You're a truly great man Doc.

Doc: Well Jane I don't know about that, but it doesn't seem five minutes ago that I was bouncing you up and down on my knee and picking the lice out of your hair.

Jane: Thanks Doc . . . that's a lovely picture. But I'm not here to reminisce about old times. There's something I want to ask you.

Doc: Fire away Jane, I'm all ears.

Jane: It's about the preacher man who's arrived in town.

Doc: Oh yes, now I've heard about him. Causing quite a commotion from what I hear.

Jane: You hear right Doc Jennings. And I must admit I am powerfully moved by the words he says.

Doc: Powerfully moved?

Jane: Powerfully moved.

Doc: So what is this message that's got you all shaken and stirred?

Jane: It's a message of hope.

Doc: Well we could all use a little more of that in this topsy-turvy, upside down kind of world.

Jane: But it's also about a man who is coming.

Doc: Not this man of mystery I've been hearing so much about?

Jane: The very same Doc.

Doc: A man who's going to turn our lives upside down?

Jane: That's the one.

Doc: A man who knows what's what and who's not afraid to say so?

Jane: I couldn't put it better myself.

Doc: A man full of courage, honesty and love?

Jane: I can hardly wait!

Doc: But you're going to have to, aren't you Jane?

Jane: I am?

Doc: Well from what I hear Sheriff Pikestaff and Deputy Dooby asked this preacher man whether he was the one we were waiting for or not and he said 'No'.

Jane: No?

Doc: That's right – the man we're waiting for is still to come.

Jane: Oh Doc – I can hardly stand it. The drama! The tension! The waiting!

Doc: I know Jane, I know. But take it from me, drama, tension and waiting, they're all part of everyday life down here on . . . *Sunshine Beach.*

FOURTH SUNDAY OF ADVENT

Luke 1. 26–38

ADVENT SOAP – SUNSHINE BEACH 4

(Jack and Doc are standing centrally.)

Jack: I don't know Doc, I just don't know.

Doc: Look, Jack, how many years have I known you? I've brought your kids into the world. I treated you when you had that mysterious non-specific yet life threatening illness last month. When you got involved in the dramatic motor-bike crashing into a supermarket trolley incident last year which involved three tear-filled weeks of you lying on a hospital bed, your life dangling by a thread – I was the one who sat by your side. You trusted me then, I need you to trust me now.

Jack: Okay Doc, okay. Your twinkling smile and gentle winning ways have become a way of life down here on . . . *Sunshine Beach*. If you say there's nothing to be worried about with the arrival of this mysterious stranger – then I'll believe you.

Doc: That's the Jack Bannon, ruggedly handsome odd-job man that I've come to know and respect.

Jack: It's just that Lucille and Jane have got themselves all riled up about this preacher man who's come to town.

Doc: I know Jack, I know. It does seem mighty strange and full of tension but I'm sure that the one we're waiting for; the one this preacher man seems to be pointing the way towards – I'm sure this stranger who is on his way will be just what we need.

Jack: You think so Doc?

Doc: Look Jack, sometimes you've just got to trust.

Jack: You do?

Doc: Absolutely. You know Jack, you can't always see the way ahead, things just don't seem like they could ever work out. Sometimes what you're being told seems so incredible, so unbelievable that you can't see how it could ever happen.

Jack: That's pretty much how I feel now Doc.

Doc: Well Jack it's at times like this that you have to have some faith – some belief in God.

Jack: I didn't know you were a religious man Doc.

Doc: Oh, always have been Jack. Always have been. And there's not many things in this topsy-turvy world that I know for sure, but there is one.

Jack: Oh yeah Doc, and what's that?

Doc: It's just this – God needs people of faith, people who will say 'Yes', and just get on and do what God wants. You don't need to be a rocket scientist, you just need to believe. It's not always going to be easy, sometimes what God asks is going to seem impossible, crazy. But what God needs is for us to say 'Yes'.

Jack: Saying 'Yes' to God . . . I like the sound of that.

Doc: I knew you would Jack, and when we do that the most incredible, wonderful things can happen, because it's then that God comes to earth.

Jack: It sounds amazing Doc.

Doc: It is Jack, even more amazing than daily life here on . . . *Sunshine Beach*.

CHRISTMAS DAY

Luke 2.8–20

WHAT A NIGHT!

(Santa and Rudolph are on stage.)

Santa: What a night Rudolph – I'm shattered.

Rudolph: You're telling me Santa. I'm getting too old for this.

Santa: Racing around the world in one evening certainly isn't getting any easier.

Rudolph: And I swear that sleigh is getting heavier every year.

Santa: That's because it is.

Rudolph: You know, I knew there was something wrong. It's because we're making more deliveries isn't it?

Santa: Well it's not just that. The demands are getting heavier every year as well.

Rudolph: Kids are never satisfied are they? Little rotters everyone of them.

Santa: Anyone would think Christmas was a competition about how much money could be spent.

Rudolph: And the presents people ask for! Battle Man Sam and his tactical nuclear missile launcher – how Christmassy!

Santa: Or the Crimp and Bead Sandy doll with her Malibu Beach house complete with Jacuzzi, luxury sports car and wardrobe full of the very latest designer label clothes.

Rudolph: The one I hated was the 'My Little Hijacker' set, plane, bombs, demands and batteries included.

Santa: Or what about 'Titanic: Sink or Swim', the board game?

Rudolph: People eat too much.

Santa: Drink too much.

Rudolph: Spend too much on presents they can't afford.

Santa: It's all very sad.

Rudolph: People just don't think do they?

Santa: Only about themselves.

Rudolph: There's so much love that could be shared.

Santa: Joy that could be given.

Rudolph: The thought of a baby born in a stable.

Santa: The idea of God come into the world.

Rudolph: When you think about it it's incredible. God, the creator of everything, coming down into creation. It's a wonderful thing.

Santa: Bit of a scary kind of revolutionary thing too.

Rudolph: I suppose so.

Santa: I mean if God really has come to earth . . .

Rudolph: Then humans had better take that seriously and change their lives.

Santa: And that's far too difficult.

Rudolph: Far easier to believe in characters like you and me.

Santa: Or snowmen.

Rudolph: Or red robins.

Santa: I'm afraid, Rudolph, we don't pose much of a threat.

Rudolph: No, we're far too easy going.

Santa: We don't make people think about God and religion.

Rudolph: That's funny that – you being a Saint an' all.

Santa: About as funny as my aching back – come on Rudolph, let's have a cuppa.

FIRST SUNDAY OF CHRISTMAS

Luke 2.22–40

INCARNATE

(Jerome and Roberto are Catholic monks and are standing centrally.)

Jerome: I'm sorry Brother Roberto, I just can't let you do this.

Roberto: But Father Jerome, have you seen the back streets of the city? Young boys, young girls with nothing to do, trouble around every corner.

Jerome: Which is exactly why I cannot let you go Roberto. Look, I know you want to help them.

Roberto: I want to be with them. To stand alongside them.

Jerome: I realize that, but have you any idea of the danger you'd be putting yourself in?

Roberto: I know that there is violence . . .

Jerome: Not just violence Roberto, four murders in the last month alone.

Roberto: Imagine, then, the danger those young people are in. No hope, preyed upon by gangs, drawn into crime, their lives destroyed in every way possible.

Jerome: And I would never forgive myself Roberto if you went to minister to those young people and something happened to you.

Roberto: In other words Father Jerome you are not prepared to take the risk.

Jerome: No I am not.

Roberto: But surely our faith is in a God who takes risks all the time?

Jerome: That is not the point.

Roberto: It is exactly the point. How can these young people believe that God cares for them, that God loves them, if they cannot see and feel that love for themselves?

Jerome: And what if they turn on you Roberto?

Roberto: Then they turn on me, but at least I will have shown them something of God's love. How can I help these young people, Father Jerome, unless I live with them? Stand by them? Feel what they feel. Experience what they experience?

Jerome: So you take the risk. You go down to those God forsaken back streets with their filth and grime and poverty and disease. You try to befriend those young people that you care so much about. They are not interested. Not interested in you or the Church. They do not want to know.

Roberto: That is only because they have never been shown. And I repeat, Father Jerome, I am ready to take the chance, ready to risk all for those young people. They deserve better than they have, they deserve hope. They deserve to know that God identifies with them, that God loves them.

Jerome: And the only way for that to happen is for them to see you living their life. All right, all right, you have worn me down. You may go.

Roberto: Thank you Father Jerome. Thank you.

Jerome: Do not be too quick to thank me Roberto – living their life, sharing their griefs and pains, is going to bring you much heartache.

Roberto: I will not let you down.

Jerome: I am sure you won't. But I think we will both discover, Brother Roberto, how much pain there is in true love. You are like a son to me and if anything happens to you it will break my heart, God speed. *(Roberto exits.)*

SECOND SUNDAY OF CHRISTMAS

John 1. (1–9) 10–18

HERE IS THE NEWS

(Two newsreaders are sitting centrally.)

Newsreader 1:	Good morning.
Newsreader 2:	Good morning, here is the news.
Newsreader 1:	I am a child of God.
Newsreader 2:	I'm sorry?
Newsreader 1:	I am a child of God.
Newsreader 2:	Aren't we meant to be talking about interest rates?
Newsreader 1:	Yes, I'm sure we are.
Newsreader 2:	Followed by a story about a potential strike amongst postal workers?
Newsreader 1:	Oh, probably.
Newsreader 2:	So why are you talking about being a child of God?
Newsreader 1:	Because this is more interesting.
Newsreader 2:	It is?
Newsreader 1:	Oh yes, and it's a bit of good news for a change.
Newsreader 2:	Good news?
Newsreader 1:	Of course. Don't you get a bit tired of telling people bad news?
Newsreader 2:	What are you talking about?
Newsreader 1:	Well look at tonight's news – after the postal workers' strike we've got a story about a murder in Colchester, a feared armed uprising in Indonesia and flooding in Devon. It's miserable.
Newsreader 2:	But that's how life is.
Newsreader 1:	It needn't be. Life can be enriching and exciting and fun.
Newsreader 2:	But then it wouldn't be news.
Newsreader 1:	That's rather sad isn't it? Let me ask you a question. Are you happy?
Newsreader 2:	I beg your pardon?
Newsreader 1:	Well we've known each other for five or six years – read bad news to the nation every night week in and week out – after all that, are you happy?
Newsreader 2:	I'm not sure that's a question I can answer.
Newsreader 1:	Look, I'm not trying to trick you. Before we get on to all the bad news tonight I just wanted to tell people that I am a child of God.
Newsreader 2:	And that's a good thing is it?
Newsreader 1:	It's wonderful.
Newsreader 2:	It all sounds a bit religious to me.
Newsreader 1:	Why are you so frightened of that? Are you afraid I might be right?
Newsreader 2:	No it's not that.
Newsreader 1:	My problems haven't all magically disappeared or anything like that. It's just my life has a focus, a centre it was missing before.
Newsreader 2:	It just sounds very demanding.
Newsreader 1:	No – it's about being freed to see life as it really is.
Newsreader 2:	So where does that leave today's news?
Newsreader 1:	Do you think we ought to get back to it?
Newsreader 2:	I think we do, yes.
Newsreader 1:	I just wanted to give people a little hope.
Newsreader 2:	People don't want hope, they want news . . . *(Reads)* Fifteen people are still being held hostage in Algeria tonight as tensions rise . . . *(Freeze.)*

SUNDAY BETWEEN 7 AND 13 JANUARY INCLUSIVE

Mark 1.4–11

THE PHONE-IN

(The DJ is sitting on one side – the caller on the other.)

Mike: You're listening to All Talk Radio on 57.4 FM and I'm your host for the next hour, Mike Savage. We're talking about all that's new and exciting here in the Jordan area and I've got Mandy on the line. So Mandy, what do you want to say?

Mandy: Oh, hello Mike, hello Mum. Actually Mike I wanted to talk about the traffic problem we've got down by Jordan's shore at the moment.

Mike: Ah yes, I gather it's been pretty crowded down there the past few days.

Mandy: Crowded isn't the word Mike. It's not the word at all. You can't move, you can't breathe. It takes an age to get anywhere; it's awful, that's what it is, awful. We used to be a nice quiet community down here. It's a residential area you know.

Mike: So why the sudden rush to Jordan's beautiful shores Mandy?

Mandy: Well it's that man isn't it? Unkempt weirdo.

Mike: Whoah, that's pretty strong. Who are we talking about? What's causing all the hassle?

Mandy: Well I don't like to criticize, I mean we were all students once weren't we?

Mike: Well, not everyone, but I know what you mean.

Mandy: About three weeks ago this bloke calling himself John popped out of nowhere. Long hair, wearing the most disgusting set of rags you've ever seen. And as for his diet, well don't even get me started on what I've seen him eating.

Mike: But I don't see why one harmless hippie is causing traffic gridlock.

Mandy: He's preaching, Mike.

Mike: *(Sarcastically)* Well that really explains it.

Mandy: No, I mean really powerful. He calls people sinners and vipers and all sorts. Ordinary, decent people who never said boo to a goose.

Mike: Doesn't sound much of a turn-on to me.

Mandy: And then there's the water.

Mike: The water?

Mandy: Yeah, he dunks them under the water – says it's to cleanse them of their sin and wickedness.

Mike: And people are lapping this up?

Mandy: Oh absolutely. There are crowds down here every day. They start turning up early in the morning – queuing up to get a better view.

Mike: And you're telling me that all he does is tell them how terrible they are then wash them?

Mandy: That's it.

Mike: Well I've heard it all now folks. People flocking to be told how useless they are, getting dipped in river water by some mystery preacher. Just a sign of the times perhaps, or is this the build-up to some greater madness still to come? None of us really thinks we're full of sin do we? Surely we're all just average folks trying to make a living? Why don't you ring in and share your views on 55532187?

SUNDAY BETWEEN 14 AND 20 JANUARY INCLUSIVE

John 1.43–51

COLD CALL

(Fran is sitting on one side talking on a phone. Robert sits on the other side.)

Fran: Good evening, is that Mr Barker of 23 Sycamore Drive?

Robert: It is.

Fran: I wonder whether I could have a moment of your time?

Robert: Well actually I'm rather busy at the . . .

Fran: Good. I'm calling from 'Follow Jesus Now'. Have you ever thought about becoming a disciple of our Lord and Saviour?

Robert: Well I . . .

Fran: Can I ask you this sir? Do you currently, or have you ever been to church?

Robert: Well I used to go.

Fran: Used to sir? Well that's not very good is it?

Robert: Well I suppose not but . . .

Fran: Did you know sir that several churches in your area are running special missionary activities at the moment particularly for sinners like you?

Robert: Wait a minute, that's a bit harsh.

Fran: Would you like me to sign you up sir? If you like rock music then the band 'Wretched Sinner' are playing at St Michael's on Thursday night next week. Tickets are very reasonably priced at £17.50. Shall I put you down for two or three?

Robert: No.

Fran: Well what about our speciality evening – Sylvester Trout and his Amazing Spoons of Faith? I hear he's very good. And that one might be more in your price range. Tickets start at an incredible £7.80.

Robert: I don't think so.

Fran: Well there's always Gracie Pointer and her Homely Gospel Homilies, an evening of fun and inspiration for all the family and not at all sentimental. Family tickets available at the give-away price of £26 for four.

Robert: I'm really not interested.

Fran: If I might say so sir, your negative attitude is not very helpful and contrary to the standard of gospel love – I shall pray for you.

Robert: Look I'm actually quite interested in finding out more about Jesus.

Fran: You are?

Robert: Yes but you've not told me anything about it. All you've tried to do is sell me things.

Fran: Well I er . . .

Robert: Look, how do you find it? Do you find faith easy? Difficult? What's your honest opinion?

Fran: Ooohh, well . . .

Robert: I'm wanting to give my all, but I want to be sure it's the real thing. I want to be challenged to a real commitment to something that's going to change my life. Can you do that?

Fran: Ahh well Mr Barker. Thank you very much for that interesting set of questions. Can you just hold the line a moment while I get my supervisor?

Robert: If it's not personal to you I don't want to know. Goodbye.

SUNDAY BETWEEN 21 AND 27 JANUARY INCLUSIVE

Mark 1.14–20

HELLO, I MUST BE GOING

(James and Dan enter deep in conversation.)

Dan: So then, James, I'll see you later then.

James: Well actually Dan, I don't think I'm going to be able to make it.

Dan: What do you mean, 'not make it' – you always join us down at the beach for some wine at the end of the day.

James: Well, not today Dan. I really ought to go home and spend some time with Ruth.

Dan: Uh-oh – have you two had a row? Keeping the wife happy eh?

James: Actually, no we haven't had a row, but I think we may be about to have one.

Dan: What have you been up to? You naughty boy.

James: It's nothing like that Dan. I've got to tell Ruth that I'm going away and I just don't know how she's going to handle it, that's all.

Dan: You're what?!

James: Going away Dan – do I have to tell you *all* my business?

Dan: That's what childhood friends do. Remember, 'no secrets'. And there's no need to bite my head off.

James: Oh, look Dan, I'm sorry. It's just that some pretty incredible stuff has happened today and I don't know how I'm going to tell Ruth about it, that's all.

Dan: What's going on James? You've always told me everything.

James: You know that guy who was down at the boats today?

Dan: Yeah, I've seen him around.

James: Well his name's Jesus – he's a preacher.

Dan: That's all Galilee needs, another travelling do-gooder.

James: Dan, this one's different.

Dan: Oh yeah, how so? He going to give us money is he? Or kick out the Romans? How about putting food on the table?

James: Will you stop? He is different. There's something in his eyes.

Dan: Oh, it's his eyes.

James: Yes, and his words. They cut through you like a knife, they move you.

Dan: Well what with the words and the eyes – who could resist?

James: I couldn't. I'm going with him.

Dan: You're WHAT?!

James: He leaves town tomorrow and I'm going with him.

Dan: Are you mad? What about the business? You're surely not going to leave it to John to look after are you?

James: No, because John's coming with me.

Dan: I need to sit down. Have you lost your mind?

James: No, I think I might finally have found it.

Dan: So where are you going?

James: He didn't say.

Dan: How long for?

James: He didn't say that either.

Dan: James, I just hope you know what you're doing. *(They exit talking.)*

SUNDAY BETWEEN 28 JANUARY AND 3 FEBRUARY INCLUSIVE

Mark 1.21–28

AUTHORITY

(Rebecca enters. Benjamin is sitting centrally.)

Rebecca: How are you feeling dear? A little better?

Benjamin: *(Rather pathetic)* Yes, I think I am a little better thank you.

Rebecca: That's good, only we wouldn't want you spreading those nasty germs around would we? Probably best that you didn't come to synagogue this morning although they were all asking after you.

Benjamin: That's nice of them.

Rebecca: Isn't it just? But you're going to be sorry you weren't there. You missed such a commotion. Mrs Goldstein had to be given smelling salts.

Benjamin: Whatever happened?

Rebecca: Well there were some new faces at the service this morning. Such a nice looking young man and his little band of helpers. 'Disciples' I think he called them.

Benjamin: It's always good to see new faces.

Rebecca: That's exactly what I said. 'Let him speak' I said. Well it's got to be better than the usual words of wisdom that we get.

Benjamin: Silas tries hard mother.

Rebecca: He's a fool Benjamin and you know it. You are twice the man he his. Anyway, this nice young man says he'd be happy to have a word with us all. And when he opened his mouth and spoke, oi, it was wonderful. Wonderful, you could almost feel the message coming down from heaven. The words were so powerful and he said them with such authority. Like he personally knew their truth.

Benjamin: It sounds extraordinary.

Rebecca: Oh it was, Benjamin, it was. I was just sorry you couldn't be there. Unlike some other people I could mention.

Benjamin: Don't tell me Eli was there.

Rebecca: He certainly was. And he said the strangest thing. He burst in at the back and shouted out – ooh it sent shivers down my spine.

Benjamin: So what did he say then?

Rebecca: 'Jesus' he says – that's the young man's name – 'Jesus, what do you want with us? I know who you are – God's Holy One.'

Benjamin: Are you sure that's what he said?

Rebecca: Look, I'm old, but I'm not deaf. Anyway, Jesus turns round, calm as you like, and just says 'Come out of him.' Well Eli shakes, gives the most awful cry, and then collapses on the floor, quiet as a mouse.

Benjamin: So what on earth does all of that mean?

Rebecca: I don't know. But Mrs Cohen said what if Eli was right? What if Jesus really is the Holy One?

Benjamin: Mother, you can't be serious.

Rebecca: Perhaps not. But you weren't there Benjamin. I've never seen such power, such easy authority. As though he naturally expected everything to obey him. You mark my words, we haven't seen the last of Jesus.

Benjamin: I just wish I could have been there.

Rebecca: I know. Let me make you some nice hot broth dear. *(Benjamin winces.)*

SUNDAY BETWEEN 4 AND 10 FEBRUARY INCLUSIVE

Mark 1.29–39

EXPECTATIONS

(Two actors are standing centrally.)

One: Words.
Two: Hands.
One: Bodies.
Two: Pressing down on you.
One: Searching you out.
Two: Grabbing.
One: Reaching.
Two: Clawing.
One: Heal me!
Two: Touch me.
One: Transform me.
Two: Turn my life around.
One: Let me feel your power.
Two: Come on Jesus, I know you can do it.
One: Just one word is all I need.
Two: A smile.
One: A hand laid on my head.
Two: I don't ask for much.
One: No more than anybody else.
Two: My need is just as great as theirs.
One: Just one more, Jesus
Two: I've been waiting all day.
One: I can hardly walk.
Two: Give me your time.
One: Give me your power.
Two: Give me your love.
One: I don't expect miracles.
Two: But I do expect healing.
One: After all you're meant to be special aren't you?
Two: That's what I've heard.
One: From everybody else.
Two: So show me.
One: Display your power.
Two: Let me see what all the fuss is about.
One: Give me a good show. *(Slight pause)*
Two: I expected more, to be honest.
One: He wasn't what I thought.
Two: It's all a little bit disappointing.
One: But then comes the burning thought.
Two: The uncomfortable question.
One: We expected a lot of him.
Two: But we didn't stop to wonder.
One: Or ask.
Two: Did he expect anything of us?

SUNDAY BETWEEN 11 AND 17 FEBRUARY INCLUSIVE

Mark 1.40–45

THANK YOU

(Two story-tellers come forward – speaking as they walk.)

Voice 1: This is the tale of Gretchen Small.
Voice 2: She was the kindest person anywhere at all.
Voice 1: She loved little children, visited the poor.
Voice 2: 'Be the best person you can be' was her lifelong law.
Voice 1: If you were ill there was no need to shout.
Voice 2: Gretchen was there to tend to your gout.
Voice 1: She constantly went the extra mile.
Voice 2: She was loving, she was kind, there was no guile.
Voice 1: Then one day, to Gretchen, came a man.
Voice 2: He said, 'You know my dear I'm a very great fan.'
Voice 1: 'I've heard of your good works, thought you were a fable.'
Voice 2: 'Please you must help me if you are able.'
Voice 1: The man told Gretchen his very sad tale.
Voice 2: He really was ill and all cures had failed.
Voice 1: Gretchen was terribly moved by his plight.
Voice 2: 'I'll help if I can – it's only right.'
Voice 1: She showed the man love. Cared night and day.
Voice 2: His disease was terrible. It made people say . . .
Voice 1: 'Uerrghh! You're horrible, keep out of our sight.'
Voice 2: All the poor man wanted was to walk in the light.
Voice 1: His twisted limbs were all most people could see.
Voice 2: But Gretchen was different and went down on her knees.
Voice 1: She bathed the man's sores, did all that she could.
Voice 2: He was overwhelmed to find somebody good.
Voice 1: He began to feel better, felt the need to repay
Voice 2: All the kindness and love that he'd felt each day.
Voice 1: However, Gretchen was certain – her voice it was clear
Voice 2: 'I want no one to know what happened here.'
Voice 1: 'I long to be helpful, enjoy sharing love.'
Voice 2: 'Want to point people to my Father above.'
Voice 1: 'But if you draw attention to what I have done'
Voice 2: 'There'll be people all over me, no place to run.'
Voice 1: 'So please, don't tell of what's happened to you'
Voice 2: 'Just go out and live a life that is new.'
Voice 1: I'm afraid to say that the man did not do that.
Voice 2: His good news could not be kept under a hat.
Voice 1: He trumpeted his healing far and near.
Voice 2: And people pressed round Gretchen wanting to peer.
Voice 1: At this wonderful young woman with a gift of healing.
Voice 2: They couldn't care less what she was feeling.
Voice 1: The man didn't realize what he had done.
Voice 2: He wanted to share that his life was now fun.
Voice 1: And that is the tale of Gretchen Small.
Voice 2: Whose own life is, sadly, no longer a ball.

SUNDAY BETWEEN 18 AND 24 FEBRUARY INCLUSIVE

Mark 2.1–12

DO YOU BELIEVE IT?

(Reg and Jacob are sitting in a television studio.)

Reg: Good evening folks, welcome to *Do you believe it?* A programme where we look at the, frankly, ridiculous things people claim and pour on liberal quantities of scorn and doubt. And have we got a ludicrous claim for you tonight. Meet Jacob.

Jacob: Hello Reg.

Reg: Evening Jacob. You're looking very well this evening.

Jacob: I'm feeling very fine thank you.

Reg: No aches or pains?

Jacob: Fit as a fiddle.

Reg: Not even a twinge or two?

Jacob: Uhhhh . . . no.

Reg: Which is rather odd isn't it Jacob?

Jacob: What do you mean?

Reg: Well forgive me for mentioning this but don't you claim to have been a complete and utter invalid when the sun rose this morning?

Jacob: Indeed I was.

Reg: In fact I wouldn't be too far off the mark if I said that this morning you were completely paralysed.

Jacob: That is correct.

Reg: Hasn't anybody ever told you that paralysed means not being able to move? And didn't you walk into our studios this evening? I mean if this is an insurance scam Jacob I think you've just blown it.

Jacob: It is absolutely true Reg that this morning I couldn't move at all. Indeed I was confined to bed.

Reg: So supposedly something miraculous has happened?

Jacob: Not supposedly – it has.

Reg: And you're going to tell me that the new wonder-man healer Jesus is something to do with this are you?

Jacob: Jesus healed me, yes.

Reg: So he came to see you did he?

Jacob: No, I have very good friends who took me to see Jesus.

Reg: If you don't mind me asking, how?

Jacob: They carried me there on my bed. But when we got there the room was so crowded that we couldn't get anywhere near. So my friends hoisted me up onto the roof, dug a hole in it and lowered me down so that I could see Jesus.

Reg: This story gets better by the minute. We're now adding wanton vandalism to the list of far-fetched events.

Jacob: You're obviously having problems believing all of this Reg.

Reg: You bet I am.

Jacob: Well let me introduce you to the four friends who took me to see Jesus, the crowd of fifty-six people who were crammed into that little room and the five teachers of the law who also witnessed the whole thing. *(He gestures.)*

Reg: *(Completely taken aback)* Oh.

SUNDAY BETWEEN 25 AND 29 FEBRUARY INCLUSIVE

Mark 2.13–22

PASSING THE BLAME

(Two elderly women enter and sit down.)

Irene: I was just having a chat with Phyllis over there.

Dora: Oh, is that your friend? I didn't see her there.

Irene: Oh yeah, she's just sat down over there, but I'll sit here.

Dora: Well if you want to sit by her . . .

Irene: No, I'm fine here.

Dora: *(Fishing in her pockets)* Do you want a mint?

Irene: Oh ta. *(Opens newspaper and reads.)* Have you seen this here?

Dora: No, what?

Irene: About this girl with the two young kiddies? Oh it's awful. She spends no time with them, no time at all.

Dora: Doesn't she?

Irene: No. It's wicked.

Dora: Oh dear.

Irene: People don't think do they?

Dora: No they don't. You're right.

Irene: She's probably out at all times of the day and night.

Dora: Coming back at all hours.

Irene: How the kiddies are meant to cope I don't know.

Dora: They'll be running wild.

Irene: Playing truant. Doing drugs.

Dora: The paper says all of that does it?

Irene: Well not in so many words, but you can tell.

Dora: That's right, you can always tell.

Irene: It reminds me of our Janice and the mess she's made of her life.

Dora: Oh it's an absolute mess isn't it?

Irene: I told her. I said, 'If you keep carrying on like that you'll have no one but yourself to blame.' But did she listen to me? Her own grandmother?

Dora: I don't s'pose she did.

Irene: She did not. Just kept hanging around with that good-for-nothing Phil. And his family, well they're terrible Dora, absolutely terrible. Layabouts the lot of them.

Dora: Oh dear.

Irene: I said, 'Can't you see the kind of people you're hanging around with?'. 'Leave them well alone,' I said.

Dora: But of course she won't.

Irene: You're right there Dora love and no mistake.

Dora: It's a terrible state the country – isn't it?

Irene: Teenage mothers.

Dora: Crime and violence.

Irene: People just don't care any more.

Dora: There's so much wickedness.

Irene: They all deserve to rot in jail.

Dora: Now that we've put the world to rights we'd better be getting on.

Irene: You're quite right, the Ladies' Fellowship will have started without us.

SUNDAY BEFORE LENT

Mark 9.2–9

CHANGING LIVES

(Two TV presenters are on stage.)

Gloria:	Well hello there and welcome back to *Changing Lives*. Here's our transformations' expert Theodore Ruskin.
Theodore:	Greetings.
Gloria:	Now Theodore before the break we had a look at the life of this week's guest, Trudy from Weston-super-Mare. What did you make of her?
Theodore:	Oh Gloria love. Where to start? Where to start? It's all so desperate.
Gloria:	Surely there was something that you can work on?
Theodore:	No it's all too, too horrible. We're going to have to go back to basics.
Gloria:	I see. So what about her clothes?
Theodore:	Well all of the nasty little things that she's wearing at the moment have got to go. They're hideous. We're going to have to get her quickly to the most expensive fashion boutiques London has to offer and spend obscene amounts of money on a completely new wardrobe for her.
Gloria:	What kind of clothes will you be looking for?
Theodore:	Black ones.
Gloria:	Black?
Theodore:	Nothing but black.
Gloria:	I see. What about her overall appearance?
Theodore:	That needs to be transformed too. I don't know how she can walk out of the house in the morning looking the way she does.
Gloria:	And I guess that will need lots of money too.
Theodore:	Oh but of course. New hair, new make-up, new posture, new everything, darling. We can get away with nothing less.
Gloria:	And her living space?
Theodore:	Well it's a quaint little terrace house in a seaside town if you like that kind of thing but really what she needs is a studio apartment in Kensington.
Gloria:	But isn't that going to be horribly expensive?
Theodore:	Of course, but this programme is watched by millions of people every week. We're the second most popular programme this channel makes which means we've got all the money we want.
Gloria:	I sometimes think about that Theodore.
Theodore:	Think about what dear?
Gloria:	Well, why exactly do you think we are so popular? I mean we're not very nice to people are we?
Theodore:	Of course we're not. But then we're not very nice people are we?
Gloria:	No I suppose we're not.
Theodore:	Look Gloria, think of all the other makeover shows on the telly. New hairstyles, new homes, new gardens, new cooking skills – why do people want all of that? Because they don't like their lives the way they are that's why. They feel like their lives should be better than this, need to be transformed, and they turn to us for help.
Gloria:	But what if they found some*body* who could *really* transform their lives?
Theodore:	Then, my dear, you and I would be out of a job. Now come along, Trudy needs our help to turn her life around.

FIRST SUNDAY IN LENT

Mark 1.9–15

THE LENT CASES – 1 TEMPTATION

(Inspector Riley and PC Clegg are sitting centrally.)

Riley: So then Clegg, what do we know?

Clegg: They're going to be late, Inspector Riley.

Riley: Late, what do you mean late?

Clegg: It'll be about an hour.

Riley: Do they know that we have a major murder investigation going on? Do they realize that time is of the essence? Do they have the faintest idea how vital they are to the smooth running of this enquiry?

Clegg: Well they did say that they'd have the jam doughnuts ready by half past.

Riley: What about those maple pecan Danish pastries that I like so much?

Clegg: Not until tomorrow.

Riley: This is ridiculous Clegg. I need my baked goods in the morning. I need doughnuts concealing jammy centres, I need currant buns, I need big chocolate chip cookies, I need chocolate éclairs oozing cream.

Clegg: Don't forget the caffeine sir.

Riley: Well it goes without saying PC Clegg that I also need coffee by the bucketful – and none of your decaffeinated nonsense. Is that clear?

Clegg: 100 per cent sir.

Riley: This is not a good start to the day Clegg, not a good start at all.

Clegg: I can quite see that Inspector Riley.

Riley: So where are we with the case then?

Clegg: Another three break-ins last night sir – again all of them taking the TV set, computer and hi-fi system.

Riley: Temptation, PC Clegg, is a terrible thing.

Clegg: Pardon sir?

Riley: Well think about it – forty years ago there was hardly any burglary, now there's loads of it, why?

Clegg: I have no idea sir.

Riley: What do they teach you in Police Training College these days? It is because, Clegg, forty years ago nobody had anything that was worth stealing, whereas today houses are groaning with extremely nickable stuff.

Clegg: And the thieves cannot resist the temptation.

Riley: That is correct – we'll make an officer of you yet.

Clegg: Of course you'd know all about that sir wouldn't you?

Riley: What Clegg?

Clegg: Temptation sir, I mean all of those baked goods in the mornings.

Riley: You're treading on very thin ice son. And anyway – I could give up my pastries any time I wanted to. I just choose not to.

Clegg: Oh look sir, a pig flying past the window.

Riley: Look Clegg, every day you and I are beset – beset I say – with pesky little things called temptations. How we stand up to those temptations, what we do with them, is a mark of the kind of people we are. I am an Inspector therefore I am more able to stand up to temptation than most ordinary mortals. Now do me a favour and see whether those doughnuts are ready.

Clegg: Right away sir.

SECOND SUNDAY IN LENT

Mark 8.31–38

THE LENT CASES – 2 HEARING DIFFICULT NEWS

(Riley and Clegg enter talking.)

Riley: Now then PC Clegg I know you think I'm a hard man. A tough, hard as nails, cynical police officer.

Clegg: Well sir I . . .

Riley: No, no don't try to deny it. I know what people say about me.

Clegg: You do?

Riley: Oh yes, 'That Inspector Riley, he's a hard, hard man. He wouldn't know sensitivity if it came up and bashed him over the head.'

Clegg: Well sensitivity is hardly likely to do that sir.

Riley: Don't disagree with me when I'm pontificating son.

Clegg: Sorry sir.

Riley: Well there's more under this cold, heartless exterior than you would think.

Clegg: I'm sure there is sir.

Riley: A warm, cuddly, teddy bear of a man with a heart soft as something that's very soft indeed.

Clegg: I never doubted it sir.

Riley: Which is why PC Clegg, as part of your training, we are going to talk about the most difficult thing a police officer has to do.

Clegg: What's that then sir?

Riley: The breaking of difficult news.

Clegg: Ah . . .

Riley: Indeed 'ah' – having to tell people hard news, information that they would rather not hear is extraordinarily tough.

Clegg: I don't want to have to do it sir.

Riley: Indeed PC Clegg, none of us wants to have to do it. We'd all rather let people carry on as though nothing terrible was ever going to happen to them.

Clegg: What's so bad about that sir?

Riley: It's not the truth is it? The truth is that horrible events sometimes happen.

Clegg: So how do people react sir?

Riley: Well in all my years on the force I've seen many different reactions to bad news, but I suppose the most common is disbelief.

Clegg: Disbelief sir?

Riley: Exactly. The person you are telling literally cannot or does not want to believe what you've just told them – so they don't.

Clegg: They just pretend something else?

Riley: They'll say, 'You must be mistaken, you must have got it wrong' – anything but the truth.

Clegg: But I suppose people have to be told.

Riley: Absolutely Clegg. You can't hide the truth forever. Sometimes hard things have to said and heard. You just hope that some day the person who is hearing all of this will understand.

Clegg: Difficult to know what words to use.

Riley: And difficult to know when to break the news Clegg my boy – in the end you have to ask yourself, are people ready to hear the truth?

THIRD SUNDAY IN LENT

John 2.13–22

THE LENT CASES – 3 ANGER

(Riley and WPC Canning enter talking.)

Riley: So what have we got Canning?

Canning: Well sir I have to say I don't think it's very straightforward.

Riley: Oh yes, and why's that?

Canning: Well I just have a sneaking soft spot for him sir.

Riley: A soft spot?

Canning: Yes sir.

Riley: Oh well ladies and gentlemen we must let the prisoner free immediately, it's not that he didn't commit a serious crime of vandalism, it's just that WPC Canning has a soft spot for him.

Canning: I can sympathize with him sir.

Riley: Oh can you? And that makes it all right does it?

Canning: I'm not saying that. It's just that I can understand why he was angry. It almost seems justified somehow.

Riley: Justified?

Canning: Oh come on sir, haven't you ever felt so angry about something that you felt like you wanted to do some violence?

Riley: Never.

Canning: Well I feel sorry for you then sir.

Riley: What?

Canning: Well if you're telling me that you've never cared so deeply about something that you'd commit violence to protect it, then I feel sorry for you.

Riley: I don't need your pity Canning. The fact is that this man was caught red-handed in the act of destroying another person's property. He took an iron bar to the windscreen of a car, smashing it to pieces.

Canning: A car that we know belongs to the most ruthless loan shark in the town sir.

Riley: I know that.

Canning: A man who we know is responsible for terrorizing more people in this area than any other, we've just never been able to pin anything on him.

Riley: I also know that.

Canning: A man who has made the lives of hundreds of people miserable and full of fear.

Riley: That's enough Canning.

Canning: No – with all due respect sir, it isn't enough. Haven't you heard of righteous anger? Of a feeling that runs so deep you have to do something about it? Of a sense of justice and love for people that is so strong that sometimes it explodes?

Riley: That's as maybe but he's still caused a public disturbance.

Canning: Maybe it's about time somebody did sir.

Riley: But we can't let it go unpunished.

Canning: He did it out of love, because he saw people being hurt.

Riley: I know.

Canning: He did it to make a stand. To let people know somebody is on their side. Perhaps if we'd been prepared to take action he wouldn't have needed to.

FOURTH SUNDAY IN LENT

John 3.14–21

THE LENT CASES – 4 SACRIFICIAL LOVE

(Inspector Riley is sitting. PC Clegg is standing.)

Riley: So tell me Clegg, what is our job as police officers?

Clegg: Well Inspector Riley sir, our job is to catch criminals.

Riley: That is one of our jobs yes.

Clegg: And then when we have them sir we have to get them to confess, sweat it out of them under the lights. A bit of good cop, bad cop kind of thing. Never let up, keep them guessing, keeping the streets safe for little children and puppy dogs everywhere.

Riley: *(Rather worried)* Yes, quite.

Clegg: Bringing the villains down, locking them inside and throwing away the key; always getting our man or woman.

Riley: Calm down Clegg.

Clegg: Sorry sir, got a bit carried away there.

Riley: I can see that. And you also seem to have missed the point.

Clegg: Oh not again sir.

Riley: Yes indeed. For the apprehension of criminals is but one of the many areas of the hurly-burly of modern life that police officers get involved in.

Clegg: There are also high-speed chases in police cars with the sirens blaring sir.

Riley: Indeed Clegg, but I had something else in mind entirely. Have I ever told you the story of Nathaniel Hammond?

Clegg: I don't believe you have sir.

Riley: Well, it was one rainy Wednesday night in November and a 999 call came in from the phone box on West Parade. Seems as though there'd been an electrical fault at 34 West End View and there was a fire.

Clegg: Oh I remember this one sir, it was all over the local paper.

Riley: And so it should have been Clegg. In twenty-four years on the force I've never seen anything like it. Seems there were four people in the house, ten-year-old Nathaniel Hammond, his mum and his two younger sisters.

Clegg: Charlotte and Harriet if I remember rightly sir.

Riley: You do indeed Clegg. Well done. The fire ripped through the house and by the time we got there things were very serious indeed. I pulled up in the squad car just behind two fire tenders.

Clegg: Oooh how exciting sir. I wish I could have been a fireman.

Riley: I wish you could have been a fireman too Clegg, but that's beside the point. No sooner had we got there than the front door opened and there stood little Nathaniel in his pyjamas carrying his unconscious six-year-old sister Charlotte.

Clegg: What a brave little kid.

Riley: There's more. Before anybody could stop him, he went back into the house and came out with Harriet. He also told the rescue workers which room his mum was in. It was incredible, he was nearly overcome with the smoke and he had second degree burns, but he kept on going.

Clegg: Love sir.

Riley: Love that is prepared to give anything, to go to any lengths. Sacrificial love Clegg. Never underestimate its power.

FIFTH SUNDAY IN LENT

John 12.20–33

THE LENT CASES – 5 THE COST OF DOING RIGHT

(PC Clegg and WPC Canning walk on.)

Clegg: But it's human instinct isn't it?

Canning: That doesn't make it right Richard.

Clegg: I'm not saying it's right, it's just that I can understand it.

Canning: I've had this very same argument with Inspector Riley.

Clegg: And what did he have to say for himself?

Canning: Oh – the usual. Sexist and non-committal.

Clegg: Well, Susan, I certainly think most people would want to protect themselves.

Canning: So what you're saying is, most people are cowards.

Clegg: When it really comes down to it, yes I think they are.

Canning: That's not exactly very optimistic is it?

Clegg: Maybe not – but you put yourself in the same situation. You're faced with a choice – the right thing, which is going to help loads of people but which is going to cause lots of pain and heartache for you. Or doing nothing – which is going to give you a quiet life.

Canning: Let's not forget that doing nothing would be the *wrong* thing to do.

Clegg: Well I'll give you that, but it often doesn't feel like it's the wrong thing – it just feels like keeping the peace.

Canning: Okay then, let's take a simple case. You work in an office.

Clegg: Most of the time it feels like I do.

Canning: Leaving police paperwork aside for one minute, you work in an office and you know that one of your superiors is helping themselves to loads of office supplies. Do you tell anybody?

Clegg: Absolutely not.

Canning: Richard, you're a police officer.

Clegg: I know. But I also know I'd get into trouble if I ratted on them so I wouldn't.

Canning: A great upholder of the law you are. Let's take another example – a friend of yours is in trouble. Not with the law or anything like that – just serious trouble. The only way they can get out of that trouble is if you take the blame on their behalf.

Clegg: This is a friend we're talking about here?

Canning: Yeah – a good friend. Do you take the rap for something you didn't do or let your friend get into serious trouble?

Clegg: I don't know.

Canning: What do you mean – you don't know?

Clegg: Well it depends on all kinds of things doesn't it?

Canning: Like what?

Clegg: Like what kind of trouble I was going to get into.

Canning: So if the stakes were too high you'd back out.

Clegg: I'm afraid I would, and most people would do the same.

Canning: Well I'm glad you're not my friend then.

Clegg: I'm just saying that most people wouldn't pay that kind of cost.

Canning: Well I certainly hope somebody would. *(They exit talking.)*

SIXTH SUNDAY IN LENT

Mark 11.1–11

THE LENT CASES – 6 CROWD CONTROL

(Inspector Riley is sitting. Clegg enters.)

Clegg: *(Waving a football scarf)* Here we go, here we go, here we go.

Riley: Clegg, what on earth do you think you're doing?

Clegg: Ah now Inspector Riley, nothing that you can do or say sir, not even your famously dour face can dampen my spirits today.

Riley: Don't tell me . . .

Clegg: Yes you guessed it, I'm on match duty!

Riley: It's been a long time coming.

Clegg: You're not kidding. It was 1927 the last time we got this far in the Cup.

Riley: Having a Premiership team come to our little town is quite an occasion.

Clegg: And I'm going to be there to see it. Yay!

Riley: Being completely professional at all times of course.

Clegg: Oh of course, you know me sir. Never one to let the moment go to my head. Cool, calm and totally unbiased at all times.

Riley: So you're not going to get carried away?

Clegg: Me sir? Never.

Riley: You're not going to let a crowd of 28,000 rattle you?

Clegg: No way.

Riley: You're going to keep your mind on the job at all times?

Clegg: You know me sir.

Riley: Indeed, that's why I'm worried.

Clegg: Oh that's a bit unfair, quality policing is my middle name.

Riley: Well I just hope so because crowds can be fickle creatures.

Clegg: I'm aware of that sir.

Riley: Up one minute, down the next.

Clegg: I've had the training sir.

Riley: Yes, well Clegg I'm afraid there's nothing the training can do to prepare you for what a crowd is capable of. It can turn on you in seconds. Be your best friend one minute and baying for your blood the next. It's frightening.

Clegg: I can cope with it sir.

Riley: That's where you're wrong Clegg. Nobody can cope with it, or control it or understand it.

Clegg: Now you're making me nervous.

Riley: Good, because you should be. It's all about expectations. The crowd wants to feel good, they want to win, and if they don't then they get disappointed, or even angry, and that's when you need to watch your back.

Clegg: I'll be very careful sir.

Riley: You do that Clegg because that crowd will be cheering and shouting when you arrive, but if things don't turn out the way they want there'll be trouble – you mark my words.

Clegg: Never let your head get turned by the big occasion eh sir?

Riley: Just be aware and be careful.

Clegg: Wish me luck sir.

Riley: Luck, Clegg, has nothing to do with it.

EASTER DAY

Mark 16.1–8

YOU DID WHAT?

(Two Roman soldiers are standing centrally.)

Maximus: Legionnaire Quintus Severus, so glad you could join me.

Quintus: Yes sir Centurion Maximus sir, I came as soon as I got the summons.

Maximus: *(Sweetly)* Only I wasn't sure you'd be able to come. I mean the duties of a legionnaire are so taxing aren't they? We march you around all day in this terrible heat, we give you those horribly heavy weights to carry on your back. It must be very tiring.

Quintus: Well actually, sir, it can be a little tiring, yes.

Maximus: I should say so. And then, if that wasn't enough, we make you do those pesky guard duties on top.

Quintus: Ah yes . . .

Maximus: *(Suddenly angry)* Guard duties that you did so well, Quintus Severus, that the dead body that you were guarding managed to get up in the middle of the night and waltz right out of its tomb!

Quintus: I can explain sir.

Maximus: I don't want to hear it. You would have thought that guarding a dead body was not a difficult thing to do. It's hardly going to try and escape is it?

Quintus: No sir.

Maximus: I mean, what's it going to do? Walk out of its tomb?

Quintus: But sir . . .

Maximus: Do you have any idea what Pilate is going to do to me when he finds out what has happened?

Quintus: I don't suppose it will be very pleasant sir.

Maximus: No, Quintus Severus, it won't. But I console myself with the thought that whatever horrible punishment our beloved Governor has dreamed up for me it will be as nothing compared with what I am going to do to you.

Quintus: I am sorry sir.

Maximus: 'Sorry' does not even begin to make amends for what you have done. Have you any idea who was in that tomb?

Quintus: Jesus of Nazareth sir.

Maximus: Yes indeed, Jesus of Nazareth. While I do not pretend to understand the religion of the Jews, I do know one thing – if there was one person's dead body that needed to stay where it was, it was his. Why even now his followers are probably coming up with all kinds of lies about his post-death appearances.

Quintus: But surely a man doesn't rise from the dead sir.

Maximus: I know that Quintus Severus and you know that. But I wouldn't put it past the followers of Jesus not to know that little law of physics at all.

Quintus: So what do we need to do sir?

Maximus: You need to get out there Quintus Severus, take as many men as you need, and find that body!

Quintus: Where shall I look sir?

Maximus: I don't know – I've never looked for a dead body before.

Quintus: But what if he's not dead sir?

Maximus: Don't be ridiculous, of course he's dead. Now find him!

SECOND SUNDAY OF EASTER

John 20.19–31

HAVING DOUBTS

(Two actors are standing centrally.)

One: We can understand you know.

Two: Oh yes indeed, fully understand.

One: It must have been terrible.

Two: Frustrating.

One: Disappointing in the extreme.

Two: Not to have been there.

One: To have missed out on it all.

Two: And I can just imagine what the others were like.

One: Do you think they were sensitive?

Two: Prepared not to talk about it in his presence?

One: Aware of the pain he must be feeling?

Two: I don't think so. More like . . .

One: 'Thomas, he's risen! I've seen him!'

Two: 'You should have been there Thomas – it was incredible!'

One: 'You really missed out there Thomas!'

Two: Guaranteed to make you feel better.

One: It's no wonder that he was cross.

Two: Angry.

One: Feeling a little put out.

Two: Left on the sidelines.

One: It's easy to sympathize.

Two: Poor old Thomas.

One: Hard done to.

Two: Alone.

One: Like everybody else got invited to the party and you got left out.

Two: Intemperate words were said.

One: Heated words.

Two: Words which would be very easy to regret at a later date.

One: Be careful what you wish for Thomas.

Two: You might just get it.

One: And then what will you do?

Two: What happens when all your doubts are answered in one fell swoop?

One: When you're invited to make good on your claims.

Two: When you're told to reach out and touch?

One: I guess it leaves you looking a little silly.

Two: Not to mention embarrassed.

One: Perhaps he was just overwhelmed.

Two: Overjoyed to see that the others were right.

One: Moved beyond imagining.

Two: You can understand Thomas.

One: Who doubted.

Two: But for him as well as us.

One: There comes a time when we must stop our doubting . . .

Two: And just believe.

THIRD SUNDAY OF EASTER

Luke 24.36b–48

THEY WON'T BELIEVE IT

(Rory – a writer – is sitting typing. Jennifer enters.)

Jennifer: So how's it coming then?

Rory: Don't ask.

Jennifer: What do you mean, don't ask?

Rory: I mean just that, don't ask.

Jennifer: But I have just asked so you might as well tell me.

Rory: Well if you must know I'm beginning to think I've made the biggest mistake of my life. Nothing works. The characters lack motivation, there's no real plot in the second act, and the dialogue is awful.

Jennifer: Oh come on it can't be that bad.

Rory: Well actually yes it can.

Jennifer: But that bit that you showed me last week was really good.

Rory: We were both mistaken – it's rubbish.

Jennifer: What will it take to fix it?

Rory: How about a box of matches?

Jennifer: I'm sorry, I will not believe it's as bad as you seem to think.

Rory: The real problem is the ending.

Jennifer: So what's the issue then?

Rory: Well I know how it needs to end. I know what's got to happen. It's just that nobody's going to believe it.

Jennifer: Make them believe it.

Rory: It's not that easy. The vastly charismatic teacher is killed by the very people he was trying to help.

Jennifer: That sounds okay.

Rory: His followers, completely overcome by grief at the loss of one they loved so much, suddenly begin to see him again.

Jennifer: What, like a ghost or something?

Rory: I don't know.

Jennifer: What if he was more than a ghost – an actual physical presence?

Rory: But that's just the point isn't it? The more real I make him the less people are actually going to believe it.

Jennifer: Surely that doesn't matter.

Rory: What do you mean?

Jennifer: Well if that's the way that this story has to end, if everything leads up to this point, then people will either believe or they won't. But in the end at least you'll have been true to the story.

Rory: But I want people to believe it.

Jennifer: What's more important – telling the story as it has to be told or having people believe you?

Rory: I never knew this was going to be so difficult.

Jennifer: Sometimes you've just got to tell what you understand to be the truth, and if people believe you that's great, but if they don't at least you know that you've been true to yourself.

Rory: Okay stand back then. Let's give this another go. *(He starts typing.)*

Jennifer: I can't wait to see how it comes out.

FOURTH SUNDAY OF EASTER

John 10.11–18

A GOOD SHEPHERD

(Janice and Walter are sheep and are standing centrally.)

Sheep 1: It's a good life this, isn't it Walter?

Sheep 2: It certainly is Janice. A great life and no mistake.

Sheep 1: Being a sheep is a pretty cool thing to be.

Sheep 2: Even wrapped up in all this wool.

Sheep 1: Exactly.

Sheep 2: Nibbling grass all day.

Sheep 1: Not a care in the world.

Sheep 2: Counting the other sheep before you drift off to sleep.

Sheep 1: It's just as well we've got a good shepherd isn't it?

Sheep 2: What do you mean?

Sheep 1: Well, our shepherd, he's good isn't he?

Sheep 2: Is he? You mean there are bad shepherds?

Sheep 1: Oh yeah. Haven't you heard?

Sheep 2: No I don't think I have.

Sheep 1: Well my cousin Dora, she got in with a really bad flock.

Sheep 2: She didn't!

Sheep 1: She did. Out till all hours of the day and night. Constantly getting attacked by wolves. Forever being led into rocky ravines by mistake.

Sheep 2: It sounds terrible.

Sheep 1: It was Walter, it was. You see the shepherd didn't care.

Sheep 2: You'd have thought he'd have been worried.

Sheep 1: Well you would have thought that, but you'd have been wrong. It was just a job to him. He didn't have any feelings for his sheep at all.

Sheep 2: That's so sad.

Sheep 1: It is really. Dora had to put in for a transfer to another flock in the end. All the sleepless nights and the worry, she couldn't handle it anymore. Her wool went all floppy.

Sheep 2: I'm not surprised.

Sheep 1: She didn't feel safe you see. Was never sure there wasn't a wolf prowling somewhere nearby.

Sheep 2: Our shepherd's lovely isn't he?

Sheep 1: I tell you what – I've always felt safe while he's around.

Sheep 2: He's so kind.

Sheep 1: And generous.

Sheep 2: And loving.

Sheep 1: He'd never lead us astray.

Sheep 2: Certainly not.

Sheep 1: And we're safe from attack.

Sheep 2: He'd lay down his own life to protect us.

Sheep 1: And we're always led to green pastures.

Sheep 2: Juicy grass all the way.

Sheep 1: It's a great life isn't it?

Sheep 2: Well, he is the good shepherd Janice.

Sheep 1: Walter, he's the best shepherd.

FIFTH SUNDAY OF EASTER

John 15.1–8

THE LIBRARY

(The librarian is standing behind a counter. A reader enters.)

Librarian: Good morning madam and what can I do for you this morning?

Reader: *(Looking around anxiously)* Well actually I think I might have made a terrible mistake. I'm sorry, I'll go.

Librarian: Now, now madam. I'm sure I can help you. What seems to be the trouble?

Reader: Well I'm new to the village you see and I was told that this building was the library, but I can see that I've been misinformed. So I'm sorry to have troubled you. I'll be on my way.

Librarian: No madam, you were indeed informed correctly. This is the village library, and I am the librarian.

Reader: I'm sorry to sound a little dim. But isn't a library supposed to have books in it?

Librarian: Ah yes, books, CDs, newspapers, magazines, tapes. We are at the cutting edge of the information superhighway.

Reader: But I'm afraid I don't see any.

Librarian: See any what madam?

Reader: Books, newspapers, magazines, tapes, CDs, any hint of the information superhighway having made its way to Little Norton.

Librarian: Ah yes. It's that obvious is it?

Reader: I'm afraid so yes.

Librarian: Oh dear.

Reader: So do you have any?

Librarian: Any what?

Reader: Any books?

Librarian: How can I put this? . . . No.

Reader: None at all?

Librarian: None at all.

Reader: No tapes, CDs, magazines, newspapers?

Librarian: No, no, no and no.

Reader: You're not a very good library are you?

Librarian: We used to be. We had bookcases stretching as far as the eye could see.

Reader: So what happened?

Librarian: We cut ourselves off from Head Office at County Hall and suddenly all our funding, all our book supplies, stopped.

Reader: So let me get this straight. You are a branch library that is in no way connected to the County Library system.

Librarian: That is correct. We're completely cut off.

Reader: By your own actions?

Librarian: Well we didn't like them.

Reader: You'll have to forgive me, but I think I'll take my reading needs elsewhere. Perhaps to a library that actually has something to read.

Librarian: You know, a lot of people say that.

Reader: I wonder why? Goodbye. *(Exits.)*

Librarian: *(Calling out)* But we have got some very comfortable reading chairs.

SIXTH SUNDAY OF EASTER

John 15.9–17

RALPH AND JIM ON LOVE

(Ralph and Jim are sitting centrally.)

Ralph: It's a many-splendoured thing innit Jim?

Jim: What's that then Ralph mate?

Ralph: Love, Jim, love. It's a many-splendoured thing.

Jim: I suppose it is Ralph, yes. I suppose it is.

Ralph: But difficult.

Jim: Oh yes, nobody's denying that. Many-splendoured, yet very difficult. It's both of those things at the same time.

Ralph: Take my Sandra for example.

Jim: A lovely wife Ralph.

Ralph: None lovelier Jim mate. It was our anniversary recently.

Jim: Was it Ralph? You should have told me, I'd have got you a card.

Ralph: Don't you worry about that Jim my son. The problem was that on the day of our anniversary me and Sandra had a bit of an argument.

Jim: Oh dear. On your anniversary? That's not too good.

Ralph: It isn't too good at all – an' it was all over what we were going to do to celebrate it.

Jim: Oh yes?

Ralph: You see I'd got tickets to watch United play.

Jim: A good evening out that.

Ralph: That's what I thought Jim, but it turns out that Sandra had more the candle-lit dinner kind of thing in mind.

Jim: Oh – I don't s'pose she was too happy then.

Ralph: None too happy at all mate. In fact she stormed off in a bit of a huff. Told me I was about as romantic as a soggy tea towel.

Jim: Well they're not very romantic Ralph.

Ralph: They're not known for it Jim, no.

Jim: But that's the thing with love. I mean you love football don't you?

Ralph: I do mate – there's no mistaking that.

Jim: But you also love Sandra. So which comes first?

Ralph: A good question Jim. Another good question is this – how much should you be prepared to give up for the thing that you love?

Jim: I don't know Ralph, how much?

Ralph: I don't know either Jim mate – I was hoping you might be able to help me out on that one.

Jim: I'm afraid I've never been very good at relationships.

Ralph: No – they certainly take a lot of time.

Jim: And energy.

Ralph: And commitment.

Jim: I tell you Ralph, love sounds like an awful lot of hard work.

Ralph: It is mate – but it's worth it.

Jim: Is it?

Ralph: Oh yeah, but there's a lot of sacrifice involved.

Jim: It costs a lot then does it?

Ralph: Oh yeah Jim mate, it can cost the earth.

SEVENTH SUNDAY OF EASTER

John 17.6–19

THE AGENT

('K' and Hamilton Bland are standing centrally.)

K: Good morning Agent 005.com, it's good to see you've finished your basic training.

Bland: The name's Bland, Hamilton Bland.

K: Yes, very good. Have they given you all the latest equipment?

Bland: Indeed they have K. Z branch have given me every gadget they have. Including this. *(Shows his wristwatch.)*

K: It's not . . . ?

Bland: Yes K, it's the new existential watch.

K: I'd heard rumours they were working on it but I never dreamed they were this close to a finished article.

Bland: Yes indeed. Not only does it tell the time but it asks you where you are in your life, and what steps you are going to take to achieve happiness.

K: Excellent. Those boffins at Z branch never cease to amaze me.

Bland: Well K, I'm eager for my first assignment. Hamilton Bland needs some action. Where are you going to send me, Paris? Monte Carlo? Cairo?

K: 23 Park Road, Croydon.

Bland: Croydon?

K: Is there something wrong with Croydon, Bland?

Bland: No ma'am, nothing wrong with Croydon at all. It's just not very exotic is it?

K: Oh I don't know, I've heard that Saturday nights can get pretty exciting.

Bland: But what do you want me to do there ma'am?

K: Live a Christian life, follow the teachings of Jesus.

Bland: Is that it?

K: What do you mean is that it? It's the most difficult thing you can ask anyone to do. Be forgiving, loving, generous, a seeker after justice and truth. Most people find it impossible.

Bland: Most people aren't Hamilton Bland ma'am.

K: No, and thank goodness for that.

Bland: Pardon?

K: Well you're hardly the most humble person I've ever met. This is not an easy mission Bland. In most cases we ask you to blend in with the background, not be noticed, be like everybody else. But this mission is different.

Bland: How so K?

K: If you're going to be a Christian – a real follower of Christ – you're going to stand out. Your actions, your words are going to provoke strong reactions, people will not always find you an easy person to have around.

Bland: It sounds challenging.

K: That's the most intelligent thing you've said this morning. Frankly Bland you're not up to the job, nobody is. But thank goodness Christians have some pretty powerful help.

Bland: What kind of help?

K: God. Now pack your bags and get going. Croydon awaits!

PENTECOST

Acts 2.1–21

TRANSFORMING

(Jenny and Lenny enter from the back.)

Lenny: *(Talking as he walks)* Morning everybody, morning. How are we all then?

Jenny: It's good to see you all here.

Lenny: Glad that you responded to our invitation.

Jenny: 'Cos we know how busy you all are.

Lenny: And we really appreciate you giving up your time like this on a Sunday morning.

Jenny: I mean after all, you could have gone to the car boot sale.

Lenny: Or the footie practice.

Jenny: Or down the supermarket.

Lenny: All very important things.

Jenny: So we're glad you came here to listen to us. My name is Jenny.

Lenny: And I'm her associate, Lenny.

Jenny: And I don't think you're going to be disappointed by what we have to say to you this morning.

Lenny: No indeed. In fact I think you're going to feel this morning was time very well spent.

Jenny: Very well spent indeed.

Lenny: Let me just ask you this, ladies and gentlemen. Do you feel tired?

Jenny: You do don't you? I can tell. Tired, listless, worn out.

Lenny: You just wish your life could be transformed.

Jenny: Given a sense of purpose and direction.

Lenny: You want to feel full of energy and life.

Jenny: Full of a power that doesn't seem to come from you at all.

Lenny: Well I can tell you this morning ladies and gentlemen that this very morning . . .

Jenny: Here in this little bottle.

Lenny: We have the answer to all your problems.

Jenny: In this bottle we have Lenny and Jenny's Liquid of Life. It's guaranteed to lift you up.

Lenny: To turn your life around.

Jenny: To give you meaning and purpose when all there was before was an empty hole.

Lenny: And at £74.99 I think you'll agree it's a bargain that you just can't miss out on.

Jenny: Now I know there are going to be some religious types who are going to say it's only God who can transform your life.

Lenny: It's God what sends the Holy Spirit to turn your life around.

Jenny: Well I'm sorry but doesn't that just sound a little bit far-fetched?

Lenny: Especially when you can have this special Liquid of Life that also acts as a hair-restorer for under £75?

Jenny: Now who would you rather trust ladies and gentlemen?

Lenny: Almighty God?

Jenny: Or Lenny and Jenny with this once in a lifetime offer.

Lenny: Terms and conditions apply.

TRINITY SUNDAY

John 3.1–17

SO, WHAT DID HE SAY?

(Nicodemus is standing centrally. Esther enters.)

Esther:	So, come on then, out with it. What did he say?
Nicodemus:	I'm not sure I want to talk about it.
Esther:	Not sure you want to talk? That's rubbish – you're a member of the Council, you spend your life talking.
Nicodemus:	Yes, and if they were ever to find out where I was tonight . . .
Esther:	But they're not going to are they? And even if they did you could come up with some plausible reason why you were there. You could say you were just sounding Jesus out. Trying to find out more about him.
Nicodemus:	I suppose so. It just feels like a very dangerous game I'm playing at the moment.
Esther:	And of course your life has been remarkably danger-free up until now.
Nicodemus:	What's that supposed to mean?
Esther:	Well you're hardly known for your rash acts of daring-do are you? To tell you the truth I'm finding all of this quite exciting. Now what did Jesus have to say for himself?
Nicodemus:	Riddles.
Esther:	Pardon me?
Nicodemus:	You're the one who was so keen to know what he said. He spoke in riddles, nonsensical, ludicrous riddles.
Esther:	I don't understand.
Nicodemus:	Neither do I. You'd have thought that if his teaching was meant to be popular, accepted by all, then he'd have been a bit easier to understand.
Esther:	Well try one on me. Perhaps I'll understand.
Nicodemus:	All right – he said no one can see the kingdom of God unless they have been born again.
Esther:	Born again? What kind of nonsense is that?
Nicodemus:	That's just what I said.
Esther:	Well it must mean something or he wouldn't have said it.
Nicodemus:	You have a wonderful knack of stating the obvious.
Esther:	Well did you ask him?
Nicodemus:	Yes I asked him what it meant, but I'm afraid I might have come over as a little aggressive.
Esther:	You? Impossible!
Nicodemus:	Well anyway he said we must be born of water and spirit.
Esther:	Spirit? What's that? Haven't we got enough to worry about with God?
Nicodemus:	I don't know Esther. All I know is that Jesus has a completely fresh way of talking about God, it's as if he has access to a whole new relationship.
Esther:	It all sounds a bit strange to me.
Nicodemus:	But exciting too. As if we needed to rethink all the old ideas.
Esther:	But what's wrong with the way things are?
Nicodemus:	Apparently everything.
Esther:	It all sounds a bit of a mystery to me.
Nicodemus:	God always has been Esther. A wonderful, frustrating, beautiful mystery. And I'm not sure we're meant to understand.

SUNDAY BETWEEN 24 AND 28 MAY INCLUSIVE

Mark 2.13–22

GIVE IT UP

(Joan and the minister enter, talking.)

Minister: Now then Joan I think great things are possible for this church.

Joan: Oh so do I Revd Hawkins, so do I.

Minister: Call me Simon, please.

Joan: Oh, I'll try, but you know how difficult I find that.

Minister: Now you know the church meeting said that they wanted to take radical new steps to move forward.

Joan: Indeed yes.

Minister: They wanted to look at every aspect of our church life as an outsider would look at it. Ask difficult questions about whether these things were really meeting the needs of the community we're surrounded by.

Joan: Quite right.

Minister: There would be no sacred cows, no stone left unturned.

Joan: I'm with you 100 per cent.

Minister: If something needed to be closed down, some piece of work needed to stop, we'd do the brave thing.

Joan: I agree absolutely. Except for the choir.

Minister: I'm sorry?

Joan: Well all this talk about radical change, transformation – you can do anything you like except you can't do anything with the choir.

Minister: Is there a reason for that?

Joan: We've had a choir at our church as long as I can remember. And I'm in it – so you can keep your hands off.

Minister: But there are only six of you.

Joan: Oh but we're ever so faithful.

Minister: But wouldn't it be better if you led the singing from within the congregation? Gave them some confidence?

Joan: No.

Minister: But whatever happened to radical change?

Joan: Well, as I've said, I'm behind you all the way. I'm as much for complete change as the next person. Just don't touch the choir.

Minister: Tell me Joan, what message do you think the choir communicates to people from outside?

Joan: That this church has a strong musical tradition.

Minister: With six of you?

Joan: With six of us.

Minister: But you're not actually very good are you?

Joan: We try very hard.

Minister: That's not the same thing.

Joan: Look, you can argue all you like but we're not changing.

Minister: So we carry on as before?

Joan: Yes.

Minister: No transformation? No change?

Joan: Some things, Revd Hawkins, never change.

Minister: I'm beginning to see that.

SUNDAY BETWEEN 29 MAY AND 4 JUNE INCLUSIVE

Mark 2.23–3.6

I DON'T BELIEVE IT

(Two actors enter.)

One: Unbelievable.

Two: I agree, absolutely unbelievable.

One: I mean we do have standards to keep up.

Two: Certain levels of behaviour that have to be maintained.

One: We're not ordinarily the kind of people who would complain.

Two: No, we're quite ordinary folk.

One: Just looking for a quiet life.

Two: We're not the sort who are forever writing letters to the newspapers.

One: 'Yours Angrily of Bethsaida.'

Two: The sort of letters that start off 'Why, oh why, oh why?'

One: We wouldn't dream of it.

Two: Well, not normally anyway.

One: But sometimes something happens that just has to be commented upon.

Two: Occasionally people just go too far.

One: Way too far.

Two: I mean how would you like it?

One: Yes, how would you like it?

Two: If a group of people just waltzed past your house . . .

One: On a Sabbath . . .

Two: Oh yes, the Sabbath no less . . .

One: Eating corn.

Two: Not just eating it of course.

One: Oh no – they'd picked it first.

Two: In broad daylight.

One: As brazen as you like.

Two: Corn-picking.

One: On the Sabbath.

Two: We were stunned.

One: Shocked.

Two: Scandalized.

One: How could they?

Two: Such blatant law-breaking on such a holy day.

One: And the worst thing is, these people claim to be religious.

Two: They're almost doing it to make a point.

One: Yes – their leader . . .

Two: One Jesus of Nazareth by name.

One: Claimed that the Sabbath was made for us.

Two: Almost as if it's meant to be freedom-giving.

One: Well that's plainly ludicrous.

Two: Yes. That's just an excuse for law-breaking and loutish behaviour.

One: Well it's not going to happen in our neighbourhood.

Two: Not if we can help it.

One: There's going to be no enjoyment on the Sabbath while we're around.

Two: We're writing an angry letter to the paper . . . 'Why, oh why, oh why? . . .'

SUNDAY BETWEEN 5 AND 11 JUNE INCLUSIVE

Mark 3.20–35

WHOSE SIDE?

(Two devils enter, talking.)

Devil 1: Have you heard?

Devil 2: Heard what?

Devil 1: Oh, it's too wonderful for words.

Devil 2: What is?

Devil 1: If I hadn't heard it for myself I'd never have believed it.

Devil 2: What are you talking about?

Devil 1: I mean I know the humans are stupid, but even I never thought they'd be this dense.

Devil 2: Will you just tell me what's going on?

Devil 1: Oh yes, sorry. It's just so incredible I got carried away.

Devil 2: So what's happening?

Devil 1: Well you know I've been up on earth recently?

Devil 2: Keeping an eye on what the Son of Light is up to, yes.

Devil 1: I've been watching him now for weeks now and he's so good it sickens me.

Devil 2: I can imagine. Healing the sick . . .

Devil 1: Befriending the poor.

Devil 2: Sharing love everywhere he goes. Positively horrible.

Devil 1: It is pretty grim, yes. Well, he was travelling along today when some humans came up to him. You know, the stuck-up religious kind.

Devil 2: Oh I love them. More interested in their own standing in the world than in helping anybody.

Devil 1: So worried about how things are done that they never think about justice or forgiveness.

Devil 2: There's quite a lot of them down here aren't there?

Devil 1: Lots. Enjoying a little warm hospitality.

Devil 2: So what did these humans have to say to the Son of Light then? They're finally beginning to realize who he is are they? Because that would be catastrophic.

Devil 1: No, not a bit of it. In fact this is the good part – it's quite the opposite. They think he's one of us.

Devil 2: They WHAT?

Devil 1: You heard me right. They think he's one of us. They're convinced that all the stuff he's doing is an elaborate trick to deceive them.

Devil 2: But don't they see how good he is?

Devil 1: Apparently not. They even think that the power he's showing comes from down here.

Devil 2: This is too good. He's doing good works and they're calling it evil.

Devil 1: And we get the credit.

Devil 2: They really are incredibly dumb aren't they?

Devil 1: It takes the breath away. He tried to convince them but they wouldn't listen.

Devil 2: We hardly need to do anything at all do we?

Devil 1: Just sit back and watch the fun. *(They laugh.)*

SUNDAY BETWEEN 12 AND 18 JUNE INCLUSIVE

Mark 4.26–34

STEADY GROWING

(A young man and an older woman enter.)

Robert: You don't remember me do you?

Alice: I can't quite place you.

Robert: It's me, Robert Winslow.

Alice: *(Startled)* Robert – is that really you? I'd never have recognized you.

Robert: Well it has been nearly twenty years now.

Alice: Has it really been that long?

Robert: I'm afraid so. Trinity Sunday School.

Alice: Yes – happy times.

Robert: I'm afraid I didn't make them very happy for you though.

Alice: Oh you weren't so bad.

Robert: That's very kind, but my memory is a little different.

Alice: You were quite headstrong in those days.

Robert: Loud, obnoxious, rude and very unpleasant are the words I'd use.

Alice: Well you didn't really want to be there did you?

Robert: Mum made me go every week – kicking and screaming. I hated her for it.

Alice: You weren't a very happy boy.

Robert: No. Which is why I wanted to see you again – to thank you.

Alice: Thank me?

Robert: I just wanted you to know that it worked. All that love and gentleness and patience that you showered over me – it worked.

Alice: But that was twenty years ago.

Robert: I know. I also know I wasn't very grateful at the time. You must sometimes wonder whether any of the seeds you sow really amount to anything. I want you to know that they do. You didn't see very much of me after the age of about eleven.

Alice: I was very worried.

Robert: They were a bad time – my teenage years. I drifted from one thing to another, did some pretty stupid things – things I'm not very proud of.

Alice: It happens to lots of people Robert.

Robert: I know. But I kept thinking there must be something better, something more worthwhile I could be doing. I kept thinking of you. I don't remember all the stories you told us. But I do remember you – your kindness and gentleness, your love. And I began to wonder why I'd drifted away from something so good. So I've come back.

Alice: Come back?

Robert: I've found somebody wonderful, we're very much in love, we've started going to church, and we're getting married in the autumn.

Alice: Oh Robert that's wonderful.

Robert: I'm glad you think so because I'd like you to come.

Alice: I'd be delighted.

Robert: I'd also like you to sign the registers as a witness.

Alice: Oohh I don't know what to say.

Robert: Say yes – and keep sowing seeds. It might seem hard work at times but you never know what's going to come up.

SUNDAY BETWEEN 19 AND 25 JUNE INCLUSIVE

Mark 4.35–41

INSURANCE

(Quintus is sitting. Andrew enters.)

Quintus: Welcome to Quintus and Sons, we insure anything and everything. How can I help you?

Andrew: Well I think I might be looking to insure a boat.

Quintus: Oh yes, what kind of boat? Passenger craft, pleasure?

Andrew: No, it's a fishing boat actually.

Quintus: Oh.

Andrew: What do you mean, oh?

Quintus: Well, fishing. You do know it's the most dangerous work possible don't you?

Andrew: Well I wouldn't say that . . .

Quintus: Yes, yes, more people lose their lives in fishing accidents than in gladiatorial combat – it's a proven fact.

Andrew: But my friends and I are very careful. We've been doing this for years.

Quintus: It doesn't really matter how careful you are does it? Out there on the lake anything can happen. A storm can blow up from nowhere without a moment's notice, and there you are stuck in the middle of it. Lightning flashing, thunder booming, the wind howling, waves towering over you, rain lashing the boat . . .

Andrew: Yes, thank you. I get the idea.

Quintus: I've known fishermen who were so keen to bring home the bacon . . .

Andrew: Fish actually.

Quintus: It's just a figure of speech.

Andrew: I'm Jewish.

Quintus: Oh, sorry. They were so keen to bring home the fish that they stayed out too long, ignored the warning signs and they were never seen again.

Andrew: Well as I've already said – my friends and I are very careful.

Quintus: I've only got your word for that haven't I?

Andrew: So what are you telling me?

Quintus: I'm telling you that your premium is going to be high.

Andrew: How high?

Quintus: Let me write it down for you on this scrap of parchment. *(He writes.)*

Andrew: *(The paper is pushed across the desk.)* What?!

Quintus: I did tell you fishermen aren't a very good risk. You get out on that lake and not even the gods can help you.

Andrew: Look, I have faith in my colleagues, I have faith in myself. I was born out on those waters. Nothing frightens me or takes me by surprise. And I have complete faith in my God to protect me.

Quintus: Do you now?

Andrew: What's that supposed to mean?

Quintus: It's my experience that when the chips are really down most people panic.

Andrew: Not me. I would never panic.

Quintus: Be that as it may – the premium still stands.

Andrew: This is daylight robbery.

Quintus: *(Smiling)* I know – but you'll not find anybody else to help you.

SUNDAY BETWEEN 26 JUNE AND 2 JULY INCLUSIVE

Mark 5.21–43

ACTION TIME ON COURAGE

(Action Time *is a children's TV programme. Chris – the presenter – and Jairus are sitting on a sofa.*)

Chris: Hello everybody! Welcome to *Action Time*! Jane can't be with us in the studio this week because she's off filming somewhere exotic and super-special that I can't tell you about. How come she gets to do that and I have to sit in this dingy studio? Anyway – on this week's show we take another of *Action Time*'s amazing trips back in time to meet a character from history. This week we're going to meet somebody who showed huge courage and faith, Jairus.

Jairus: Hello everybody.

Chris: Now Jairus, you've got an incredible story to tell about your daughter?

Jairus: Well yes, I suppose I have. I'm the ruler of the local synagogue.

Chris: That sounds very important.

Jairus: Well, it has its moments. And my daughter, she'd been sick for some time. We had no idea what the problem was, we just knew it wasn't getting any better.

Chris: You need to remember kids that this was before the days of great medical advances like aspirin and plasters with little pictures on.

Jairus: Then came a terrible day – my daughter got worse and it became obvious to us she was dying.

Chris: That must have been awful.

Jairus: It was. We had no idea what to do. She was so precious to us, and we were just sitting there helpless as her life ebbed away.

Chris: So what did you do?

Jairus: I just left the house, I couldn't stand it any more. I was wandering around hardly knowing what I was doing when I heard the noise of a large, excited crowd and I suddenly remembered Jesus was due in town that day.

Chris: Jesus?

Jairus: Yes, a travelling preacher and healer. I'd heard good reports of him from the neighbouring towns. And at that point I suddenly knew what I had to do. So I marched right up to him, pushed through the crowd that was pressing around him . . .

Chris: You must have been desperate by this time.

Jairus: I wasn't going to let anybody get in my way.

Chris: You knew that Jesus wasn't really approved of by the Pharisees.

Jairus: Yes, I knew that – I also knew my daughter was dying and I would do anything to try and help her. The next few minutes are all a bit of a muddle to me. I do know at one point it looked as though we were going to be too late – that she'd died. I would not wish the feelings I had at that moment on anybody.

Chris: But Jesus had other ideas?

Jairus: He just said, 'She's sleeping, don't worry.' And somehow I knew everything was going to be all right.

Chris: And everything was . . . your daughter's better?

Jairus: Running around the house like nothing had happened.

Chris: Jairus – thank you for sharing your story of courage with us.

SUNDAY BETWEEN 3 AND 9 JULY INCLUSIVE

Mark 6.1–13

WE'RE GOING OUT!

(Two characters are standing at a table.)

Jim: Now are you perfectly clear what's going to happen?

Chloe: Perfectly.

Jim: At exactly 13.45 you will deploy team A from Trinity Church Hall and move with all due speed along Privet Drive.

Chloe: Check.

Jim: You will fan out in an easterly direction armed with nothing but a handful of glossy colour pamphlets and invitation cards.

Chloe: Check.

Jim: You will attempt to engage members of the general public in conversation. Have you memorized your tried and tested conversation starters?

Chloe: I have. 'Beautiful day isn't it? Have you been washed in the blood of the lamb?' And the second one, 'That shopping looks heavy, have you thought about casting your burdens on the Lord?'

Jim: Ah yes, they never fail. You are about to embark on the most wonderful thing a person can do – attempting to bring another person to a knowledge of Jesus. Now, are there any questions before you go?

Chloe: When should I start quoting Scripture?

Jim: Not until at least three minutes into the conversation.

Chloe: I have to admit I'm a bit nervous.

Jim: Nerves are for wimps and weeds, not for you.

Chloe: Yes, but what if nobody wants to talk to me?

Jim: Make them talk.

Chloe: But what if the person seems hassled or upset? Wouldn't it be better to offer to help them carry their bags or ask them what the problem is?

Jim: No, no, no. Our job is to save souls not carry shopping bags.

Chloe: I just thought if we were helpful . . . started where people's obvious need was . . .

Jim: Did you not listen in the training sessions? It's a war out there. We go in hard, don't take any prisoners, and don't stop till we're successful. Is that clear?

Chloe: I just thought some kindness might help. You know, carrying another person's burden . . .

Jim: Is not something that we are interested in. We're about lifting the burden caused by sin. Have you got that?

Chloe: Yes sir.

Jim: Now, let's go through the check-list. Tracts, invitations cards and Bible?

Chloe: Check.

Jim: Pencil, prayer card and packed lunch.

Chloe: I've got everything. Are you sure I can't just listen to what people are saying? Let conversation start naturally?

Jim: Absolutely not. It's my way or the highway.

Chloe: Surely it should be God's way?

Jim: God's way *is* my way. Now off you go.

Chloe: Yes Dad – see you later. Bye.

SUNDAY BETWEEN 10 AND 16 JULY INCLUSIVE

Mark 6.14–29

CONSEQUENCES

(The mood should be dark and conspiratorial – two actors enter.)

Judith: So it's true then? He's done it?

Simon: Of course he's done it – he's a weak-minded fool.

Judith: I can't believe he agreed to it.

Simon: When you're drunk in front of your friends and a pretty girl throws herself at you, you'll promise almost anything.

Judith: I gather she put on quite a show.

Simon: Oh it was spectacular all right. Herod couldn't take his eyes off her. But that kind of thing always comes at a price.

Judith: And of course heaven forbid he should lose face in front of his friends.

Simon: Even though it costs somebody their life.

Judith: *(Pause)* Herodias is behind all this of course.

Simon: Well John hardly made a secret of his dislike of her did he?

Judith: And now he's going to die.

Simon: I just wish there was something we could do.

Judith: You know how dangerous that could be.

Simon: Still, John needs our help. Think of all he's done for us, how he's opened our eyes to what's around us. It's taken real courage to do that.

Judith: I know, I know. It's just that I don't think I've got that kind of courage. I mean think of what Herod could do to us . . .

Simon: So we abandon our friend because we're frightened, is that it?

Judith: It's just so difficult . . .

Simon: We give up on all that we know to be right because of pressure. I don't see John doing that, do you?

Judith: But John's not like that.

Simon: And we are, is that it?

Judith: Look it's all very well for you to stand here now and spout great words of courage but I don't see you marching into Herod's chamber and demanding he change his orders.

Simon: I'm sorry – I just feel so useless.

Judith: So do I.

Simon: I mean we should be better than this shouldn't we? Here's a clear case of right and wrong, a case where we know what we should do, just the kind of case that John's been talking about, and we can't bring ourselves to do anything about it.

Judith: He never said it would be easy.

Simon: I just wish I could have a tiny amount of his courage.

Judith: Look, if we go to Herod all we're going to do is make him more angry. What good will it do if we're killed as well? We can continue to work for change here, continue to fight against corruption.

Simon: Oh yeah – we can do all of those things. So how come I feel like I've just caved in, made excuses, taken the easy way out?

Judith: It's all that we can do.

Simon: And how does that make us any better than Herod himself? It looks to me like we're exactly the same.

SUNDAY BETWEEN 17 AND 23 JULY INCLUSIVE

Mark 6.30–34, 53–56

IT'S TOO CROWDED!

(Clifton Moore – movie superstar – enters, followed by A. J.)

Clifton: Quick A. J. shut the door. They're mad I tell you, mad.

A.J.: It's just your adoring fans Mr Moore.

Clifton: I know that, and I am thankful to them. Where would I Clifton Moore, Hollywood superstar, be without the loyal army of fans whose screams and adulation have propelled me to where I am today? And where am I today A. J.?

A.J.: $20 million a picture Mr Moore.

Clifton: Exactly. But the demands are getting too great. I need my personal, private space after all.

A.J.: Indeed you do Mr Moore.

Clifton: A place of peace and quiet where I can contemplate my greatness.

A.J.: No one deserves it more than you Mr Moore.

Clifton: I get sacks of mail from sad little housewives in Idaho. They all want something from me A. J.

A.J.: They do indeed.

Clifton: Some little piece of light to brighten up their otherwise dull, monotonous and incredibly humdrum lives. Isn't that right A. J.?

A.J.: You hit the nail right on the head Mr Moore.

Clifton: And I give them that light. My own colourful and exciting exploits on the screen and off are the food and drink of tabloid editors all over the world.

A.J.: They follow you everywhere sir.

Clifton: They do indeed. The public, A. J., they're like sheep without a shepherd, sheep without a shepherd.

A.J.: That's very biblical sir.

Clifton: It is?

A.J.: Absolutely Mr Moore. Jesus once used the phrase when he was pressed around from all sides by large crowds.

Clifton: A bit like me then?

A.J.: Well I wouldn't say you and Jesus had a great deal in common Mr Moore.

Clifton: And why not?

A.J.: Well, he was the saviour of the world Mr Moore. And you're . . . you're just a film star.

Clifton: JUST! JUST! There is no 'just' in the movie business A. J.

A.J.: No sir, of course not. But the reason people run around after you is because they've seen you in the movies, they think you're rich and glamorous.

Clifton: And indeed I am A. J.

A.J.: But Jesus – they ran after him because they loved what he had to say. He told people stories that explained their lives, he healed people, he told them about God.

Clifton: Hmmm. So how did Jesus deal with the crowds A. J.?

A.J.: He talked to them, he loved them, he gave all that he had to help them.

Clifton: What, like signed photographs?

A.J.: Not even close Mr Moore. Not even close.

SUNDAY BETWEEN 24 AND 30 JULY INCLUSIVE

John 6.1–21

SO PROUD

(Judith is standing centrally. Rachel enters.)

Rachel: Judith, quick, come here. News I have for you, such news – oh it makes a mother's heart swell with pride.

Judith: What is it now? Your little Matthew a musical prodigy is he?

Rachel: No, although you never know.

Judith: Your Andrew single-handedly took on a bunch of thieves?

Rachel: No, no. Although he's brave as a lion. No, it's my Benjamin.

Judith: So what's he been up to?

Rachel: You'll never guess. He fed five thousand starving people.

Judith: Your Benjamin?

Rachel: Yes.

Judith: The one with the acne and the limp?

Rachel: Don't mock the afflicted, he gets it from his father, God rest his soul.

Judith: He fed five thousand people?

Rachel: So he tells me.

Judith: This I've got to hear.

Rachel: Well he went out to listen to that wandering preacher.

Judith: You mean Jesus?

Rachel: That's the one. Well I asked him how long he was going to be out, and he said, 'Oh, not long, about an hour or two.' And I said to him, 'Benjamin,' I said, 'these preachers always go on longer than you think they're going to. They get carried away by the sound of their own voices and before you know it your tummy is rumbling, it's half past two in the afternoon, and you've had nothing to eat.'

Judith: Well I can't argue with you there.

Rachel: Anyway I said to him, 'Listen to your mother' I said, 'she knows what's best.' So I packed him up a nice packed lunch to take with him just in case. A nice couple of fresh fish and you know my beautiful, famous barley loaves, well he took five of those as well because you know he's got such an appetite on him.

Judith: So what happened?

Rachel: Well it seems like I was the only one who had foresight in the food department. Jesus went on for hours, everybody got carried away and forgot what time it was and before you know it, they're all out there in the middle of nowhere with nothing to eat. So my Benjamin – he always was such a generous boy, such a kind-hearted, loving lad – he offers his little packed lunch to one of the followers of Jesus.

Judith: Oh yes, and what then?

Rachel: Well then everything gets a bit hazy in my Benjamin's mind.

Judith: Surprise, surprise.

Rachel: Apparently, Jesus took my loaves and the fish and blessed them, everybody was fed, and there were twelve baskets of leftovers.

Judith: *(Laughing)* I'm sorry Rachel – even I'm not falling for that. You've been out in the sun too long. Go home, have a rest, put your feet up, and the next time you've got a story for me, make sure it's believable.

SUNDAY BETWEEN 31 JULY AND 6 AUGUST INCLUSIVE

John 6.24–35

SIGNS AND WONDERS

(Two actors are standing centrally.)

One: The world is an incredible place.

Two: Full of technological wonders . . .

One: Marvels of science . . .

Two: Astounding new medical breakthroughs . . .

One: So wonderful and grand . . .

Two: That we don't really need a supreme being any more – because we've got us.

One: So if you're there great God . . .

Two: Give us a sign.

One: Because everybody else has.

Two: A wonderful sign of your power and grace would do.

One: Something nicely spectacular.

Two: Really grand so nobody could be in any doubt . . .

One: That you are God. *(Pause)*

Two: The world is a surprising place.

One: People feel better about themselves than ever before.

Two: And if they don't there are lots of self-help groups.

One: To help us understand ourselves.

Two: And make sure we blame our failings on other people.

One: What need do we have of God . . .

Two: When the answers are so obviously within ourselves?

One: We can believe what we like and make our own salvation.

Two: And if we don't like the spiritual world we've constructed for ourselves that's okay . . .

One: It's our world – we can just change it.

Two: Now if you're there God . . .

One: You'd better give us sign . . .

Two: Something really grand and attention-grabbing.

One: After all we live in a world that is so noisy that a quiet voice would get drowned out in all the din.

Two: Yes give us a sign God.

One: A grand sign.

Two: A wonderful sign.

One: A sign that nobody would be able to dispute or deny.

Two: You've got to do it God.

One: Everybody else does.

Two: Shows their strength and power.

One: We want you to do that too.

Two: All we need are some miracles . . .

One: So that we can believe in you.

Two: *(Pause)* And yet we do not see you or hear you.

One: And pardon us gracious God but we are beginning to wonder . . .

Two: Whether we are looking in the wrong places . . .

One: Or demanding the wrong things.

SUNDAY BETWEEN 7 AND 13 AUGUST INCLUSIVE

John 6.35, 41–51

BREAD

(The shopkeeper is standing centrally. A customer enters.)

Shopkeeper: Good morning madam, can I help you?

Customer: Well I hope so. I want to get some bread.

Shopkeeper: Then you are in luck good lady for this is indeed a bread shop.

Customer: Oh wonderful.

Shopkeeper: Yes, yes. We can provide you with just the loaf you need to make your taste buds tingle. White or brown, sliced or unsliced, wholemeal, granary or organic or a mixture of all three. French sticks or farmhouse loaves, bread baps or finger rolls. We've got it all madam. Tomato and basil flavoured loaves, speciality breads, ciabatta or focaccia.

Customer: Steady on a bit.

Shopkeeper: Don't worry madam it was not my intention to be rude. We have wholegrain or wheat germ, we've got bread sprinkled with flour or with those little seeds that get in between your teeth. It is all completely freshly baked on the premises as you can tell by the delightful aroma that pervades the very air around us.

Customer: You've got a lovely way with words.

Shopkeeper: Thank you madam, I've always fancied myself something of a silver-tongued flatterer. Now madam what kind of loaf can I fix you up with?

Customer: Well, I'd like some bread of life please.

Shopkeeper: I'm sorry?

Customer: Bread of life.

Shopkeeper: I'm not quite sure what you're getting at. Our bread is fresh but I wouldn't say it's alive. You might well know that yeast – one of the key constituents of bread – is alive in its own little way, until we bake it of course – then it's dead.

Customer: I'm sorry, you seem to have misunderstood me.

Shopkeeper: Ah good, I was beginning to get a trifle perplexed.

Customer: I don't want bread that's alive, I want the bread of life.

Shopkeeper: I'm afraid I still don't quite catch your drift.

Customer: Well I'm sure the bread you sell is lovely.

Shopkeeper: There is none better.

Customer: I'm sure. But nonetheless after eating it one will, eventually, get hungry again and need to eat more bread.

Shopkeeper: That's the general idea, yes.

Customer: What I'm looking for is the bread of life. Spiritual food. After eating of this bread you will never be hungry again. It will fulfil all your needs.

Shopkeeper: I'm sorry madam but if I sold bread like that I'd put myself out of business wouldn't I? Nobody would need to come back to my shop again. It would be a fool who sold bread like that.

Customer: Not sold – I'm reliably informed it comes free of charge.

Shopkeeper: It's being given away? That does it – this must be some kind of hoax – come on, get out of my shop. Away with you. Bread of life indeed, and free of charge. Get out, go on. Wasting my time. Bread that fulfils all your needs – what kind of fool would give that away for free?

SUNDAY BETWEEN 14 AND 20 AUGUST INCLUSIVE

John 6.51–58

FLESH AND BLOOD

(Two actors stand centrally.)

One: Bread.
Two: Wine.
One: Flesh.
Two: Blood.
One: Ordinary and sacred.
Two: Everyday and touched by God.
One: Month in and month out.
Two: Year after year.
One: Very ordinary people.
Two: Just like us.
One: Have knelt at rails.
Two: All over the world.
One: And held out their hands.
Two: Just a simple act of receiving.
One: From tiny villages in Nepal and Madagascar.
Two: To huge cities in Brazil and Russia.
One: The action has continued.
Two: Every second of every day.
One: Bread is broken.
Two: Wine is poured.
One: From monasteries in Bulgaria.
Two: To prisons in Mexico.
One: The story has gone on.
Two: Just as it has for hundreds of years.
One: People holding out their hands and being given bread.
Two: People reaching out and receiving wine.
One: A very ordinary action in many ways.
Two: Nothing special.
One: Hardly spectacular.
Two: And yet faithful people have continued to do so for 2,000 years.
One: Why?
Two: Because this is no ordinary event.
One: In the taking of bread and wine.
Two: People time and time again.
One: Have discovered God.
Two: Sometimes crashing into their lives in power and splendour.
One: Sometimes in silence and whisper, barely noticed.
Two: This meal where bread and flesh combine.
One: And blood and wine converge.
Two: Is life.
One: And health.
Two: And joy to us.
One: For at this table Christ meets us at the point of our need.
Two: And takes us home.

SUNDAY BETWEEN 21 AND 27 AUGUST INCLUSIVE

John 6.56–59

CELEBRITY CHEF!

(Standing behind a table are Ros and George – celebrity chef.)

Ros: Good morning everybody and welcome to this week's edition of
         Celebrity Chef, and this week we have George Fatigoucho in the kitchen.

George: *(A real personality!)* Hello viewers!

Ros: So what have you cooked up for us this week George?

George: Well Ros, you know there are a lot of chefs on television nowadays?

Ros: There certainly are.

George: And I don't want to knock any of my colleagues – really I don't – but not
         one of them compares to my brilliance in the kitchen.

Ros: That's a fairly big claim George.

George: And one that you know to be right. My imagination, my brilliance, my
         charisma are all second to none.

Ros: Yes indeed.

George: My meals are heaven on a plate.

Ros: Well your cooking is quite nice.

George: Nice? Nice? That is not a word that can be used to describe my cooking!
         Astounding, brilliant, magnificent – these are all worthy words to express
         the wonder of what I put on the table. Nice is not a word that could be
         used.

Ros: Well I think I'd use it.

George: So you don't think much of my cooking eh?

Ros: I think you have your off-days.

George: What?

Ros: Take what you cooked for us last week – if you can call it cooked – three
         artichokes on a plate with a chopped-up tomato.

George: That was sheer brilliance.

Ros: Oh it was not. It was hardly enough to keep a hamster alive. People want
         real food, nourishing good cooking that's going to equip them for what
         they've got to do – not a cracker with a slither of pineapple on the top.

George: That meal was sheer genius.

Ros: It was sheer something.

George: I've never been spoken to like this in all my life.

Ros: Well perhaps you should have been. But that's the problem isn't it?
         We're bombarded with so many people telling us they're experts that we
         tend to believe them. I'm sorry, but I don't believe you're an expert at all.

George: How dare you!

Ros: Quite easily really. People need real food, real nourishment; something
         that's going to equip them for their lives, not the kind of excuse for food
         that you serve up.

George: You are a Philistine!

Ros: Perhaps I am, but I know one thing, it's a tough world out there and I
         need something that's going to help me cope with it, not the kind of
         excuse for nourishment that you come up with.

George: I'm leaving!

Ros: Not if I leave first – I'm off for some real food. Bye. *(She exits quickly.)*

SUNDAY BETWEEN 28 AUGUST AND 3 SEPTEMBER INCLUSIVE

Mark 7.1–8, 14–15, 21–23

PRIORITIES

(Two characters are sitting at a table writing letters. One is dressed very simply, Two is in a suit.)

One: Dear Sir or Madam . . . Yes that's a good start . . . I have never met you before and you don't know me. Why should you know me? It is just that my family and I for twenty years have worked very hard to grow the best coffee to make you and your company rich. My name is Ricardo and I work in one of the plantations your company owns in Peru. I was wondering whether you would like to know something about how your company workers live in this country? I am sure that all you want is the happiness and welfare of your workers. You must have so many people whose lives and health depend on the decisions you make every day. I have to tell you that life is very hard here in my country. I work very long hours and get paid very little money. The work is difficult and as I get older I am less and less able to work as hard as I used to. I look towards the future and I worry very much. I am sure that your company has a very good pension scheme in your country but here there is nothing. When I am no longer able to work I will have to depend on my children to look after me. They too work in the plantation because that is all there is here. I cannot see any way in which our future will become better. Recently our manager told us that our wages would be cut. There is a worldwide surplus of coffee he said and the price has dropped. I think we will go hungry this year. That is why I write to you for I am sure that you do not know of our plight. If you did you would do something about it, because I am sure that your loyal workers mean a great deal to you.

Two: Dear Ricardo, Thank you very much for your letter which reached me here in Coffee House two months ago. I am sorry that I am only now getting round to answering your queries but my family and I were enjoying a holiday in Mauritius getting in a little scuba diving. Have you ever done that? I can really recommend it. Our priorities here at Costalot Coffee Corporation have always been and always will be fat dividend cheques for our share holders. I'm sorry if that sounds a little brutal but life is hard sometimes – in fact that's something you know about already. Let me see if I can explain the worldwide coffee trade to you, Ricardo, in small words that you will understand. You grow coffee. You need to grow that coffee as cheaply as possible so I can sell it at as much of a profit as I can in order that I can continue to go on holidays to exotic destinations all over the world and live in a small mansion in Surrey. You seem to think that my priority ought to be the welfare and happiness of my work force. So it is Ricardo – so it is. Only the other day I gave the not insubstantial sum of £4.50 for the work of Oxfam. Some business people, Ricardo, want to change the world, improve the environment, transform business practice – all I want to do is make lots of money and do that as quickly and painlessly as possible. So my priorities are clear and I think very good ones. They're just slightly different from your priorities. Isn't it odd that we both work for the same company. Yours sincerely, Sir Jocelyn Moneybags.

SUNDAY BETWEEN 4 AND 10 SEPTEMBER INCLUSIVE

Mark 7.24–37

RALPH AND JIM ON BEING OPEN

(Ralph and Jim are sitting centrally.)

Ralph: You know what Jim mate . . . I've been thinking.

Jim: Have you Ralphy boy? What you been thinking about then eh?

Ralph: Well Jim mate I have been wrapping my not insignificant grey matter around the issue of being open.

Jim: Being open?

Ralph: That's what I said Jim.

Jim: What, like the Chinese take-away's open? 'Cos they're like open all the time in't they?

Ralph: No, not like the Chinese take-away.

Jim: Well what about that new corner shop? 'Cos like they're open from 7 in the morning till 11 at night.

Ralph: No Jim mate – as usual you have misunderstood my meaning.

Jim: Oh, sorry about that Ralphy boy.

Ralph: That's all right Jim, I just have to get used to the fact that you're a bit slow on the take-up, that's all. When I said 'open', I meant openness of the mind and spirit. Being open to new an' surprising things.

Jim: What like Watford winning the Cup? 'Cos that would be a new an' a surprising thing wouldn't it?

Ralph: It would indeed Jim. But I'm thinking even more broadly than that.

Jim: Wow.

Ralph: Absolutely wow! What I'm thinking about is how prepared are we to open our minds to possibilities that we'd never even thought of before?

Jim: Like ITV putting *Coronation Street* on on a Saturday night.

Ralph: Well there is that, but there's also the issue of prejudice as well.

Jim: There is?

Ralph: You'd better believe it. Everyone of us has little prejudices in our heads – ways of thinking about other people, pictures and ideas that pop into our heads without us even realizing it sometimes.

Jim: That always happens when I think about my mother-in-law.

Ralph: It always happens when *I* think about your mother-in-law as well.

Jim: So all this is a bad thing then is it Ralph?

Ralph: Well of course it is. It stops us being open to what's really happening around us. It closes us off to amazing possibilities because we can't see them.

Jim: I suppose you're right.

Ralph: I know I'm right Jim mate.

Jim: 'Cos like God could want us to see an' understand all kinds of new and exciting things about other people.

Ralph: But we're too blind to see them.

Jim: It's a bit worrying when you think about it really, 'cos we've probably missed so much.

Ralph: I think we've all just got to be really open to seeing new and wonderful truths about the world around us Jim mate.

Jim: I'll certainly try Ralphy boy, I'll certainly try.

SUNDAY BETWEEN 11 AND 17 SEPTEMBER INCLUSIVE

Mark 8.27–38

WHO IS HE?

(Sal is a tabloid editor. Hal is a reporter.)

Sal: So, Hal, tell me you've got something. We've got a paper to get out and four hours till the deadline.

Hal: Well Sal, it's difficult . . .

Sal: Difficult? Difficult? Difficult is how you're going to find life when you're out of a job because you didn't get me this story.

Hal: Well he won't commit himself.

Sal: I don't care if he won't commit himself. The readers of the *Daily News* have a right to know who this guy is. Did you go back to Nazareth? Talk to a few old dears there, dig up a past girlfriend? There must be somebody who wants to dish the dirt on this guy.

Hal: Look, I went to Nazareth, just as you said, but they're just surprised that he's doing anything like this. They're pleased for him really.

Sal: Pleased for him. That's nice. Unfortunately 'nice' doesn't sell newspapers, sensational scandal does. So what have we got so far?

Hal: Well there are all kinds of rumours going round about him.

Sal: Rumours – that's good. What kind of rumours?

Hal: Well some people say he's Elijah back from the dead.

Sal: Gimme a break – that stuff's so old it's got wrinkles. What else is there?

Hal: Some people think he's John the Baptist.

Sal: What, the guy Herod had killed? Back from the dead? Hey, that wouldn't be a bad angle. 'You thought he had his head on a plate, but John the Baptist escaped and is alive and well.' But do we believe it?

Hal: That's never stopped you before.

Sal: I know. What can I tell you? I'm getting a conscience in my old age. Wouldn't that be a terrible thing? Is there anything else?

Hal: Well I did some digging around amongst his followers.

Sal: And? I mean they've dropped everything to traipse round after this guy, they must have some idea of who he is, right?

Hal: Well yes and no really.

Sal: Oh, that's really helpful.

Hal: It's just that they know he's special, they just can't quite put their finger on why. Except . . .

Sal: Yes?

Hal: It's probably nothing. I just get the feeling that they know who he is really, it's just that they're frightened of saying it out loud.

Sal: What do you mean?

Hal: You know when you were in school and the teacher asked a question and you were pretty sure you knew the answer but it sounded so far-fetched that you didn't want to say it just in case everybody thought you were stupid? I think it's something like that.

Sal: But that would imply that there's something *really* special about this guy.

Hal: I think there might be.

Sal: You've got a week Hal. I want everything. If this guy's hiding something our readers have a right to know what it is. Now get going. *(Hal exits.)*

SUNDAY BETWEEN 18 AND 24 SEPTEMBER INCLUSIVE

Mark 9.30–37

THE GREATEST

(Commentator and politician are sitting centrally.)

Smarmy: Welcome to *Election Night Special*, I'm your host, Smarmy Talker, and we're here with the absolute loser of tonight's competition of ideas, Jenny Goodperson.

Jenny: Hello.

Smarmy: Well, the electors have spoken haven't they Jenny?

Jenny: I'm afraid they have, yes.

Smarmy: And they really didn't like what you had to say.

Jenny: It appears not.

Smarmy: You are definitely not the greatest politician here today – in fact you're the worst.

Jenny: I suppose you could look at it that way.

Smarmy: I do, Jenny, I do. So I suppose you'll be changing your policies now?

Jenny: Why would I do that?

Smarmy: Well, not to put too fine a point on it, the electors obviously didn't like what you had to say. And they did like what Sir Winston Backhander put before them.

Jenny: And that's a reason to change what I say is it?

Smarmy: Well, duh, he's an MP and you're not – you do the maths.

Jenny: So it's all about getting elected is it?

Smarmy: Of course it is, it's politics.

Jenny: And it's not about telling the truth or standing up for what you believe in?

Smarmy: Absolutely not. Sir Winston did not become one of the country's greatest MPs by sticking to ideals. He works out what the voters want and then gives it to them. He's jumped on every bandwagon there is going.

Jenny: And that's greatness is it?

Smarmy: Look you keep on asking me questions, I'm the interviewer.

Jenny: I'm sorry; I just thought that telling the truth, whether it's what people want to hear or not, was the important thing.

Smarmy: Look, you're never going to be a great politician with that kind of view.

Jenny: Apparently not.

Smarmy: Don't you want to be the greatest?

Jenny: Not really, no. I want to do a good job.

Smarmy: So while Sir Winston is enjoying a fat expense account and a London apartment, you'll still be in your pokey little two-bedroom flat with running damp trying to change the world.

Jenny: What can I say? It's a glamorous life.

Smarmy: I just don't understand you.

Jenny: I don't think the voters did either.

Smarmy: So don't you feel any twinge of jealousy as Sir Winston motors off in his chauffeur-driven limousine?

Jenny: No, I'm quite happy for him to be the greatest. As long as I can continue my work here.

Smarmy: Well folks, there you have it. She doesn't want your sympathy or your vote – all she wants is to be faithful – this is Smarmy Talker, and you've been watching *Election Night Special*.

SUNDAY BETWEEN 25 SEPTEMBER AND 1 OCTOBER INCLUSIVE

Mark 9.38–50

OUTSIDE INFLUENCES

(The judge is seated centrally. The accused enters.)

Judge: Judith Margaret Jones, you stand accused by some rather self-righteous do-gooders of not being a Christian. How do you plead?

Accused: Not guilty m'lud.

Judge: Well, let us look at the evidence. It says here that you did not attend a meeting of the Wednesday Fellowship Group based at your local church – do you have a good reason for this?

Accused: I was doing some volunteer work at the local Night Stop Hostel m'lud.

Judge: Miss Jones, while that might be considered very worthwhile work, is it really right that you should neglect Christian fellowship?

Accused: I believe on this occasion yes. I'm not against other people going to Fellowship Group, honest I'm not, I just felt I could do more good where I was on this particular Wednesday.

Judge: I see. *(Pause)* You are further accused of not attending the church's Bring and Buy Coffee Morning the following Saturday.

Accused: I was rattling a can for a local cancer charity outside the supermarket. They were short of volunteers so I did a couple of hours for them.

Judge: Do you not think the *church* needs to raise funds to keep its doors open Miss Jones?

Accused: I'm sure it does m'lud and the Bring and Buy Coffee Mornings are always well supported. I just thought my time was better used elsewhere. All the folk who work for the cancer charity know I'm a Christian, they were very happy to see me there and I don't think that does the church any harm.

Judge: Perhaps. The third charge is perhaps the most serious of all. You stand accused of not being at church for morning worship two Sundays ago. Do you have something to say for yourself?

Accused: I was not at my local church m'lud, that's true.

Judge: Oh dear, oh dear.

Accused: I was at the local hospital chapel attending their morning service with my mother-in-law. She's a patient at the moment. She wanted to go to church but didn't want to go alone so I said I'd go with her.

Judge: I see.

Accused: Do you? Do you really see?

Judge: I beg your pardon?

Accused: Look, I'm trying to be a Christian the best way I know how. It may not be very conventional. I may not be at all the meetings I'm meant to be at or jump through all the hoops that people feel they'd like to see me get through, but I feel I'm being as faithful as I can, and if that's a crime then I'm sorry. I'm trying really hard at this – it's just not easy.

Judge: Miss Jones calm yourself. I think you're doing exceptionally well.

Accused: You do?

Judge: Indeed I do. You mustn't let yourself get worried about one or two busybodies who think they have the copyright on what makes a good Christian. You keep going just the way you are. To be honest, the church could do with one or two more like you. Case dismissed.

SUNDAY BETWEEN 2 AND 8 OCTOBER INCLUSIVE

Mark 10.2–16

CHILDREN

(Gwendolyn and Anastasia approach from the back.)

Gwendolyn:	Do you know what?
Anastasia:	I bet you'll never guess!
Gwendolyn:	No I bet you never will.
Anastasia:	Gwendolyn – beautiful Gwendolyn – and I are sisters.
Gwendolyn:	Yes indeed, indeed, lovely Anastasia and I are sisters!
Anastasia:	*(Turning to face Gwendolyn)* Hello beautiful sister Gwendolyn.
Gwendolyn:	Hello entrancing sister Anastasia!
Anastasia:	You know, darling sister, that the thing we hate most in all the world is about to shatter the peace of our lives?
Gwendolyn:	You couldn't possibly mean . . . ?
Anastasia:	I'm afraid I do.
Gwendolyn:	Oh horrible, too horrible.
Anastasia:	Yes, our little nephew and niece the Prince Roderick and the Princess Celia are coming to visit.
Gwendolyn:	If there is something I hate more than a pimple spoiling my otherwise flawless complexion, it is children.
Anastasia:	Particularly children of the ages five and eight.
Gwendolyn:	They should be locked away somewhere and not allowed out until at least the age of eighteen.
Anastasia:	They always want you to play with them.
Gwendolyn:	Or talk with them . . .
Anastasia:	Or shower them with attention.
Gwendolyn:	It is perfectly disgusting.
Anastasia:	They're forever asking questions.
Gwendolyn:	And expecting us to know the answers.
Anastasia:	They chatter incessantly . . .
Gwendolyn:	When all *we* want to do is listen to ourselves.
Anastasia:	They bounce around early in the morning, shouting and screeching.
Gwendolyn:	Just when we need our beauty sleep.
Anastasia:	I hate children.
Gwendolyn:	I loathe them.
Anastasia:	I detest them.
Gwendolyn:	You know, dearest sister Anastasia, I can hardly believe that we were children ourselves once.
Anastasia:	I am almost certain, wonderful sister Gwendolyn, that we were not.
Gwendolyn:	We certainly have nothing to learn from them now.
Anastasia:	Oh absolutely not.
Gwendolyn:	We are not childlike in any way.
Anastasia:	In any way at all.
Gwendolyn:	We are far more realistic,
Anastasia:	Worldly wise, hard-hearted . . .
Gwendolyn:	And cynical.
Anastasia:	Isn't being a grown-up wonderful, beauteous sister Gwendolyn?
Gwendolyn:	It certainly is, dazzling sister Anastasia.

SUNDAY BETWEEN 9 AND 15 OCTOBER INCLUSIVE

Mark 10.17–31

WHO WANTS TO BE A VERY RICH PERSON INDEED?

(Game show host and contestant enter from opposite sides.)

Host: Welcome back folks, and I cannot believe how tense it is here in the studio. Can you believe how tense it is Lindsey?

Lindsey: No I can't believe how tense it is Grant.

Host: Neither can I. Here's the situation . . . Lindsey here is one question away from being a very, very rich person indeed. Isn't that right?

Lindsey: Oooh, yes it is.

Host: She's answered fifteen questions correctly so far and has £750,000 in the bank. But she can gamble it all for a crack at our final question and the chance to win £3 million! Would you like £3 million Lindsey?

Lindsey: Oh yes.

Host: Of course you would. Who wouldn't? All that lovely loot – yours to do what you want with. All of it absolutely tax-free. Just think of what you could do with that amount of money. I mean – it's almost half my salary! You could buy an incredible house, a luxury car, go on the holiday of your dreams – the possibilities are endless. Tell me Lindsey, what would you do with all that cash?

Lindsey: I'd give it away Grant.

Host: *(Pause)* I'm sorry, what was that again?

Lindsey: I'd give it away.

Host: You mean you'd give *some* of it away. I can understand that – perhaps to a home for sick animals or something like that.

Lindsey: No Grant, I'd give it *all* away.

Host: All of it?

Lindsey: That's right.

Host: Every penny of the £3 million cleverly extorted from the general public through massively expensive phone line questions?

Lindsey: That's it. There are a couple of charities working with issues of poverty in the Third World that will be a lot better off after tonight's quiz.

Host: Well I'm sorry then, but I'm not going to ask you the question.

Lindsey: What?

Host: Look, this whole programme is based on the concept of sheer unadulterated greed for money. Now if you're not going to play the game properly and show money the rich respect that it deserves then I'm sorry, but we're not going to ask you the question at all.

Lindsey: But I've got a right . . .

Host: You've got no right at all. No right not to take money seriously. No right not to be selfish. No right not to be greedy. I'm sorry but we can't have you standing here and knocking the very basis of our society.

Lindsey: But I answered all the questions properly.

Host: Yes but little did we know then that you were some kind of lunatic. Imagine being prepared to give away £3 million – you must be mad.

Lindsey: So it's mad not to let money rule your life?

Host: Of course it is, and if you were rich like me you'd know that. Now get out before we have you kicked out. Go on! *(Ad lib as she exits.)*

SUNDAY BETWEEN 16 AND 22 OCTOBER INCLUSIVE

Mark 10.35–45

AND THE ARGUMENT GOES ON

(James and John are standing centrally.)

James: So if you're so clever, you tell me what he meant then.
John: All right then I will.
James: Well come on then, I'm waiting.
John: I would if you'd give me a chance.
James: Or perhaps it's just that I'm a better disciple than you.
John: I can't believe you're off on that tack again.
James: Holier, more faithful . . .
John: Look we've only just got into trouble for arguing about that.
James: Oh, *(Pause)* yeah, you're right.
John: For what it's worth, I think he was talking about suffering.
James: Well that's obvious, 'Can you drink from the cup I'm going to drink from?' . . . anybody could see he's talking about suffering.
John: And I think he's saying he's going to suffer in some way.
James: Well the Pharisees hate him.
John: The Sadducees detest him.
James: My Auntie Joan thinks he's a bit of a weirdo too.
John: So suffering is inevitable in some way.
James: But it won't be anything too extreme will it?
John: Oh no, probably just a rap over the knuckles for bad behaviour.
James: Perhaps a few months in a Roman jail.
John: Just to make a point.
James: Then they'll let him go.
John: And everything will be the same as it was before.
James: But better 'cos they'll have made their point.
John: Which means we'll probably be left alone.
James: So that means Jesus was saying 'Can you . . . that is you and me . . . suffer in the way that I'm going to suffer?'
John: And the answer to that is a resounding 'Yes'.
James: I'm really good at suffering.
John: And I'm even better at suffering than you are.
James: What do you mean you're better at suffering than I am?
John: Well I am. Even at school you were a bit squeamish.
James: I was not.
John: Oh you were a real wimp. You couldn't suffer for more than a few seconds. Whereas me – my pain threshold is huge. If you're talking suffering, I'm your man.
James: That is *so* not true. I still remember when that kid dropped a spider down your back – you were crying for a month.
John: I was not. I can suffer more than you can.
James: I'm far better at suffering than you.
John: You are not.
James: Am too.
John: *(Pause)* You don't think we've missed the point of what he was on about?
James: Nah! How could we have done that?

SUNDAY BETWEEN 23 AND 29 OCTOBER INCLUSIVE

Mark 10.46–52

ANOTHER ONE

(Simeon is sitting at a table. Saul enters.)

Simeon: Ah Saul, come in, I've just been reading your latest reports. Very lucid, very good indeed. I think we're not far off having Jesus just where we want him.

Saul: I'm afraid there's been another one sir.

Simeon: Another what?

Saul: Another healing sir. Just yesterday – I've got the details here.

Simeon: Does this man not know when to stop?

Saul: I'm afraid he doesn't seem to sir, no.

Simeon: So what is it this time? Demons cast out? Deaf people hearing? Lame people walking?

Saul: No sir, it's a blind man being able to see again.

Simeon: Oh that's not terribly original. Haven't we seen one of those before?

Saul: Yes sir, several.

Simeon: So then, give me the boring details.

Saul: The man's name is Bartimaeus, blind Bartimaeus.

Simeon: Oh good, he even has a nickname. I'll give Jesus this much, he does know how to pick them.

Saul: Yes sir, except apparently in this case Bartimaeus picked Jesus.

Simeon: How do you mean?

Saul: Well it appears that Jesus and his rabble were travelling through Jericho. This blind beggar made such a din as Jesus was passing by that the crowd pushed him forward to be touched by the master.

Simeon: Why are these people always hanging around? Don't they have jobs to go to?

Saul: I know, there are seemingly a limitless supply of hard luck cases for Jesus to take an interest in, and an adoring crowd to watch and provide background colour.

Simeon: It boils my blood Saul, it really does. How people could be so gullible is beyond me. And no doubt some kind of healing took place?

Saul: I'm afraid so. If the reports are to be believed Jesus asked this Bartimaeus what he wanted.

Simeon: Oh I wonder what the answer to that one was?!

Saul: Exactly. He says, 'Rabbi I want to see' and the healing is set up.

Simeon: It's so obvious Saul – that's what really angers me. Anyway with your latest reports I think the end is nigh for our little thorn in the flesh from Nazareth. We've got enough evidence now. The days of Jesus are numbered.

Saul: I'm just glad to have been of use sir. The people need to have their eyes opened to what is right in front of them.

Simeon: They do indeed, Saul, they do indeed. You know as well as I do that there are none who are so blind as those who will not see.

Saul: Which means we will need to force people to see.

Simeon: And you're just the one to enable that to happen. I foresee great things for you Saul of Tarsus, great things indeed.

SUNDAY BETWEEN 30 OCTOBER AND 5 NOVEMBER INCLUSIVE

Mark 12.28–34

CALL CENTRE

(Two people are sitting by telephones, facing forward.)

One: *(Dialling)* Hello, is that heaven?

Two: Good morning, yes, this is the heaven switchboard. My name is Michael, how can I be of service?

One: Well I'm really wanting some advice.

Two: If you want guidance on how to live your life press 2 now, if you want to know how many angels fit on the head of a pin please press 3, for all other enquiries please press 4.

One: Oh no please don't go. I actually wanted to talk to a person not a recording.

Two: Of course. I'm an angel, will that do?

One: Wonderful.

Two: Good, now what can we help you with?

One: Well I've been a Christian for about three months now.

Two: Excellent, how are you finding it?

One: Oh it's going well I think.

Two: We had the most brilliant party when you joined up you know. A real blow-out. You should have seen it.

One: What, a party, just for me?

Two: Absolutely. We just love it when people like you understand what it's all about.

One: Ah, well that's what I'm calling about.

Two: Oh, is there some kind of trouble?

One: Well I'm not sure I'm doing it right.

Two: Doing what right?

One: The whole Christian life bit. I mean are there rules I should be following? Things I should be doing?

Two: We've really got only one rule both up here and down there.

One: Oh yes, and what's that?

Two: Love.

One: Love . . . that's it?

Two: You wanted more?

One: It just doesn't seem to be very much really.

Two: Well we wanted to keep things simple, but you'll find it's not as easy as it looks. To be loving to all the people you meet, friend and foe – it's quite difficult.

One: Oh I'm sure. I can think of one or two people already that I'm going to have trouble with.

Two: Yes . . . I know. The trick is to make sure you love *God* fully first and then love for the people that God has created sort of falls into place.

One: Right, thank you.

Two: We do offer help as well you know.

One: You do?

Two: Oh yes, well it's very difficult to do all this by yourself. One might almost say impossible. Let me transfer you to Holy Spirit help services and they'll get right on it. Goodbye . . . thank you for calling heaven today.

SUNDAY BETWEEN 6 AND 12 NOVEMBER INCLUSIVE

Mark 12.38–44

THE COLLECTION

(Brian is sitting at the front. Conscience is behind him and to one side.)

Brian:	Ah, the collection.
Conscience:	Excellent, the collection.
Brian:	Who said that?
Conscience:	I did.
Brian:	And who are you?
Conscience:	Oh just your conscience, don't mind me.
Brian:	I don't intend to.
Conscience:	No, I've noticed. So, what are you putting in the plate this week?
Brian:	I'm giving what I normally give.
Conscience:	And how much is that?
Brian:	What I can afford.
Conscience:	Oh well that could cover a multitude of sins. Come on, what are you actually giving?
Brian:	*(Showing an amount of money to Conscience)* This.
Conscience:	*(Not impressed)* Last of the big spenders eh? And that's all you can afford is it?
Brian:	It's more than Miss Johnson's giving.
Conscience:	She's ninety-seven years old! And anyway, if you really want to know the truth, she actually gives rather more than that.
Brian:	*(Embarrassed)* Well I have a lot of commitments.
Conscience:	Such as?
Brian:	Loads of direct debits, bills, I've got savings accounts to put money into, pension payments to make, a mortgage to meet, hire purchase commitments.
Conscience:	So let me get this straight – you say you give all you can afford, right?
Brian:	Right.
Conscience:	And it turns out that what you can afford is the money you've got left after you've spent everything else.
Brian:	Well, yes. Isn't that what everybody does?
Conscience:	Not really, no.
Brian:	Well I'm sorry I'm not the perfect little Christian.
Conscience:	It's not a matter of that. It's a matter of being really thankful, truly overwhelmed by gratitude and wanting to give some of that back.
Brian:	I'm thankful.
Conscience:	I'd hate to see you when you're grudging.
Brian:	All you're trying to do is make me feel guilty.
Conscience:	Well if the cap fits . . . What I'm really trying to do is to help you see that what you give here should be the first thing you think about, not the last.
Brian:	But that would mean changing all my priorities round.
Conscience:	Surprise, surprise.
Brian:	But I'm happy with my life the way it is.
Conscience:	That's not the question though, is it?
Brian:	It isn't?
Conscience:	No, the question is – is God happy?

SUNDAY BETWEEN 13 AND 19 NOVEMBER INCLUSIVE

Mark 13.1–8

END TIMES

(Two officers on the bridge of a starship.)

Lester: Captain Thaddeus T. Lester of the starship *Quirky* – Captain's log star-date 31 point 45 point 467 and three tenths. I don't know how much longer we can go on like this. My gallant crew and I have been travelling through the same gaseous nebula for three months now and still no sign of the other side. My ability to over-act is sapped dry. How much more of this can any of us take?!

Splot: Calm yourself Captain. You must think logically.

Lester: Ah, Mr Splot, my trusted second-in-command. How do you remain so focused and at peace in the middle of the most terrible threat we have ever faced?

Splot: Simple Captain, I practise the old earth art of crochet.

Lester: Crochet?

Splot: Yes, have this lovely woolly hat I've been working on *(Produces hat)*.

Lester: Thank you. But how is this hat going to protect us from a fate worse than death? Pure boredom? I'm not sure Splot, but I think the end is nigh.

Splot: The end Captain?

Lester: Yes, Splot, old friend. The end of life, meaning, purpose, everything. Goodbye my pointy-eared colleague – it's been good working with you.

Splot: I think it maybe a little premature to be predicting the end Captain.

Lester: You think so?

Splot: In my extensive study of earth's history, Captain, it appears to me that humans have always felt that whenever they faced difficult times they have always thought the end of the world was imminent.

Lester: They have?

Splot: Indeed from Nostradamus onwards humans have loved to predict that 'the end is nigh'. Of course it never actually happens.

Lester: No, our long-range scanners would have told us.

Splot: Yes, that vast array of flashing lights and displays we have must tell us something.

Lester: So let me get this right Splot. You're telling me the end of all things is almost certainly not here yet.

Splot: No Captain, I'm telling you that it is a big mistake to try and predict when the end will be, because you'll almost certainly get it wrong and then you'll end up looking stupid, which in your case wouldn't be too difficult.

Lester: I think I see Splot.

Splot: Good because I'm not going to try to explain it to you again.

Lester: I suppose Splot, old chum, that we should leave the end of all things in the capable hands of God.

Splot: That would almost certainly be best sir.

Lester: 'Cos God knows, right?

Splot: That would be my deduction sir.

Lester: If we asked nicely do you think he'd tell us?

Splot: No sir.

Lester: Darn. Then all we've got left is my acting ability. Full ahead, Warp 7!

SUNDAY BETWEEN 20 AND 26 NOVEMBER INCLUSIVE

John 18.33–37

KINGSHIP

(King and Bert process down to the front.)

King: Greetings good subjects, greetings indeed. You all know me, King Reginald XXIII, and this is my wise royal adviser, Bert.

Bert: Yes, yes. Good morning.

King: I've come here today to share with you something of what it means to be a king.

Bert: Oh good grief, have you?

King: Yes, I thought you knew.

Bert: No, I imagined we were coming to open a supermarket or something.

King: Well this is a nice surprise for you isn't it then? My thoughts on being a king.

Bert: Well that shouldn't take too long.

King: Thank you very much. A king should always be kind and thoughtful towards others.

Bert: Is that it? Have you finished now?

King: No, not quite. A king should also be gentle and wise.

Bert: Right, can we be off home?

King: Why all the rush wise adviser Bert?

Bert: Well, the fact is you're not actually a very good king are you? So why these good people here should take the blindest bit of notice of anything you say is quite beyond me.

King: I'm sorry, but I think I'm a very fine king indeed.

Bert: Oh you are not. I've been doing some reading.

King: You haven't have you?

Bert: I have. Now I know what you think a king should be, all pomp and circumstance. Purple robes, fur-lined crowns, dripping with jewellery, all that kind of stuff.

King: Well it does sound rather regal doesn't it?

Bert: But what about a king who doesn't want power, at least not in the way the world sees it? A king who lives and dies without ever owning a house, yet alone a palace?

King: This person hardly sounds like a king at all.

Bert: Oh it gets better. This king doesn't have any army to send into battle, he doesn't have any fancy clothes, and the crown he wears is a bunch of thorn branches pressed deep into his scalp.

King: Eurgh! It sounds awful.

Bert: But this king doesn't need any of the trappings that normal kings have because he has more power in his little finger than you'll ever have. His kingdom is heaven and his domain is the universe.

King: This is all sounding very strange.

Bert: Imagine a king that takes every idea that you have ever had about kingship and turns it upside down. A man who is the least likely looking king that you've ever seen.

King: This man sounds very dangerous, Bert, very dangerous indeed.

Bert: Oh he is, Your Majesty, Jesus is the most dangerous king you'll ever meet.

YEAR C

FIRST SUNDAY OF ADVENT

Luke 21.25–36

RALPH AND JIM ON THE END OF THE WORLD

(Two characters sit on stage at a table.)

Ralph: I don't understand it Jim mate.

Jim: What's that then Ralph?

Ralph: The end Jim.

Jim: Oh . . . the end of what Ralph . . . your latest book? . . . Thursday's *Coronation Street*? . . . what?

Ralph: No . . . the end of all things Jim.

Jim: Oh . . . how's that then?

Ralph: Well, you know Jim. What's going to happen like at the end of time? Where are we heading? Will creation end with a huge bang or a bit of a whimper?

Jim: You've been thinking about that?

Ralph: I have, Jim mate, I have.

Jim: Well that's a bit depressing innit? I mean you could be thinking about sausages or cream cakes or James Bond films. But you're thinking about the end of everything.

Ralph: I s'pose it could be deemed by some to be a bit of a downer Jim mate – it could indeed. But when you've got a great intellect like mine then these random thoughts just sometimes get in and won't go away.

Jim: So what have you decided about the end Ralph?

Ralph: Good question Jim. I've looked at all the evidence, weighed up all the theories, consulted all the scientific documentation, and come up with a truly startling conclusion.

Jim: What's that then Ralph?

Ralph: Nobody knows Jim mate.

Jim: Oh well that's a bit of a shocker.

Ralph: I thought so Jim. Not even Mystic Meg was prepared to give a definitive theory about how the end of all things was going to take place.

Jim: Oh, what a disappointment. 'Cos you could have hoped for something a bit more dramatic than that. Like – the world's going to end on Thursday so you'd better do your supermarket shopping now.

Ralph: It is true, Jim, that I was a little saddened by this lack of knowledge in the scientific community. But it has led me to one conclusion.

Jim: And what's that then Ralph?

Ralph: Well, I've decided that if all of this is the case then absolutely every thought we have, every action we take is like really important. Everything matters.

Jim: How'd you figure that then?

Ralph: Well, it could happen at any time couldn't it? The end of the planet. The end of you or of me.

Jim: Well there's a cheery thought.

Ralph: But it's true Jim. It could happen at any time, as the Good Book says.

Jim: What Good Book's that then? John Grisham? Jeffrey Archer?

Ralph: No, the Bible you plonker. You cannot tell the times or the seasons – so everything that you do or say or think could be your last.

Jim: Scary thought Ralph.

Ralph: Scary indeed Jim . . . buy us a pint willya?

SECOND SUNDAY OF ADVENT

Luke 3.1–6

AGENTS ANONYMOUS 1

(Two characters appear from opposite directions moving furtively.)

Agent 01: The brown cow faces north.

Agent 02: Eh? *(Realizing it is a secret password)* Oh yeah . . . but only in the sunset hour on a Thursday.

Agent 01: I do wish you'd learn the secret password properly 02. I mean our very lives could be in danger. Utmost secrecy at all times is vital to our mission. You know that.

Agent 02: I'm sorry 01. I just forgot. My mind's been on other things – my sciatica hasn't half been playing up recently. By the way – do you want a cup of tea and a nice digestive biscuit?

Agent 01: No you fool – not when we're on duty.

Agent 02: Cor, you take everything so seriously – don't you?

Agent 01: Yes I do. If we're going to report back to the Pharisees with the right information we can't afford to make any mistakes. Now what have you found out?

Agent 02: Well it's fascinating – absolutely fascinating. The hold he has on the crowds, the message he preaches – it's incredibly powerful. I really got quite carried away. And you know that's not normally like me. Not at all. No. I mean you know me. Am I the sort to get easily carried away? No I don't think so. Mr Unflappable – that's me, but he really is very moving.

Agent 01: If I didn't know any better I'd say you'd allowed yourself to become personally involved.

Agent 02: Oh no, no, not me. But you've got to admit it's riveting stuff. I mean just looking at him. The wild eyes, the clothing, the whole desert man aesthetic – very powerful. And then there's the message.

Agent 01: Ah, yes. Now I'm interested to hear about this.

Agent 02: Well, I was on the edge of one of the crowds. He calls people out of the cities you know, to riverbanks. And ooh it was a hot day. Anyway – the message is very simple. Turn away from your sins he says. Turn your back on your old life. And there's all these people standing there lapping all this up. And they're all sorts – these people – young, old, rich, poor. All equally moved. It's electric – I mean you could cut the atmosphere with a knife. Then he says 'Be baptized and God will forgive you.' Well there's silence for a long time. I mean you could hear a pin drop. Then this elderly fellow steps up and he goes quietly down to the water and John dips him under. Then there's another person and another, and before you know it half the crowd are down there. And they're coming back crying tears of joy. It was incredible.

Agent 01: This is worrying, very worrying.

Agent 02: You're telling me. It looked so unhygienic.

Agent 01: No you fool. Our masters are going to want to know about this straight away.

Agent 02: Oh, yes, indeed. Do you think they'll arrest him?

Agent 01: They might do. But that's not what I'm concerned about. The thing I'm worried about is what all of this is building up to. Come on. *(Exit.)*

THIRD SUNDAY OF ADVENT

Luke 3.7–18

ROBERT AND KATY ON ADVICE

(Robert and Katy are two seven-year-olds played by adults.)

Robert: Wotcha Katy *(Wipes nose)*.

Katy: Wotcha Robert *(Wipes nose)*.

Robert: I see your mum and dad have let you out again after the chocolate cake incident then.

Katy: Yeah. But there's still chocolate cream filling to be washed out of the cream corded settee. *(Sniggers)*

Robert: *(Sniggering)* Well it's nice to leave your mark on the world innit?

Katy: Yeah – that's what I thought. I mean at least *I'm* safe and all right.

Robert: Y'know I don't understand adults sometimes.

Katy: Well they're a foreign species ain't they?

Robert: I mean – they criticize us for the things we do but they do some pretty strange stuff themselves.

Katy: You know when we go to church on Sundays my mum's always telling me to be quiet, and then there she is talking to loads of people before the service at the top of her voice. 'Oh Katy's been so naughty this week, I don't know what I'm going to do with her.'

Robert: Yeah my dad does the same thing. He keeps on saying really mean things about Mrs Baxter at No. 43 – like what a bad temper she's got, and how he hates her yappy little dog. But then, when he was talking to Mrs Baxter in the shops the other day, I reminded him of what he'd said and he gave me a clip round the ear. And when we got home he gave me a real telling off. I don't understand it.

Katy: It's best not to try and understand grown-ups. They say one thing and do another all the time.

Robert: My auntie's always reading the advice columns in magazines. You know, people write in with all their problems and then some really clever person, who probably lives in London in a really expensive house and gets loads of money, tells 'em what to do with their lives.

Katy: Cor, that sounds like a good job. I could do that.

Robert: Don't be daft. You have to go to big school to get a job like that.

Katy: Nah, I bet it's not that difficult.

Robert: Okay, let's give it a try then. *(Puts on adult voice)* Dear Katy, I have so many clothes at home that I really don't know what to do with them. It's such a difficult choice in the morning deciding what to wear. And yet I keep on buying more – what shall I do?

Katy: Dear Worried, if I were you I'd give a load of your clothes away to the big metal boxes from the Salvation Army outside the supermarket. The end.

Robert: Hey that's really good. Where'd you learn to do that?

Katy: I guess I must have picked it up from all the church services Mum takes me to. Jesus and that John the Baptist guy were always talking about how you should live an' being kind and generous.

Robert: Oh right.

Katy: Course Mum and her friends never do anything about it. They just listen and then have a good old gossip after the service. Adults eh?

FOURTH SUNDAY OF ADVENT

Luke 1.39–45

THE NEWS

(Two women enter from opposite directions.)

Hannah: Sarah, Sarah. It's good to see you, how are you?

Sarah: Well, I can't complain, my Samuel is as useless as ever around the house. He does nothing I tell you, nothing. I told him, 'Samuel, I don't know why my mother (God rest her soul) ever insisted on us getting married. She must have been having an off-day or something. She would never have inflicted this kind of misery on me intentionally. And my sinuses, they're terrible, it's like having a couple of bits of cotton wool shoved up your nose. And my feet . . . don't get me started on my feet. But enough about my horrible life, how are you Hannah?

Hannah: Well, Sarah, my Eli is doing his mother proud, so proud. He has bought home the nicest girl. She comes from a good family and she is intelligent and clean. I told him, 'You move quickly with this one eh? Girls like her don't come along very often.'

Sarah: And will he act on your advice?

Hannah: *(Sternly)* He better had if he knows what's good for him.

Sarah: Talking about couples – have you seen Mary and Joseph recently?

Hannah: Let me think . . . yes I saw Mary in the market just yesterday. Why, is there something wrong?

Sarah: How did she look to you?

Hannah: Why? How should she look? Like a girl who is about to get married, that's how she looked. You're being very mysterious Sarah and I still have no idea what you're getting at.

Sarah: It's probably nothing.

Hannah: What's nothing? She's ill isn't she? I knew it. Some terrible fever has struck her down. Oy, so young and full of life and vitality, it's tragic.

Sarah: Will you be quiet? It's nothing like that. At least I don't think so. It's just that she's been acting rather strangely recently.

Hannah: She has?

Sarah: Yes, haven't you noticed? This whole trip to Elizabeth's – it was all very rushed, very strange. And I'm hearing odd reports from a friend of mine about Zechariah. He's suddenly playing the strong silent type – doesn't say a word apparently. And then there's Joseph.

Hannah: Joseph too. Is he sick?

Sarah: Not sick exactly no. But he's going around looking worried. Very worried indeed, as if he had the cares of the whole world on his shoulders.

Hannah: Well he has got to travel to Bethlehem for the Census – maybe it's just that.

Sarah: No, there's more. Something's going on, I just can't put my finger on what.

Hannah: You worry too much Sarah. Mary is a lovely girl. So kind and gentle and loving – and very soon now we're going to have a beautiful wedding. Won't that be nice?

Sarah: Yes, it will. At least I hope so. I just can't shake this feeling that something really important is going on right under our very noses.

CHRISTMAS DAY

Luke 2.8–20

THE GIFT

(Two people stand talking on the phone, but not to each other.)

Roger: I don't believe it. The children have been up since half past five this morning they were so excited. They were very good – they tried not to wake us up, but I could hear this excited whispering coming through the wall. Then they started giggling as they opened their stocking presents. And as soon as they'd started playing – well, that was it.

Anne: I tried really hard to make Christmas special, but it's not been easy. A few old decorations that my mother gave us, a little bit of tinsel – that's about it. I got the gas bill two weeks ago, and what with that cold snap in November it was more than I thought. That meant that I didn't have as much to spend on presents as I'd hoped. No stocking this year – still he was really excited when he got out of bed this morning.

Roger: I tell you, the main present opening session was a nightmare. Jimmy's only three and the vision of fifteen large packages lined up for him was more than his little eyes could cope with. All his aunts and uncles, all his cousins, his grandparents, they've all given him huge presents. He's sitting there now surrounded by so much stuff it looks like the front window of a rather well stocked toy shop. Heaven knows where we're going to put it all. He's so bewildered he doesn't know which thing to play with first.

Anne: He had three presents to open – which was nice. My mother gave him a little something – though she's been ill recently and can't get out to the shops much. Next door gave him a selection bag of chocolate bars which he loved, and I gave him a sweat shirt which he put on straight away – I'd have liked to have given him toys really, but he needed something practical and I can't afford both. Still – he seems really happy.

Roger: And then there was lunch. Turkey with all the trimmings, sausages, sausage meat, bacon, four different vegetables, two different types of potato, sage and onion stuffing. Christmas pudding, Christmas cake, mince pies, satsumas – I'm telling you I can hardly move. We sat twelve people down to eat you know.

Anne: Well you know our oven's not very big, and anyway with only two of us there wasn't much point in going overboard. We had some turkey – just a cheap cut and some potatoes and peas. He's not one for Christmas pudding, so we had some cakes afterwards.

Roger: I tell you it was the afternoon that seemed to drag. We sat watching telly for a while with the kids playing with their presents but then one of Amy's toys broke and there was much stamping of feet and crying – awful.

Anne: We sat and had a lovely time in the afternoon. We played a game together then went out for a walk – it was wonderful – cold but bright.

Roger: You know after a day like today I really wonder what Christmas is about. All that stuff about babies in mangers and peace on earth and goodwill to all – what's all that got to do with what I experienced today?

Anne: It was better than I could have hoped for really. I was dreading today but it's gone really well – I feel at peace somehow – like Christmas has really happened. Anyway, must go. Bye. *(They exit.)*

FIRST SUNDAY OF CHRISTMAS

Luke 2.41–52

THE VISITOR

(Two rabbis sit side by side.)

Samuel: So Benjamin, now that a week has passed, what do you think?

Benjamin: What do I think about what?

Samuel: *(Exasperated)* What do I think about what? I swear you say these things on purpose just to vex me. What do you think about the boy? What are your thoughts? How do you feel about him? Was he just a hoax? Some kind of elaborate trick? I mean his parents seemed genuine enough in their anger. But perhaps there is something else going on, something we haven't spotted. I mean – how could one child know so much? Be so well versed in even the most obscure parts of Scripture?

Benjamin: Oh, you mean our little visitor.

Samuel: Yes I mean our little visitor. Nice of you to finally arrive in the conversation Benjamin my boy, I was beginning to think you would never make it. But here you are – and you're only several ideas late. Again.

Benjamin: I'm sorry Samuel, but I don't see why you're making such a fuss.

Samuel: Well let me put it simply for you then. If that boy was genuine we have been in the presence of one of the greatest minds the world has ever seen.

Benjamin: And he had such a nice smile too.

Samuel: *(Frustrated)* Yes he had a nice smile, he had a wonderful smile, he had the most beautiful smile I have ever seen, but what does that matter?

Benjamin: I think it matters rather a lot. Knowledge without humility can be rather an ugly thing.

Samuel: Yes, I suppose you're right. What staggered me though was not only the knowledge he displayed but the questions that he asked. Such deep, profound, probing questions; questions that could illuminate the mind without even finding answers.

Benjamin: Well as you say, his parents seemed genuine enough in their concern and worry.

Samuel: Frantic I'd say. The poor things, fancy travelling so far just to turn round and have to retrace your steps.

Benjamin: I rather fancy that finding their son was a more important issue to them than wearing out another pair of sandals.

Samuel: Of course, of course. So anyway, Benjamin, what do you think?

Benjamin: You keep on asking me these questions and I'm not sure what you expect in response. Yes we have been in the presence of a quite remarkable child. A child, who displayed wisdom and humility and humour and a quiet authority. I was amazed. As were we all I think.

Samuel: So then? Do we trace him? Find out where he comes from? Invite him to come back? Offer him further teaching? Try and discover whether we have been tricked?

Benjamin: Samuel, we will do none of these things.

Samuel: Why ever not?

Benjamin: Because, Samuel, if I am right, last week we were permitted to see something of the glory of God, and when you experience that gift you don't try to keep hold of it, you give thanks for the wonder and let it go.

SECOND SUNDAY OF CHRISTMAS

John 1.10–18

WORDS

(Two people stand facing the congregation.)

Voice 1: The world is full of words.

Voice 2: Big words.

Voice 1: Small words.

Voice 2: Happy words.

Voice 1: Distinguished words.

Voice 2: Foreign words.

Voice 1: *(Getting excited)* Onomatopoeic words.

Voice 2: What?

Voice 1: Sorry.

Voice 2: Words that are so full of love they give you goose bumps.

Voice 1: Words that are so full of hatred they send a shiver down your spine.

Voice 2: Some people are very good at using words.

Voice 1: Politicians using silvery words to persuade you that they are right.

Voice 2: Advertisers using words to persuade you to buy.

Voice 1: Ah, those magical words . . .

Voice 2: 'Two for the price of one.'

Voice 1: Some people aren't very good with words.

Voice 2: They never quite know what words to say.

Voice 1: 'Gracious, you do look ill.'

Voice 2: 'Oh, thanks a lot!'

Voice 1: Some people rather like the sound of their own voices.

Voice 2: Too many words come tumbling out.

Voice 1: One after another.

Voice 1: Each one weaker.

Voice 2: And less needed . . .

Voice 1: Than the last.

Voice 2: Other people hardly say anything at all.

Voice 1: But when they do speak . . .

Voice 2: What power!

Voice 1: Yes, words are powerful.

Voice 2: They can move to tears.

Voice 1: They can inspire to action.

Voice 2: They can declare love.

Voice 1: But there is one Word that is different.

Voice 2: That has the power to change lives.

Voice 1: All by itself.

Voice 2: That can still storms.

Voice 1: Just like that!

Voice 2: That can bring forgiveness and salvation.

Voice 1: In an instant!

Voice 2: This is a Word that is so powerful that it spoke and creation took place.

Voice 1: It is a very special Word.

Voice 2: The Word is . . .

Voices 1 and 2: Jesus.

SUNDAY BETWEEN 7 AND 13 JANUARY INCLUSIVE

Luke 3.15–17, 21–22

GREATER THAN I?

(A teacher speaks to a small child – both played by adults.)

Miss Seaton:	Now then Gerald, about your part in our little play. I would like you to take on the vital role of John the Baptist.
Gerald:	Cor Miss, a vital role. That sounds really important. Does he have lots of brilliant clothes to wear, like crowns an' robes an' things?
Miss Seaton:	Ah, no actually Gerald. Mrs Willis and I were thinking more along the lines of some potato sacking and a piece of old string as a belt.
Gerald:	What, no cloak?
Miss Seaton:	No cloak.
Gerald:	But I thought you said he was important.
Miss Seaton:	He is Gerald – absolutely pivotal to the plot.
Gerald:	Oh okay. So I bet he gets to eat loads of great food in front of everybody. Cream cakes and sausages on sticks, and jelly and ice cream and chips an' baked beans an' chicken nuggets, an' chips, an' fish fingers, an' chips. 'Cos that's what important people do isn't it? Eat loads of great stuff.
Miss Seaton:	Well indeed Gerald there is a scene in our little play where you eat something of the diet of the great man himself.
Gerald:	Cool! Chocolate an' chips here I come!
Miss Seaton:	Yes, we have a small plate of locusts and wild honey for you to savour.
Gerald:	Wild honey and what?
Miss Seaton:	Well, obviously they're not real locusts no, no, that would never do. We've substituted asparagus tips hollowed out and filled with crisps to make the right crunching sound.
Gerald:	You cannot be serious.
Miss Seaton:	Oh, absolutely and completely serious Gerald I'm afraid. John the Baptist's diet was a very strict one as described by the Scriptures.
Gerald:	So wait a minute, let's see if I've got this straight. You want me to play a man who you say is really important and he's wearing potato sacking tied up with string an' he's eating locusts and wild honey.
Miss Seaton:	I understand how it might sound a little odd Gerald.
Gerald:	A *little* odd! I don't want to be in your play any more. You've got me here under false pretences you have. How come he's important? He must have had hundreds of people following him.
Miss Seaton:	Oh indeed he did.
Gerald:	Great, so he's some kind of king or something. He's the guy who's in charge. Great, I get to boss loads of people around.
Miss Seaton:	Actually Gerald, John the Baptist was waiting for somebody far greater.
Gerald:	So he's not even the boss?
Miss Seaton:	No. In fact, when John was asked whether he was the boss or not he said, 'There's somebody else coming and I'm not even fit to untie his sandals.'
Gerald:	Miss Seaton, from everything you've said to me it doesn't sound as if John the Baptist was very great at all. He doesn't have nice clothes, he doesn't eat great food, he isn't in charge – exactly what does he do?
Miss Seaton:	He is the one who prepares people for the coming of the Son of God.
Gerald:	Oh. . . . Perhaps I will play him after all.

SUNDAY BETWEEN 14 AND 20 JANUARY INCLUSIVE

John 2.1–11

THE COMPLAINT

(Two characters are on stage. Silas is on the phone.)

Silas: Yes sir, I assure you we take this very seriously . . . No sir, I'm as confused as you are about what's gone on . . . Yes sir, we do try to achieve complete customer satisfaction every time . . . Absolutely, I can see how this could be very embarrassing for you . . . No sir, my wife has never been called a cheapskate in front of the town officials. Leave it with me sir, I'll follow this up right away. *(Puts phone down)* DAVID!!

David: Yes sir, coming sir.

Silas: David, do you have any idea who that was on the phone just now?

David: No sir.

Silas: It was Benjamin Jacobson, one of the most important businessmen in Cana.

David: Ah, the wedding.

Silas: Yes, the wedding. Now then David, Benjamin Jacobson is not a happy man – not a happy man at all. It appears that there were two basic problems with the wine that we sold him for the wedding of his dear and only daughter. The first problem being that it ran out.

David: You mean there wasn't enough of it?

Silas: Well I don't mean that it suddenly sprouted legs and made a quick dash for the nearest exit do I? How many jars did we send over there?

David: Eleven sir, just as you ordered.

Silas: Let me have a look at that order form . . . that's not eleven, you stupid boy, it's seventeen . . . seventeen. Oh he'll have my licence to trade for this. And here I am, I've been in the wedding trade fifteen years. Working my way up from the odd song at a Bar Mitzvah to being one of the premier wedding and special occasion organizers in the whole of Galilee. When this town wants a really good funeral who do they come to?

David: You sir.

Silas: Of course me. But not for much longer at this rate.

David: What was the other problem with the wine sir?

Silas: Ah yes – the second problem. This one is harder to understand. What wine did we send over there David?

David: The year of Herod '22 sir.

Silas: A very good year, and a good wine.

David: Indeed sir.

Silas: Then why is Jacobson claiming that it was a second rate wine compared to what came later?

David: What do you mean?

Silas: Apparently a long-haired guest calling himself Jesus did some kind of a conjuring job on a bunch of water jars. Ordinary water one minute, the best wine anybody's ever tasted the next. So good in fact that all of the guests were going on about how everybody else saves poor wine for last when everyone's blotto – but not Ben Jacobson, oh no, he saves the best until last.

David: So what's going on sir?

Silas: I don't know David – but unless we calm down Ben Jacobson pretty quickly my business is finished. Come on! *(Exit.)*

SUNDAY BETWEEN 21 AND 27 JANUARY INCLUSIVE

Luke 4.14–21

DEVILS 1

(Two devils are standing centre stage.)

Brimstone: I've not been hearing very good reports about your progress Treacle.

Treacle: I'm sorry Brimstone, it's just that this particular human is proving rather hard to crack.

Brimstone: Oh, nonsense. How difficult can it be? He's only a human when all's said and done.

Treacle: I realize that – and a rather simpering example of humankind too, but I'm afraid his friends keep praying for him.

Brimstone: Euughh! Well we've got to stop that right away. You were making such good progress on his attitudes.

Treacle: I know. I've got him making snap judgements without listening to any of the facts.

Brimstone: And having wonderfully unkind and hurtful thoughts about people he doesn't even know.

Treacle: I even persuaded him to steal a whole range of office equipment from his work place – and the best thing of all is that he doesn't feel bad about it. He's justified it to himself by believing the company is so big and rich they'll never miss it. He doesn't think it's wrong at all!

Brimstone: I would suggest that you move quickly on his thoughts. Play with his mind a little bit. Let him believe that his new-found Christian friends are all somehow faintly ridiculous.

Treacle: That won't be difficult – he already thinks their dress sense is a bit grim.

Brimstone: Oh, and another idea's just occurred to me. This one's brilliant. Let him discover that his rather bizarre, interfering, new friends are praying for him. He'll hate that.

Treacle: Why?

Brimstone: Humans detest the thought that somebody else is talking about them behind their back. Don't let him think for a moment that the prayers are for his own good. Let him dwell on the fact that these people, who he hardly knows, are suddenly in the business of speaking with the Almighty. What a threat to his pride that these painfully ordinary people could be agents of God.

Treacle: So, playing on his pride will blind him to the truth.

Brimstone: Of course it will – that's basic tempter training – I don't know, they don't train devils like they used to.

Treacle: I'm sorry.

Brimstone: Never, ever say you're sorry.

Treacle: So, let me see if I've got this right. Humans can't bear to see God at work in the ordinary and everyday.

Brimstone: Quite right, it offends their pride to realize that God's been at work under their very noses and they were too stupid to recognize it.

Treacle: And that makes them angry?

Brimstone: To be made to look foolish? It makes their blood boil.

Treacle: And as soon as that happens . . .

Brimstone: We've got them! *(Laughs.)*

SUNDAY BETWEEN 28 JANUARY AND 3 FEBRUARY INCLUSIVE

Luke 4.21–30

NEVER THEIR OWN

(Two officers are on the bridge of a starship.)

Lester: Captain Thaddeus T. Lester of the starship *Quirky* – Captain's log stardate 20 point 67 point 124 and a quarter. We have been sent on a mission to the little-known planet Acne in the Zitblast galaxy. As fortune would have it, we have on board our ship an ensign from the very planet we seek to help. However, as this ensign has never been seen on this programme up until this episode, it probably means he has been introduced simply to be killed off by the end of the show. I need to speak to my trusty second-in-command Mr Splot.

Splot: You were thinking of asking my advice Captain?

Lester: I was indeed Splot. How is it that you can anticipate my every need?

Splot: My extra-sensory perceptions are particularly acute Captain – and a full view of this week's script is also helpful. What is our new mission sir? Will we be encountering any spatial anomalies? They are my special favourite. Perhaps a dreaded virus has infested our ship, or perchance a breach of the warp core has taken place. Whatever it is, my trusty tri-corder will almost certainly make loud blipping sounds and have pretty flashing lights on it which will, in a mysterious way, tell me exactly what is wrong.

Lester: Excellent Splot. As ever your ability to dazzle me with scientific language that means nothing at all is first rate. Our mission this week, however, is slightly different.

Splot: You intrigue me Captain.

Lester: I hope so, I didn't go to the Hollywood School of Overacting in Science Fiction Dramas for nothing.

Splot: Quite so Captain. Now what is our mission?

Lester: Our mission Splot, should we choose to accept it, is to send an away team down to the planet surface to warn the inhabitants of a mysterious impending disaster. But, I am afraid Splot; there is a problem.

Splot: Isn't there always Captain?

Lester: How right you are, my trusted friend. The dilemma I am faced with is this – do I send ensign Oozy down with the away team? He is a native of the planet it is true . . .

Splot: But that may well work against us. In our travels around the universe we have often discovered a tendency amongst alien races to distrust those sent to help them – particularly those who seem familiar.

Lester: Distrust so strong in many cases that we have often been unable to help those most in need of our aid.

Splot: They could well look on Oozy as an outsider and refuse to listen to what he has to say, believing themselves superior. They may also feel that they know better than he does the way out of their problems. They may – in the words of an old human saying – tell him 'Doctor, heal yourself.'

Lester: Indeed Splot – you are wise as always.

Splot: In my experience sir, many lifeforms are terribly arrogant and even when offered the help they need to save themselves refuse to take it – especially when that help is offered in a form they think they know.

Lester: Perhaps, old friend, we need another plan. To my ready room. *(Exit.)*

SUNDAY BETWEEN 4 AND 10 FEBRUARY INCLUSIVE

Luke 5.1–11

RALPH AND JIM ON CALLING

(Two characters are sitting facing each other.)

Ralph: So then, Jim mate.

Jim: So then, Ralph.

Ralph: What's ah . . . what's new then?

Jim: Ah, I'm glad you asked me that Ralphy boy.

Ralph: So something's happened then has it Jim mate?

Jim: It has indeed Ralph – I've been thinking.

Ralph: Thinking mate . . . thinking. That's a bit dangerous innit? You know what your doctor said.

Jim: Well I've been reading the Bible, Ralph.

Ralph: Well that'll do it every time.

Jim: Do what?

Ralph: Make you think. It does that, the holy word of God. It opens your mind to new thoughts, expands your horizons with infinite possibilities, and I've found it works quite well as a door stop too.

Jim: I don't know Ralph, you're terrible you are – you've got to treat bibles with respect.

Ralph: I do mate, I do. So, what you been thinking about then Jim?

Jim: Ah well Ralph, I've been dwelling on calling.

Ralph: Calling? Calling who? Calling your bank manager? Calling your mother? Calling your home planet?

Jim: No, no you misunderstand my meaning.

Ralph: Well that's not difficult is it?

Jim: What I'm trying to get at Ralph mate, is that Jesus called people to follow him and they dropped everything they were doing. They left their homes and their families an' everything an' just followed him. There weren't any questions. They didn't say, 'Wait a minute Jesus, can I just wait to see if me number's come up on the lucky Big Number Draw, or can I just watch this Tuesday's *Eastenders* on the telly.' They said, 'Okay Jesus you're on. Let's get going.'

Ralph: Did they?

Jim: Yes Ralph they did. In fact I've searched through Holy Writ.

Ralph: Have you?

Jim: Yes indeed – and most of them didn't even ask where they were going – they just went.

Ralph: Cor, that's a bit of a stunner.

Jim: That it is Ralph mate, that it is. Ordinary guys like you an' me goin' off an' followin' God.

Ralph: What's the point you're making with all of all this then Jim?

Jim: Well I just can't help wondering why I make so many excuses. Y' know, I've got too much work on, or there's something good on the telly, or I'm going out with me mates, or . . . well quite honestly any old excuse not to hear the question.

Ralph: What question's that then?

Jim: 'Will you come and follow me?'

Ralph: An' Jim mate – is that the question that Jesus is asking you?

Jim: I don't know Ralph. That's the whole point innit, I'm always too busy to listen.

SUNDAY BETWEEN 11 AND 17 FEBRUARY INCLUSIVE

Luke 6.17–26

A NEW CODE

(Two people are standing centrally.)

Voice 1: Ladies and Gentlemen!

Voice 2: We are proud . . .

Voice 1: And humbled . . .

Voice 2: Oh yes indeed, proud and humbled . . .

Voice 1: And delighted . . .

Voice 2: *(Becoming a little frustrated)* Yes, proud, humbled and delighted . . .

Voice 1: To present for your delectation and education . . .

Voice 2: A new moral code.

Voice 1: Brand spanking new . . .

Voice 2: Mobile phone friendly and bang up to date . . .

Voice 1: For life in the fast lane . . .

Voice 2: Of the twenty-first century.

Voice 1: Happy are you who are wealthy.

Voice 2: Especially if you have a nicely diversified investment portfolio with bonds, stocks, shares, and all that other financial stuff.

Voice 1: Because you have all the insurance you need . . .

Voice 2: To look down on poor people and gloat.

Voice 1: Happy are you who are full of food.

Voice 2: Especially if it was from that rather nice Italian restaurant down the road.

Voice 1: As you sleep off yet one more night of over-indulgence . . .

Voice 2: You can doze peacefully through the cries of the starving poor.

Voice 1: Happy are you who have developed a nice thick skin now.

Voice 2: Because hardly anything that anybody says or does will get through to you.

Voice 1: And you can look at other people in their pain and distress . . .

Voice 2: And think 'What a bunch of pathetic losers.'

Voice 1: Happy are you when people fawn over you and praise you, and are envious of you and your lifestyle . . .

Voice 2: Be pleased and proud when this happens.

Voice 1: Because this is a mark of your power over others. You've really arrived in the world. Congratulations!

Voice 2: If this is a little unlike any other code of conduct you've heard before . . .

Voice 1: You're thick.

Voice 2: I say, that's a bit harsh.

Voice 1: But true . . .

Voice 2: Sadly yes. Because thousands of very rich men and women.

Voice 1: Most of them in advertising.

Voice 2: Have spent millions upon millions of pounds persuading you that all of this is true.

Voice 1: And if you're concerned about what God will think . . . don't worry.

Voice 2: He won't hold a few minor indiscretions against you will he?

Voice 1: Will he?

Voice 2: After all, it's not like he's given us an example to live by, is it?

Voice 1: Is it?

SUNDAY BETWEEN 18 AND 24 FEBRUARY INCLUSIVE

Luke 6.27–38

WINSTANLY-WALKER AND CARRINGTON-CRUMBLY

(Two characters are sitting centrally.)

W.W.: Good morning everybody – you are welcome.

C.C.: Most welcome indeed.

W.W.: We would like to introduce ourselves to you. I am Gerald Winstanly-Walker and my most learned colleague here is . . .

C.C.: Cornelia Carrington-Crumbly. And together we are . . .

W.W.: Crumbly-Walker attorneys at law – at your service.

C.C.: Now we are here at this church this morning to warn you of a most worrying state of affairs that has come to our attention.

W.W.: Indeed we are. And let me say straight off that you will not owe us a penny for our services here today.

C.C.: Well, not unless you decide to take things further and then, of course, we'll take half of everything you own.

W.W.: Oh, at least. Anyway, back to the case in hand. It has come to our attention that your spiritual leader . . .

C.C.: Jesus of Nazareth I believe his name is.

W.W.: Yes that's right. We believe that the advice this Jesus is giving you is very much against your best interests. Isn't that right Cornelia?

C.C.: It certainly is Gerald. For example we have been reading your Scriptures and it appears that this Jesus fellow actually told you that if somebody hits you on the cheek you should turn your head and let that miscreant hit you on the other cheek too.

W.W.: Well really! What a ridiculous state of affairs. I am afraid you have been advised most unwisely. You don't want the world to think of you as doormats do you? What we would advise is this.

C.C.: If somebody hits you on one cheek . . .

W.W.: Then take out a Court Order making sure that they can't step within 25 metres of you.

C.C.: Then take that person to court. We could have them up on a case of grievous bodily harm before you could say, 'Here's the other cheek.'

W.W.: Finally we would advise you to slap on a hefty claim for compensation. Loss of earnings, mental anguish, you know the kind of thing.

C.C.: You could be looking at a monetary package worth thousands.

W.W.: And the rather satisfying sight of watching someone else squirming under the full force of the law.

C.C.: Now isn't that better than two bruised cheeks?

W.W.: There's all sorts of other matters we could bring to your attention.

C.C.: Like the rather worrying advice to give away your shirt to someone who has already stolen your coat.

W.W.: And giving to anybody who asks you for something.

C.C.: Dear me. It seems to us that this Jesus character wasn't very worldly.

W.W.: No, indeed, not very worldly at all.

C.C.: He seems to have had his eyes set on somewhere else entirely.

W.W.: We hope that what you have heard this morning has interested you.

C.C.: And if so you can find our business cards at the back of the church. *(Exit.)*

136

SUNDAY BETWEEN 25 AND 29 FEBRUARY INCLUSIVE

Luke 6.39–49

SISTERS

(Two females are standing back to back – they address the audience.)

Gwendolyn: Do you know what?

Anastasia: I bet you'll never guess!

Gwendolyn: No I bet you never will.

Anastasia: Gwendolyn – beautiful Gwendolyn – and I are sisters.

Gwendolyn: Yes indeed, indeed, lovely Anastasia and I are sisters!

Anastasia: *(Turning to face Gwendolyn)* Hello beautiful sister Gwendolyn.

Gwendolyn: Hello lovely sister Anastasia!

Anastasia: Gwendolyn must be the kindest person in the entire kingdom.

Gwendolyn: Modesty prevents me from agreeing – but yes I am.

Anastasia: Except for that occasion when Cook found out that somebody had put French fries in the ice-cream, that wasn't very kind now was it Gwendolyn?

Gwendolyn: *(A little upset)* Well I'm not at all sure that it was necessary to mention that in public was it, dearest sister Anastasia?

Anastasia: No, but it was true wasn't it, lovely sister Gwendolyn?

Gwendolyn: *(Facing the audience)* Well, of course, I would like you all to know that my sweetest sister Anastasia is the most generous person in the land.

Anastasia: Ah, how true.

Gwendolyn: I would like you all to know that if it were true, but alas it is not.

Anastasia: What?

Gwendolyn: Well there was that occasion, just last week if I recall correctly, when you told that poor beggar on the street outside the palace that he was a miserable scrounger. Do please feel free to correct me if I got the words wrong, lovely sister Anastasia.

Anastasia: Well you would be beautiful if it wasn't for that huge pimple on your chin.

Gwendolyn: And you would be loving if it weren't for all those mud pies you made me eat as a child.

Anastasia: Well you snore all night long.

Gwendolyn: And you talk in your sleep.

Anastasia: I do not. I am lovely, honest, kind and beautiful. You're the one who is mean, hurtful and ugly.

Gwendolyn: Oh, what rubbish. I am trusting, generous and pretty, you are envious, spiteful and rude.

Anastasia: Really, I am surprised that you had never spotted any of your faults before – they are so obvious when compared to my strengths.

Gwendolyn: And I am equally shocked that you can be so blind to your own shortcomings when viewed next to my goodness and light.

Anastasia: Well I am sure that there is nothing wrong with me.

Gwendolyn: And I am convinced that there can be no fault on my part.

Anastasia: I really do not know what I have done to deserve such a wilful sister – as ignorant of her own faults as she is of her sister's virtue.

Gwendolyn: As usual, you have got everything completely the wrong way round.

Anastasia: I cannot stay in your presence a moment longer. I am leaving.

Gwendolyn: Not if I leave first! *(They stride off in opposite directions.)*

SUNDAY BEFORE LENT

Luke 9.28–36 (37–43)

TRANSFIGURED

(Two actors are standing centrally.)

Voice 1:   Light.

Voice 2:   Blinding.

Voice 1:   Flashing.

Voice 2:   Dazzling.

Voice 1:   Light.

Voice 2:   So powerful you can almost touch it.

Voice 1:   So dynamic that it seems alive.

Voice 2:   Washing over you, wave after wave.

Voice 1:   Soaking through every fibre of your being.

Voice 2:   Light so bright you want to look away.

Voice 1:   Light so warm you can do nothing but gaze.

Voice 2:   Awe-inspiring.

Voice 1:   Joyfully shocking.

Voice 2:   Fear inducing . . .

Voices 1
  and 2:   Light.

Voice 1:   And what do you do?

Voice 2:   When confronted with a light like that?

Voice 1:   Which one of our paltry . . .

Voice 2:   Insubstantial . . .

Voice 1:   Painfully inadequate . . .

Voice 2:   Oh-so-human responses will meet the occasion?

Voice 1:   Perhaps silence – in the presence and mystery of God.

Voice 2:   Falling down in worship and wonder.

Voice 1:   Watching and listening in reverent joy.

Voice 2:   Holy fear at spying something of heaven.

Voice 1:   All of these would work.

Voice 2:   Would be right for the occasion.

Voice 1:   Would express the proper devotion.

Voice 2:   And then there is the babbling cascade of useless words.

Voice 1:   One after another, tumbling out.

Voice 2:   Not knowing what is being said.

Voice 1:   But feeling the need to say something.

Voice 2:   However strange.

Voice 1:   It is just too much.

Voice 2:   The silence has to be filled.

Voice 1:   Excitement and wonder expressed.

Voice 2:   The experience pinned down.

Voice 1:   And we do want to stay here forever, don't we?

Voice 2:   Caught up in heaven's light.

Voice 1:   Away from the world with its problems.

Voice 2:   And pain and dullness.

Voice 1:   Oh to be able to stay here and bask in God.

Voice 2:   But that cannot be. The experience must end.

Voice 1:   And we must walk in the light of day again.

FIRST SUNDAY IN LENT

Luke 4.1–13

LAMBERTON AND PHIPPS 1

(A master and servant enter.)

Lamberton: Gosh Phipps. Has it really been that long?

Phipps: It really has sir.

Lamberton: Fifteen years?

Phipps: Yes sir. Fifteen years of faithful service.

Lamberton: And it really has been faithful service Phipps. What would I have done without you?

Phipps: It's hard to say sir.

Lamberton: Not hard for me to say Phipps, dash it all. I'd have been lost, that's what I would have been. Lost without the wisdom of your counsel and advice. But I bet there were times, eh Phipps?

Phipps: Sir?

Lamberton: Hang it all Phipps, don't come the innocent with me. I just bet there were times when you nearly lost your patience with me. Times, I'll wager, when you thought to yourself, 'That Lamberton – even though he's the second richest earl in the country, I'd like to wring his scrawny little neck.'

Phipps: I can't think of any off hand sir.

Lamberton: Well then Phipps, let me remind you. What about that time when I took a horrible, smelly old kipper and tied it to the radiator of the Rolls. It took weeks to get the smell out of the car.

Phipps: It did indeed sir. I remember it well.

Lamberton: And do you recall the occasion when I asked you to climb up that big old tree to get my ball back and then I pulled the ladder away?

Phipps: Just your little joke sir.

Lamberton: But you were up there for two days before anybody found you Phipps.

Phipps: It gave me time to think sir.

Lamberton: And I'll bet you thought to yourself, 'What a little pest that Lamberton is', eh?

Phipps: Not at all sir. That would have been to yield.

Lamberton: To yield? Yield to what?

Phipps: To temptation sir.

Lamberton: The temptation to think ill of me?

Phipps: Indeed sir.

Lamberton: And that would have been a bad thing?

Phipps: I believe so, yes sir.

Lamberton: So are you often tempted Phipps?

Phipps: I have had my fair share sir.

Lamberton: I am afraid Phipps that I have rather too often given in to the temptations that have come my way.

Phipps: That would be my observation sir, yes.

Lamberton: And yet you stick by my side, no matter what Phipps, eh?

Phipps: And try to help you be strong sir.

Lamberton: I'm not always very grateful am I?

Phipps: I'm not here to be thanked sir, I'm here to serve.

Lamberton: Nevertheless, thank you Phipps. *(Pause)* Thank you very much.

SECOND SUNDAY IN LENT

Luke 13.31–35

LAMBERTON AND PHIPPS 2

(Phipps is on stage. Lamberton enters.)

Lamberton:	Oh woe is me! Oh alas and alack! Oh, my life is not worth living!
Phipps:	Good morning sir.
Lamberton:	Ah, Phipps. Good Phipps, worthy, loyal and trusty Phipps – my life is over – just take me somewhere and put me out of my misery.
Phipps:	I gather, sir, that something is amiss.
Lamberton:	Amiss?! My heart is broken Phipps. Cleaved in two, destroyed. The reason for the sun to rise and the moon to shine has deserted me.
Phipps:	Can I take it sir that we are talking about a woman?
Lamberton:	To call her a woman is not to do her justice Phipps – she is my Diana, my morning star, the apple of my eye, the cherry on my cheesecake.
Phipps:	You certainly have a way with words sir.
Lamberton:	Yes Phipps, but what good is that when the object of all my affection will have nothing to do with me?
Phipps:	Perhaps you could tell me the name of the young lady sir?
Lamberton:	Oh, I'm sorry Phipps, you see love has addled my mind, the name of the adorable young lady in question is Penelope Fitzhugh McReuterman.
Phipps:	A name to conjure with sir.
Lamberton:	Ah, indeed Phipps, indeed.
Phipps:	And I gather sir that the young lady in question has spurned your affections.
Lamberton:	Utterly and completely. She will have nothing to do with me. I have sent her trifles of my love – flowers, jewellery, cards, chocolates. I have declared my love time and time again, and still I am rejected.
Phipps:	Is there another suitor sir?
Lamberton:	A rival for her affection? No Phipps, I don't think so. The problem with Penelope is that she seems so completely wrapped up in herself that she seems incapable of loving anybody else.
Phipps:	*(With recognition)* Ah sir.
Lamberton:	Dash it all Phipps, what do you mean, 'Ah sir'?
Phipps:	This is the worst kind of rival of all – self-love.
Lamberton:	What do I do Phipps? How do I make this unbearable pain go away?
Phipps:	If it is true love that you feel for her, sir, there is nothing that will make the pain go away.
Lamberton:	You mean I've got to put up with this? But I feel like my heart will break.
Phipps:	The ways of love have always held that potential sir. There is nothing that hurts so much as to go to someone and offer them love, only to have that offer thrown back at you.
Lamberton:	But I have offered my heart to her Phipps.
Phipps:	And it has been broken sir.
Lamberton:	Phipps, your wise and sage counsel has always been my guide. Will this rejection continue?
Phipps:	It may well do sir.
Lamberton:	But despite all of that, I love her.
Phipps:	That, sir, is the cost of love. Come along. *(They exit.)*

THIRD SUNDAY IN LENT

Luke 13.1–9

LAMBERTON AND PHIPPS 3

(Lamberton is sitting centrally. Phipps enters.)

Phipps: Good morning sir.

Lamberton: Is it Phipps? Is it really?

Phipps: Well, sir. The sun is shining. Flowers are breaking into blossom all around us, and it is unseasonably fine for the time of year. So yes sir, unless you know otherwise, I would say that it is a good morning.

Lamberton: *(Sighs deeply)* I suppose so Phipps. If you say it is a good morning, and are prepared to back it up with facts, then who am I to gainsay you?

Phipps: I know I am going to regret this question almost immediately sir but is there something wrong?

Lamberton: Ah, Phipps. You've seen through my clever attempts at disguise.

Phipps: *(Dryly)* Yes sir, you have as always cleverly hidden your true feelings.

Lamberton: How is that you know me so well Phipps?

Phipps: I have always fancied myself as something of a student of the human condition sir. If I may be so bold, what is troubling you?

Lamberton: I'm afraid I am a little pensive Phipps.

Phipps: Not still dwelling on your unrequited love for Penelope Fitzhugh McReuterman I hope?

Lamberton: No, no Phipps. Although I still yearn for her with all my heart and soul.

Phipps: As you say sir.

Lamberton: No, what causes this furrow in my brow is something else entirely. May I ask you a question Phipps? You know how I value your sage counsel and advice.

Phipps: But of course sir. I am all ears.

Lamberton: Am I a lost cause Phipps? A hopeless case?

Phipps: What do you mean sir?

Lamberton: It's just that as I look back through my life there isn't all that much to be proud of. In fact I've been, let's face it, a bit of a beast.

Phipps: Oh I don't know about that sir.

Lamberton: I do Phipps, I do. I've been mean to you on more occasions than I care to remember. I've been a bit of a rotter where Auntie Agnes is concerned as well. I'm afraid the old copy-book is well and truly blotted.

Phipps: And you think, sir, that the Almighty will be angry with you?

Lamberton: Well he's hardly going to give me a good old pat on the back is he?

Phipps: And you no doubt believe that new starts and second chances are not part of his plan.

Lamberton: Well Phipps, it's just that I've been so thoroughly beastly.

Phipps: Sir, it sounds from what you have said that you are sorry for your previous lapses of judgement.

Lamberton: Certainly am Phipps.

Phipps: Then you have repented. As I understand it sir, freedom, a second chance and a fresh start are yours.

Lamberton: What, you mean at once?

Phipps: Immediately sir.

Lamberton: Gosh, then it may be a good morning after all, a very good morning indeed.

FOURTH SUNDAY IN LENT

Luke 15.1–3, 11b–32

LAMBERTON AND PHIPPS 4

(Lamberton is reading a bible. Phipps enters.)

Phipps: You rang sir?

Lamberton: Ah, yes, Phipps there you are. How are you this fine morning?

Phipps: I do believe I am as well as can be expected sir.

Lamberton: Good, good. *(Silence, Lamberton reading.)*

Phipps: You rang sir.

Lamberton: What was that?

Phipps: You rang your bell. I came to serve your needs. It's what we do sir.

Lamberton: Oh, yes . . . did I?

Phipps: Yes. If you don't mind me saying so sir you seem rather distracted today.

Lamberton: Distracted? Yes, yes, I suppose I am. It's this book Phipps. Dashed interesting.

Phipps: And what might the book be sir?

Lamberton: Ah, yes, sorry Phipps. Rather rude of me I dare say. I'm reading the ah, thingy.

Phipps: The thingy sir?

Lamberton: Yes, the ah whatchimacallit.

Phipps: You might want to try to be more precise sir.

Lamberton: You know, rainbows and fish and serpents.

Phipps: The Bible sir?

Lamberton: That's the chappie, yes.

Phipps: And are you finding the Good Book to be helpful sir?

Lamberton: Well, yes I am actually Phipps. I've just been reading something that helps me a great deal with the conversation we were having recently.

Phipps: About your feeling rather rotten about yourself sir?

Lamberton: That's the one Phipps yes. You see I have been such a beast. Greedy and selfish and spiteful and oh, just horrid.

Phipps: I'm sure it's nothing that can't be forgiven sir.

Lamberton: Well that's just the point Phipps. I've just been reading a bit of a ripping yarn in here about a chappie who was even more rotten than me.

Phipps: Hard to believe sir.

Lamberton: I know, but it's true. Left the old family seat, took the loot, blew the lot, decided to trot on back to Pater, tail well and truly between legs, covered with embarrassment. And what do you think the father does?

Phipps: I can hardly guess sir.

Lamberton: Dashed if he doesn't rush to wayward son with open arms and welcome him home. Turns out that he was watching and waiting for the chappie to come home all along.

Phipps: That's very comforting sir.

Lamberton: I'll say Phipps. Seems like God will forgive me for past indiscretions and bad behaviour as well. I'll shout hooray and hurrah to that! . . . Say wait a minute Phipps, this page in my bible has been folded down . . . It was you wasn't it? You wanted me to read that story.

Phipps: I thought it might be of help sir.

Lamberton: You sly old dog Phipps. Well done. Well done indeed. *(Exit.)*

FIFTH SUNDAY IN LENT

John 12.1–8

LAMBERTON AND PHIPPS 5

(Lamberton is pacing back and forth. Phipps enters.)

Lamberton: Where have you been Phipps, where on earth have you been?

Phipps: I'm sorry sir?

Lamberton: You're supposed to be taking me down to the seaside in the motor to see Constance Crestfall and you're a good ten minutes late.

Phipps: I don't recall you saying that you wanted to leave by a certain time sir.

Lamberton: I did you know, I'm absolutely certain that I did. And by the way, where were you when I wanted my Sunday morning paper brought to me this morning Phipps? I mean there I was, sitting at the breakfast table, and there was the paper nestling nicely on the dresser, and did it get opened? Was it read as all good newspapers should be? No, because somebody wasn't there to give it me.

Phipps: It didn't occur to you to get it for yourself sir?

Lamberton: Why should I Phipps? That's what I've got you for isn't it?

Phipps: Obviously sir.

Lamberton: Look Phipps, this is dashed unhelpful behaviour. There are people to see, chums to meet, larks to be had. We should have been off absolutely ages ago, and we're still sitting around here. What on earth have you been up to?

Phipps: Do you really want to know sir?

Lamberton: Of course I do – what's been going on?

Phipps: I've been to church sir.

Lamberton: Church?

Phipps: Yes sir, worship.

Lamberton: And you mean we're running late for one of Constance Crestfall's excellent Sunday cheese and wine dos because you went to sing some hymns and say some prayers?

Phipps: It would appear that way sir, yes.

Lamberton: But Roger Simpkinson-Smythe has challenged me to a rematch at croquet.

Phipps: And I'm sure he will wait for us sir.

Lamberton: Dash it all Phipps that's not the point.

Phipps: Then exactly what is the point sir?

Lamberton: The point Phipps . . . the point is . . . well it's that um . . . ah . . . well I'm sure there is a point Phipps and it's a jolly good one I'll be bound.

Phipps: Quite sir.

Lamberton: No, the point is Phipps that you need to get your priorities right.

Phipps: And they would be?

Lamberton: Well – looking after me.

Phipps: You mean waiting on you hand and foot.

Lamberton: That wouldn't go amiss either.

Phipps: Well I am afraid sir that while I love to serve you my priorities lie somewhere else.

Lamberton: But Phipps I need you.

Phipps: And the creator of the universe needs me too sir.

Lamberton: *(Flustered)* Well I . . . I . . . I, oh come on Phipps we're late as it is.
(Lamberton exits pulling Phipps behind him.)

SIXTH SUNDAY IN LENT – ENTRY INTO JERUSALEM

Luke 19.28–40

LAMBERTON AND PHIPPS 6

(Lamberton enters from the back of the church.)

Lamberton: Phipps, I say Phipps. Where are you? Come on Phipps, I know you're around here somewhere.

Phipps: *(Entering)* You called sir?

Lamberton: Certainly did Phipps. Got a bit of a poser for you this morning.

Phipps: You do sir?

Lamberton: Absolutely. Well I know you're into crosswords and puzzles and studying the human spirit and all that other mumbo-jumbo that sounds like dashed hard work to me.

Phipps: Indeed sir, I do fancy myself a student of the human condition. It has always fascinated me for example that . . .

Lamberton: Yes, yes I'm sure, riveting, absolutely riveting. But my puzzle for you this morning is going to really fox you or my name isn't Eugene P. H. Lamberton.

Phipps: Very well sir – fire away.

Lamberton: Ah, yes. Hmm. Righto. Well the fact is Phipps that I've been reading the old Bible again.

Phipps: Most commendable sir.

Lamberton: That's what I thought. Anyway it's a jolly good read, frightfully inspirational.

Phipps: Saints and martyrs over the centuries have found it so sir.

Lamberton: Yes, 'spect they have. Anyway, as I was reading I came across a bit of a conundrum.

Phipps: And that would be sir?

Lamberton: Well, on the Sunday of the last week of his life Jesus rides into Jerusalem on a donkey – by the way Phipps, poor choice of transportation – he should have let me know if he was short of a bob or two, I'd have lent him the Roller.

Phipps: There was a prophecy to be fulfilled sir.

Lamberton: No doubt Phipps, but what I say is never let prophecy get in the way of personal comfort. Anyway, there are people – lots of people. And they're cheering and shouting and screaming and generally getting in a right old lather. Pleased to see Jesus – well hurrah and hooray, God bless him who comes in the name of the Lord!

Phipps: It must have been quite a sight sir.

Lamberton: And quite a din too. Anyway, by the end of that week, those cheers have changed to cries for blood, and there's a crowd screaming for Jesus to be killed. What has got me puzzled Phipps is – was it the same people in the two crowds? I mean, cheering one moment, jeering the next?

Phipps: I believe it could well have been sir. And what that tells me is that human beings then were much the same as they are now – fickle and prone to great anger when disappointed.

Lamberton: Gracious Phipps, are we really that bad?

Phipps: That far from recognizing the truth sir? Yes. And that is precisely the reason Jesus came. *(Exit.)*

EASTER DAY

Luke 24.1–12

LIFE!

(Two people enter from the back of the church and walk forward.)

Voice 1: Life.
Voice 2: Energetic.
Voice 1: Brilliant.
Voice 2: Wonderful.
Voice 1: Life.
Voice 2: Bursting out of every crevice.
Voice 1: Crashing out of caves.
Voice 2: Smashing through boulders.
Voice 1: Life that cannot be contained by our expectations.
Voice 2: Or confined by our ideas.
Voice 1: Beautiful.
Voice 2: Exciting.
Voice 1: Surprising.
Voice 2: Life.
Voice 1: And we had thought that death was all there was.
Voice 2: We had despaired.
Voice 1: Mourned.
Voice 2: Our hearts broke.
Voice 1: We could not believe what had happened.
Voice 2: But we had to believe because we had seen.
Voice 1: Life nailed up.
Voice 2: Legs broken.
Voice 1: Life taken away.
Voice 2: Dead.
Voice 1: Defeated.
Voice 2: Shut away in a cave.
Voice 1: Guarded by rock and soldier.
Voice 2: We ran away.
Voice 1: We hid.
Voice 2: We were scared.
Voice 1: It seemed that life itself had been stolen from us.
Voice 2: There was nothing we could do.
Voice 1: We were helpless.
Voice 2: But now life has exploded out of its prison.
Voice 1: Life is here.
Voice 2: All around us.
Voice 1: Inside of us.
Voice 2: And there is nothing.
Voice 1: Absolutely nothing.
Voice 2: In all of creation.
Voice 1: Or beyond it.
Voice 2: That will ever be the same again.
Voice 1: The Lord is risen.
Voice 2: He is risen indeed. HALLELUJAH!

SECOND SUNDAY OF EASTER

John 20.19–31

REACH OUT

(John 20.19–25 is read.)

Peter: You know, there are some days when I just give up with Thomas. What
            does he want? What's going to please him? He makes me so angry
            sometimes. I mean – here we are trying to tell him that the most
            incredible thing has happened. That we have seen a man come back
            from the dead. That we have seen Jesus. But will he at least join in with
            our joy? Will he be happy for us? Oh no, of course not. It's all 'I won't
            believe until I see too.' Now don't get me wrong, I'm sorry that he
            wasn't there, really I am. I'd give anything to change things so that he
            could have experienced it. It was so wonderful. I can imagine how he's
            feeling – hurt, left out, alone. You know none of us would like to be the
            one person who wasn't there. It is hard. But I'm sorry, he is labouring
            the point just a little. All of this attitude he's giving us at the moment –
            like a spoilt child. I tell you, he's in danger of ruining it for the rest of
            us. Perhaps I ought to be kinder, more understanding, not quite so
            hotheaded and judgmental. The others think I'm being a bit harsh. But
            when you've seen what we've seen. When you've experienced love and
            power and joy. When you've been as lonely and afraid as we have over
            the past few days, and then had your life – no, your universe – turned
            upside down, well then it's a little bit hard to be quiet about it. Thomas
            is a wonderful person – kind, generous, but he is so, so stubborn. Then
            again perhaps it takes one to know one. I just hope that he does see
            Jesus, because I think he really does want to believe.

(John 20.26–31 is read.)

Thomas: All right, all right, I know I was stubborn and stupid. As I look back on
            it now it's difficult to see how I could have been so dull, so bound by
            everything I knew, or thought I knew. To be honest I wanted the others
            to be right – I wanted Jesus to be alive. I was just so disappointed, so
            crushed that I hadn't seen him too. You know what it's like when all
            your friends have been somewhere or seen something really wonderful
            and for some reason or another you weren't there. And they keep on
            going on about it, they won't stop talking about how brilliant it was –
            and all that does is just rub your nose deeper and deeper in the fact that
            you didn't experience it. That somehow you missed the party that
            everybody's going on about. It was like that – only worse, because this
            really was the one thing that it would have been nice to have been there
            for. And I know I came over as stubborn – but I wanted to see Jesus so
            much. After having been told endless times about how exciting it all was
            – not to have seen him felt so unfair. And now I have – I reached out –
            these fingers reached out ever so slowly and carefully and touched him.
            I'd seen him die, and now he's alive. He's living and breathing and
            talking and telling me off, it's incredible. I am overwhelmed by what has
            happened. I can hardly get my mind around it – but it is true. I know I
            didn't believe it – but please, please don't be as stubborn as me – believe
            it – Jesus is alive.

THIRD SUNDAY OF EASTER

John 21.1–19

THE INTERVIEW

(Peter and an interviewer are sitting centrally.)

Interviewer: Good morning ladies and gentlemen and welcome to today's edition of *Face to Faith*. We have with us this morning somebody who has the most incredible story to tell of dead people coming to life, fish, and the questions which renewed faith. Welcome to our show, Peter.

Peter: Thank you very much.

Interviewer: Now let me get this straight Peter, you claim to have seen the religious leader Jesus, who we all saw nailed up on a cross, alive and walking around.

Peter: I don't claim it, I know it. He even gave us fishing instructions.

Interviewer: Fishing instructions?

Peter: That's right. A group of us found ourselves down by the shore of Lake Tiberias. It was a really strange feeling because none of us had much idea what was going to happen next.

Interviewer: Next?

Peter: Well yes. After Jesus came back from the dead he'd appeared to a number of us over a period of a few days, but we'd got the feeling that this wasn't going to go on for ever – that something else was going to happen. We just had to wait. And you can ask any of the others; I'm not very good at waiting.

Interviewer: So you were down by the lake shore.

Peter: And I was going a little stir crazy with hanging around, I just had to have something to do so I suggested we all go out onto the lake to do a bit of fishing.

Interviewer: So you all leap into a boat and go off to fish. All night I gather.

Peter: And not even a hint of fish – it was the most miserable night's fishing I'd had in a long time. There was just nothing biting at all.

Interviewer: Until, from what I heard, you had a little shore-side assistance.

Peter: Yes, this figure on the beach calls out to us and asks whether we've caught anything. Then he tells us to throw our nets over onto the other side of the boat. It seemed a strange suggestion, but there was something about his voice which inspired confidence, so we did.

Interviewer: And you caught some fish.

Peter: That's the understatement of the year. The nets were so full we couldn't even pull them back in. And that's when I realized that the person on the beach must be Jesus. So I waded ashore and joined him.

Interviewer: I gather he had some difficult questions to ask you.

Peter: Well, one question asked three times. 'Simon,' – he used that name, not the name he'd given me – 'do you love me?'

Interviewer: It must have been difficult.

Peter: You have no idea, but you see I'd betrayed him – the night of the arrest – I'd let him down. He wanted to give me a second chance, a new start, but he needed to know that I was ready. He also needed me to realize that I was forgiven, that he still had confidence in me.

Interviewer: Faith shown from both sides I'd say. Peter, thank you.

FOURTH SUNDAY OF EASTER

John 10.22–30

ALL WE LIKE SHEEP

(Two characters enter – they are sheep. Any costume should be minimal.)

Sheep 1:   Yes indeed good morrow to you all and a hey nonny nonny.

Sheep 1:   I think just a word of explanation is in order.

Sheep 2:   Just the briefest of words of introduction.

Sheep 1:   My colleague and I are – not to beat about the bush . . .

Sheep 2:   Not to put too fine a point on it . . .

Sheep 1:   Sheep.

Sheep 2:   Sheep.

Sheep 1:   Now you see you wouldn't have guessed that if we hadn't told you.

Sheep 2:   Well it isn't all that obvious is it?

Sheep 1:   Now we know what you're thinking.

Sheep 2:   Yes indeed we do.

Sheep 1:   You're thinking, 'Hang on a minute . . .

Sheep 2:   We know what sheep look like.

Sheep 1:   Woolly guys who all look the same.

Sheep 2:   Black noses with a tendency to go around in groups.

Sheep 1:   They eat grass, they make a kind of a baaing sound.

Sheep 2:   And these two don't look like sheep at all.

Sheep 1:   No, not at all.'

Sheep 2:   See, we knew what you were thinking.

Sheep 1:   Now what if we were to tell you that you were wrong.

Sheep 2:   That in fact each sheep has its very own distinct personality.

Sheep 1:   That we're all incredibly different from each other.

Sheep 2:   For example while it is true that I do enjoy baaing from time to time.

Sheep 1:   I am more of a crooner myself.

Sheep 2:   I am rather partial to a spot of crochet.

Sheep 1:   While I am a dab hand at whist.

Sheep 2:   My favourite hobbies are archery and photography.

Sheep 1:   While I enjoy a spot of gardening and do-it-yourself.

Sheep 2:   Now you never knew that about sheep did you?

Sheep 1:   And you never really cared.

Sheep 2:   To you we were all the same.

Sheep 1:   But there is one who knows us completely.

Sheep 2:   Who has called us by name.

Sheep 1:   Who has made us his.

Sheep 2:   And even though *we* sometimes feel rather ordinary, part of the crowd.

Sheep 1:   And certainly not very special.

Sheep 2:   He knows each one of us, loves us and calls us his own.

Sheep 1:   His name is Jesus.

Sheep 2:   And though we are sheep.

Sheep 1:   And therefore not meant to know all that much.

Sheep 2:   Our best guess is he does the same for you.

Sheep 1:   Known, and loved and called by name to be one of his flock.

FIFTH SUNDAY OF EASTER

John 13.31–35

LOVE

(Two characters – a man and woman – enter deep in conversation.)

Husband: Well I can't believe it.

Wife: Neither can I.

Husband: What an absolutely awful sermon.

Wife: Quite – I'm not sure we ought to go back there again.

Husband: Indeed, we ought to take our Mercedes elsewhere.

Wife: And at the beginning I thought it was going to be a nice little talk about love.

Husband: That's what I thought. It started off well enough.

Wife: Yes, lots of kind thoughts about being nice to animals and thoughtful to children.

Husband: Well, yes, as long as it's not that rabble from the school on the estate.

Wife: Oh, absolutely, they're terrible. Shouting and swearing, and they look so dirty too.

Husband: Layabouts the lot of them. But the sermon was promising – not too controversial.

Wife: Nothing too religious, just nice and sweet.

Husband: And then she had to start on about prejudice.

Wife: As if that's got anything to do with love.

Husband: Quite. What did we need to hear about tramps and beggars for?

Wife: I see enough of them when I go down to town. They're all over the place, sitting on the ground with signs propped up, or selling that newspaper thingy.

Husband: Yes, the ah . . . *The Big Issue*. Remind me to write that letter to the Council complaining – it's bringing down the tone of the neighbourhood.

Wife: It certainly is – and as for the sermon, well . . .

Husband: She seemed to think that we were prejudiced against everybody. I do not have problems with old people. That old dear who sits in front of us at church is really quite sweet. And I only blared my horn at that old man on the way back because the silly old fool was getting in my way.

Wife: He looked like he was about to have a heart attack.

Husband: Yes, it was quite amusing wasn't it?

Wife: I thought so. But really, the thought that we might be prejudiced – it's preposterous.

Husband: Not only that, but to suggest that we aren't loving – I'll have her dog-collar for that.

Wife: And to say that every time we show a lack of love it's harmful to the kingdom of God. She's gone too far. I like lots of people, except the old.

Husband: And young people – hooligans the lot of them.

Wife: And tramps and down-and-outs.

Husband: Oh, and the French.

Wife: And don't forget the working class.

Husband: Apart from them we like lots of people.

Wife: Yes, how dare she accuse us of a lack of love.

Husband: We're great adverts for Christianity aren't we dear?

SIXTH SUNDAY OF EASTER

John 14.23–29

PEACE

(Two business people – one of them talking on a mobile phone – enter.)

Suit 1: *(To other character)* I'll be with you in just a minute. *(Into phone)* Yes, buy at 28 and I'll talk to them later on. Have the suits come back from the dry cleaner's yet? Good. Ring Roger and tell him I'll be there by 3 p.m., make sure he brings the paperwork with him. I'm having a drink at 5 p.m. with Sophie then a meal with the reps at 7 p.m. I'll sign all letters in the car on the way – is the car laid on? Good. Tomorrow I'm going to need to add meetings with Damian and Finch and Sons as well as the four we've already talked about. Is lunch set up? Excellent, I'll talk to you later. Bye.

Suit 2: It sounds hectic.

Suit 1: Understatement of the year. I was up at 6 this morning, in the office by 7.30. I'd made twenty-seven calls by 9 a.m. I won't be home tonight until 10 and it's the same again tomorrow.

Suit 2: What about the weekend?

Suit 1: Well it's golf with clients all Saturday and Sunday mornings – lunch at the club house both days. Saturday night we've got a cocktail party. Sunday evening I've got a presentation to write for Monday morning, and so on.

Suit 2: I see. What about Jennifer and the children?

Suit 1: Well I schedule quality time for the kids at weekends – at least an hour each on Saturday and Sunday. I haven't seen them awake on a weeknight now for six months. Jennifer . . . well, things have been difficult recently.

Suit 2: I'm not surprised.

Suit 1: I don't know. Every time we manage to spend time in each other's company recently it seems that we're both so tired that we just end up falling asleep in front of the telly.

Suit 2: And of course you do enjoy what you're doing don't you?

Suit 1: Enjoy?

Suit 2: Yes, that sense of purpose you get after a really satisfying day's work.

Suit 1: Well I . . .

Suit 2: Don't tell me – you don't have that feeling? Why do you do it?

Suit 1: What do you mean?

Suit 2: Well what do you want to achieve? Why do you do it? It can't be for the money and the lifestyle – you're too tired to enjoy either of them.

Suit 1: But there is a sense of satisfaction.

Suit 2: In what? Spending two hours with your children each week? Being a stranger to your wife? Staying at work till all hours?

Suit 1: Well if you're going to put it that way . . .

Suit 2: I am. Look, I've only just met you but it seems to me you're almost proud of the fact that you're too busy to be human.

Suit 1: I resent that.

Suit 2: Of course you do – you have no peace.

Suit 1: And I suppose you do?

Suit 2: Ah, wouldn't you like to know? I suppose you could always follow me and find out. *(He begins to leave.)* Well, are you coming or not? *(Exit.)*

SEVENTH SUNDAY OF EASTER

John 17.20–26

SHARON AND MICHELLE ON UNITY

(The characters are sitting in a pub.)

Sharon:	*(Excitedly)* Ooo, get me a half of shandy Michelle quick.
Michelle:	So what's got you so excited then? You haven't been watching clips of Tom Cruise on the telly again have you?
Sharon:	Nah, although he is pretty tasty isn't he?
Michelle:	So . . . come on, tell me what's going on. Hey, you haven't chucked Damian at last have you? I always told you he was no good.
Sharon:	No, Damian an' I are still together – and what do you mean he's no good? Besides the eighteen tattoos he's got all over his body, an' the fact that he hasn't washed his hair for three weeks, he's lovely.
Michelle:	All right, all right, if you say so, you're dating Mr Perfect. So what's got you so excited?
Sharon:	Work.
Michelle:	Work? Are you feeling all right? They haven't been getting at you have they? Nobody likes working on a plastic toy production line. Painting all those fiddly little eye bits in. It's horrible.
Sharon:	Yeah, but we're going to change all that ain't we?
Michelle:	We are?
Sharon:	Yeah – I've formed a committee.
Michelle:	You have?
Sharon:	Yeah. See what's the main problem at work? It's not the job is it? I mean it's not brilliant, but it's okay. No, the problem at work is the way we're treated. Like dirt, like we're not important. Like they can do whatever they want to us an' we'll never complain.
Michelle:	Yeah, so?
Sharon:	Well I thought if we stand up for our rights, if we get together an' tell 'em what we think – if we show some unity, then things will improve won't they? If they see we all agree with each other then they'll take us more seriously.
Michelle:	Actually that sounds like a half-decent idea – well done Sharon.
Sharon:	Yeah, well, it's not *my* plan actually.
Michelle:	I didn't think it was. Okay, whose idea was it?
Sharon:	Rodney's.
Michelle:	Not Rodney Simpkins the Christian, from down in Packing?
Sharon:	The very same. He said it's really important to show people how united we are. He said Jesus talked about unity in the Holy Bible.
Michelle:	I dare say he did but I'm not very happy about bringing all that religious malarkey onto the shop floor, the next thing you know people will want us to start being nice to each other an' that would never do. After all, the only thing that makes work worthwhile is a nice bit of tasty gossip.
Sharon:	That is true – still, I quite like the idea of all this unity – standing together for something you believe is right – it's nice innit?
Michelle:	Well that's okay Sharon 'cos we're united in our love of shandy ain't we?
Sharon:	Oh yeah, we are, aren't we? An' there's no greater unity than that.
Michelle:	There certainly isn't Sharon, there certainly isn't.

PENTECOST

Acts 2.1–21

AGENTS ANONYMOUS 2

(Two characters enter furtively.)

Agent 01: I prefer my Egyptian beansprouts with tomatoes.

Agent 02: Eh? . . . Oh yes sorry, um . . . except when the wind blows from the south.

Agent 01: Excellent agent 02, you're getting better at this secrecy lark all the time.

Agent 02: *(Excitedly)* Yeah, and it's great fun too. I get to wear dark glasses and skulk around . . . it's so cool!

Agent 01: This is not some kind of jape that we engage in for our own benefit, 02.

Agent 02: No, but as long as we've got to do this let's enjoy ourselves a little bit, after all, the threat from the Nazarene and his followers is over. It's just a matter of time before they order us home.

Agent 01: I'm afraid, 02, that's just where you're wrong.

Agent 02: Wrong? What do you mean? I can't be wrong. We both saw him die.

Agent 01: That's as may be but the fact is that the followers of the Nazarene are back in no uncertain terms.

Agent 02: But they were broken, despairing, lost, we'd beaten them!

Agent 01: Apparently not. They were seen by upwards of four thousand people just yesterday.

Agent 02: Where? What on earth were they doing?

Agent 01: Well, the details are still a little sketchy. We're waiting for Agent Parsnip to submit his report.

Agent 02: I'm so glad they'd run out of root vegetables when it came round to giving us our agent designations.

Agent 01: Indeed. What is clear is this – the followers of the Nazarene were gathered together in some kind of upper room in the city.

Agent 02: Scared and defeated.

Agent 01: Well there are the persistent rumours that Jesus was seen walking around as little as three days after the crucifixion. Now I know we don't believe those rumours but there is some evidence that the followers of this Jesus weren't as frightened as we thought they were.

Agent 02: Okay, so what happened yesterday then?

Agent 01: Well we're not entirely sure.

Agent 02: Oh good.

Agent 01: Quite. What we do know is that suddenly the disciples of Jesus rushed into the crowd talking excitedly. But there's a problem.

Agent 02: What kind of a problem?

Agent 01: Well, it appears that they're nowhere near as timid or frightened as we thought. They're saying that Jesus is alive somehow and latest reports have them speaking with great power about something called 'the Spirit'.

Agent 02: But our profiles of the disciples don't show any ability to preach.

Agent 01: Exactly – look, we thought we were dealing with a group of scared, weak, defeated little men, but now I gather everyone in Jerusalem is talking about what's going on. You can't go anywhere without hearing people talk about Jesus and what his followers are going to do next.

Agent 02: This is disastrous. Heads are going to roll for this.

Agent 01: I know, that's why *we* need to make ourselves scarce, come on! *(Exit.)*

TRINITY SUNDAY

John 16.12–15

RALPH AND JIM ON THE TRINITY

(Ralph and Jim are sitting facing each other.)

Ralph: You know what Jim mate?

Jim: What's that then Ralph?

Ralph: The world Jim mate is full of conundrums.

Jim: Conun . . . what?

Ralph: Problems Jim mate. Perplexing issues what have puzzled the heads of wise men and women over the centuries.

Jim: So what are you doing thinking about them then?

Ralph: Oh very funny Jim, very droll I must say. I'll have you know that I've been wrapping my not insignificant brain around one of the greatest theological problems of this or any age.

Jim: What's that then? Why do churches have tea and coffee in little blue or green cups after everything?

Ralph: No . . .

Jim: Why does the queue I join at the supermarket always go slowest?

Ralph: Not that . . .

Jim: What do newsreaders say when they turn to each other at the end of the programme and shuffle those little piles of useless paper?

Ralph: No, though that is a good one. No, Jim mate, I'm talking about the problem of the Trinity.

Jim: Oh that's nice . . . what's the Trinity?

Ralph: Well traditional Church teaching 'as always held that God is three persons in one.

Jim: Come again?

Ralph: Look – there is one God, right?

Jim: Right.

Ralph: But Christians have long believed that that God operates in three different ways. As Father, Son, and Holy Spirit.

Jim: They have?

Ralph: Yes of course they have.

Jim: But wouldn't that mean that there were three Gods?

Ralph: No, just one.

Jim: Well, I think there's a bit of a problem there.

Ralph: Exactly – an' that's what I've been bending my mind around. I've been spending weeks trying to work out a way of describing what the Trinity's like – a kind of a picture if you will.

Jim: Oh, okay. That's nice.

Ralph: But really difficult – I've thought of all sorts of images but none of them really seemed to do the trick until this morning.

Jim: Oh yeah?

Ralph: Yeah – I've finally done it. I've created a picture of the Trinity. The Trinity is like three people in the same taxi.

Jim: Yeah – I s'pose. That *is* nice, but isn't the Trinity more like the same person in three different taxis?

Ralph: *(Pause)* Thanks a lot Jim mate. Thanks a lot.

SUNDAY BETWEEN 24 AND 28 MAY INCLUSIVE

Luke 6.39–49

THE BUILDERS

(A man and woman enter.)

Jerry: Good morning everybody, good morning indeed. How are you all? My name is Jerry, and this is my partner in crime . . . Geri.

Geri: That's with an 'i'.

Jerry: Yes indeed with an 'i'.

Geri: Now we have come here this morning with an offer you cannot possibly refuse.

Jerry: Of course you may have heard of us or seen our advert in the book.

Geri: We are 'Geri and Jerry with no Tom . . . foolery'.

Jerry: And we are the finest . . .

Geri: Most hardworking . . .

Jerry: Most trustworthy . . .

Geri: Cheapest . . .

Jerry: Builders you are ever going to meet.

Geri: Now I know what you're thinking.

Jerry: 'I don't have any building work I need doing', you're thinking

Geri: Well you will when we're through with you and make no mistake!

Jerry: For instance just look at the guttering and the pointing on this building – who did all of this for you, eh?

Geri: A right botched job. But we could fit you in next Thursday if you like.

Jerry: And although we don't normally give preferential rates, seeing as we like you . . .

Geri: We'll give you a hefty discount.

Jerry: That means for cash in hand we could do the job for oooh *(Scratches head)* . . .

Geri: Four thousand.

Jerry: Yeah, four thousand.

Geri: Now you may have heard one or two rumours about us.

Jerry: Yeah, one or two rumours.

Geri: There are some people who have chosen to attack our revolutionary new building method.

Jerry: Yeah, it's absolutely revolutionary.

Geri: And there are people who feel threatened by it.

Jerry: Yes, threatened indeed. But 'twas ever thus with challenging new ideas. Isn't that right Geri?

Geri: Absolutely. Now the method is this – most builders that you will have met will tell you that foundations are very important for a structure.

Jerry: But we say – that just adds extra and unnecessary expense.

Geri: Indeed, all of our buildings have been constructed without foundations of any kind. Just bricks lying on the ground.

Jerry: Well actually when Geri says 'ground' . . . sand is rather better.

Geri: 'Cos we can make sandcastles during our lunch breaks.

Jerry: Now we do wish we could take you round one of our revolutionary new homes, but I am afraid that is impossible.

Geri: Yes . . . ah impossible. You see there was a storm with high winds last night and . . .

Jerry: Well anyway. We have full faith in our exciting new techniques.

Geri: And I'm sure we leave you brim-full of confidence too.

Jerry: So we'll see you next Thursday about that guttering shall we? *(Exit.)*

SUNDAY BETWEEN 29 MAY AND 4 JUNE INCLUSIVE

Luke 7.1–10

AUTHORITY

(A king and queen enter – costume should be minimal.)

King: Ah, good morrow to you all, it is surely a pleasure for you to be here.

Queen: Yes indeed, an honour and a privilege for each and every one of you.

King: For I am King Reginald XXIII, and this is my loving wife . . .

Queen: Queen Jessica.

King: Now I know that being normal, humble, peasant folk you won't have much idea of how to behave when royalty is present.

Queen: But let me give you one or two hints and tips. You should have all stood up when we came in.

King: Yes indeed you should. A little bit of cap-doffing wouldn't have gone amiss either.

Queen: A slight bow or curtsey would have been very nice.

King: You see we don't expect very much but in our experience if you don't insist on the little things . . .

Queen: Then the bigger things soon follow suit.

King: Indeed they do.

Queen: Now as you can see we are very obviously royalty.

King: And how do you know that?

Queen: Well it's not due to the wardrobe that we are wearing.

King: No stuffy old crowns and sceptres for us.

Queen: Absolutely not. We enjoy dressing down. No, the way that you could, of course, immediately tell that we were royalty is because of our regal bearing.

King: Yes, the effortless air of authority and power that we both have.

Queen: A way of holding ourselves that says 'Yes, here indeed is somebody special'.

King: Now, being of noble birth, we have both had that kind of superiority since the day we were born. It has always come naturally to us.

Queen: Ordering people around has always been second nature.

King: I have servants – I tell them to go and do things and they go and do them.

Queen: We just assume it will happen.

King: But just the other day I was talking to one of these Christian chappies and he was telling me about a different kind of authority entirely.

Queen: Yes, about sickness healed and lives changed.

King: About grace given and death conquered.

Queen: About freedom offered and sins forgiven.

King: Well, it all sounded pretty amazing to us.

Queen: And he said Jesus had power over all these things.

King: And I said, 'Well if this Jesus fella has that kind of clout what does he base it on?'

Queen: Yes, I mean our authority is based on centuries of tradition and a little bit of abject fear. What about Jesus?

King: Well you'll never guess what he said.

Queen: No you never will.

King: Love. He said. Just love. Whatever will they think of next eh? *(Exit.)*

SUNDAY BETWEEN 5 AND 11 JUNE INCLUSIVE

Luke 7.11–17

ROBERT AND KATY ON POWER

(The characters are seven-year-olds played by adults.)

Robert: Katy, Katy. Oh come on Katy, hurry up.

Katy: I'm coming, I'm coming. Keep your hair on.

Robert: We're going to be late.

Katy: Well I don't know why we're doing this anyway – it's stupid.

Robert: I know that. But your brother's huge – I mean he must be a mile high.

Katy: He's only eleven.

Robert: Well he's big for his age.

Katy: Oh you're just scared.

Robert: Yes I am. Very scared indeed. If we don't get him those sweets he'll duff us both up – and he'll probably hit me a lot more than he hits you.

Katy: This whole thing is so unfair!

Robert: You've said that like a million times in the last two minutes.

Katy: Well it is. Just 'cos he's bigger than us he thinks he can push us around.

Robert: He can. It's called 'power'. He says what he wants an' we go and do it.

Katy: My dad says power should be used wisely and well.

Robert: Your dad says a lot of things – some of them are even right. But it doesn't mean they're going to happen does it?

Katy: Why are you getting so upset?

Robert: 'Cos I'm thinking of what your brother's going to do to my arm if we're not back in ten minutes. Face it Katy, your brother's got complete power over us.

Katy: That's the problem isn't it? Everybody's got power over us. Just because we're only small, people take advantage of us.

Robert: Yeah, it's always 'Don't touch.'

Katy: 'Don't make such a noise.'

Robert: 'Do be sensible.'

Katy: 'Don't be so childish.'

Robert: People spend all their time telling us off.

Katy: Well when I'm grown up things are going to be different.

Robert: Yeah, when I've got power I'm going to be really kind to people.

Katy: I'm going to make sure there are no hungry babies anywhere.

Robert: An' I'm going to make sure that everybody's generous.

Katy: And that nobody shouts at anyone.

Robert: If somebody was really sad I'd hold their hand and give them a big hankie so they could blow their nose and wipe their eyes.

Katy: And if anybody was lonely I'd say, 'I'll sit by you.'

Robert: And if anybody was really angry I'd give them a really big hug.

Katy: It would be nice to have the power to make all that happen wouldn't it?

Robert: My mum says Jesus was always using his power to be really kind to people – like healing them if they were sick, and loving them when nobody else wanted to. She says that's real power.

Katy: That's given me an idea. Why don't we go an' get my brother his sweets and then give him a big kiss to show him the power of love.

Robert: Oohh. He'll love that. Come on. *(Exit giggling.)*

SUNDAY BETWEEN 12 AND 18 JUNE INCLUSIVE

Luke 7.36—8.3

APPROPRIATE LOVE

(One male is sitting on stage – another enters.)

Silas: How are you then? Have you recovered from last night?

Elias: What do you think?

Silas: Look don't take your anger out on me. We were all there.

Elias: I'm sorry Silas. I just still can't believe it happened.

Silas: I'm having a bit of a hard time believing it myself.

Elias: What on earth do you think he was trying to do? Prove a point?

Silas: You seem to be working on the assumption that he set the whole thing up himself. Why would he do that?

Elias: To make us look stupid of course. To watch us cringe. He enjoyed every minute of it.

Silas: I'm not denying that he used the occasion to make a point but I'm not so sure it was as planned as you seem to think. I thought he looked genuinely surprised to see her.

Elias: Well of course he did. He's a great play-actor isn't he? You mark my words, he knew what he was doing.

Silas: You know I just feel sorry for Simon.

Elias: I know, what a complete and utter embarrassment.

Silas: I mean at least he'd offered Jesus a meal. He'd reached out in friendship. Trying to build bridges – understand why he acts the way he does.

Elias: Well he was hoping to grill him a little at the dinner table wasn't he?

Silas: A harmless attempt to try and get some answers.

Elias: I must admit I was a little bit surprised when Jesus agreed to come.

Silas: Particularly when he knew we'd be there as well.

Elias: The whole thing must have felt a bit like a set-up.

Silas: But I don't blame Simon for trying.

Elias: Absolutely not. The Galilean has been saying the most extraordinary things.

Silas: We were quite within our rights to test him a little.

Elias: But that woman . . .

Silas: Did you see what she was wearing?

Elias: Or *not* wearing to be more precise. And the smell of the perfume, her hair, the whole thing – it was just horrible.

Silas: Not only that but also all of that weeping and wailing.

Elias: I thought she'd never stop – it was really quite embarrassing. And she was all over him.

Silas: I can't believe he didn't do anything about it. He didn't even seem uncomfortable.

Elias: No, but he was quite happy for us to squirm wasn't he?

Silas: What did you make of that story he told about forgiveness?

Elias: I suppose it was quaint in its own little way. But rather provincial and, given the fact that he had a prostitute draped over his feet, rather inappropriate.

Silas: Indeed, I would have thought it should be him begging for forgiveness.

Elias: Well I can't think why he thought it had anything to say to us.

Silas: Absolutely. It was that awful woman who needed forgiveness.

Elias: Yes, she's probably had enough love to last a lifetime. *(Laughing, they exit.)*

SUNDAY BETWEEN 19 AND 25 JUNE INCLUSIVE

Luke 8.26–39

WHOLE

(Two characters are standing centrally.)

Voice 1: Now here's a problem.

Voice 2: Of the twisty turning variety.

Voice 1: What do we do when something is difficult?

Voice 2: Or hard to understand?

Voice 1: Something that comes from a world and place that's so different from ours . . .

Voice 2: That it's tough to know what to do with it.

Voice 1: I used to have that problem with algebra.

Voice 2: Did you?

Voice 1: Absolutely – I could never work out what to do with it. I'd stare at it for ages thinking that if I looked at it long enough and hard enough it would make sense.

Voice 2: And did it?

Voice 1: No. So I ignored it. Just walked away and pretended it didn't exist. I live in an algebra-free world.

Voice 2: So what about the Bible?

Voice 1: What do you mean?

Voice 2: Here's a story about some pigs and a man possessed by demons.

Voice 1: Ahhh, I love pigs – especially those little cute, furry, cuddly soft toy ones you can get. They're so sweet.

Voice 2: Yes, well these pigs all drowned.

Voice 1: They did?

Voice 2: Yes and Jesus was responsible.

Voice 1: He was? Whatever happened to gentle Jesus meek and mild?

Voice 2: Quite – it's a difficult story.

Voice 1: It sounds it.

Voice 2: Which brings me back to *your* algebra-free lifestyle.

Voice 1: It does?

Voice 2: Indeed. Here's the question. Do we look at this bible story and say, 'That's far too difficult, it raises lots of thorny problems, let's pretend it isn't there.'

Voice 1: Just like I did with algebra.

Voice 2: Exactly. Or do we say, 'The difficulties are what makes this story interesting and worth struggling with'?

Voice 1: Ignoring it doesn't make it go away.

Voice 2: Not even with algebra.

Voice 1: Okay, okay.

Voice 2: And if we do ignore it think of what we're missing.

Voice 1: And what would that be?

Voice 2: An incredibly moving, mysterious story of huge power shown and a person made whole.

Voice 1: Whole? Well that's good.

Voice 2: I guess he thought so.

Voice 1: Well then let's take up the struggle! *(They open a bible and exit together.)*

SUNDAY BETWEEN 26 JUNE AND 2 JULY INCLUSIVE

Luke 9.51–62

UP TO THE CHALLENGE

(Two characters – a game show host and contestant.)

Host: *(As over the top as possible)* Welcome back from the break folks, and you're watching, *Up to the Challenge* – the show that puts the spark in sparkle! Every week we put pesky moral problems to our contestants to see if they are up to the job of following Jesus. And here's this week's contestant, Hilary from High Wycombe!

Hilary: Hello.

Host: Now, before the break you saw Hilary get very close to our mystery star holiday prize by answering five moral dilemma questions correctly. Now we move on to our final, nail-biting round. Hilary, are you ready?

Hilary: I think so.

Host: Not too nervous?

Hilary: Well I wasn't till you just mentioned it.

Host: Great, great. I tell you folks, you can cut the tension here with a knife. Okay, so Hilary let's move on to our high-scoring questions. The first is this: what is more important, burying your recently deceased father or following Jesus?

Hilary: Oooh, it's a difficult one this one . . .

Host: I know, but take your time Hilary, we're all rooting for you.

Hilary: Is it following Jesus?

Host: Hilary you are . . . absolutely correct! Indeed it is more important to follow Jesus according to Luke Chapter 9. Well done.

Hilary: Ooh thanks, I'm so excited.

Host: As are we all Hilary. As are we all.

Hilary: I've never won anything before.

Host: Yes, yes, fascinating. And now our second and final question. Are you ready?

Hilary: Yes, I think so.

Host: Remember, don't worry, you've got plenty of time.

Hilary: Yes I know that.

Host: Good. Okay then here it is. Is it more important to say goodbye to your family or follow Jesus straight away?

Hilary: Oooo, I know this one.

Host: I'm going to have to push you for an answer Hilary.

Hilary: I thought you said I had plenty of time?

Host: Yeah well not that much time.

Hilary: It's more important to follow Jesus straight away.

Host: Hilary from High Wycombe you are rrright! Absolutely correct. You win our mystery star holiday prize, which is a weekend for one in a challengingly spartan youth hostel in the middle of nowhere.

Hilary: Oooh lovely.

Host: It is more important indeed to follow Jesus than to say goodbye to your family. In fact it's so important to follow Jesus in all things I'm not sure what you're doing on this inane game show!

Hilary: Neither am I really. Bye! *(She exits.)*

Host: What? Wait a minute Hilary. I was only joking. Following Jesus has its place but there are corporate sponsors to satisfy. Wait Hilary, come back. Hilary!

SUNDAY BETWEEN 3 AND 9 JULY INCLUSIVE

Luke 10.1–11, 16–20

TELLING THE WORLD

(Two characters enter and face the audience.)

Voice 1: I'd *like* to spread the Good News.
Voice 2: Talk about the love and power of Jesus.
Voice 1: Preach mightily to hundreds.
Voice 2: Thousands.
Voice 1: Millions of people.
Voice 2: I'd like to change lives.
Voice 1: Transform outlooks.
Voice 2: Inspire love.
Voice 1: *(Pause)* But I don't.
Voice 2: Don't you?
Voice 1: No.
Voice 2: Neither do I.
Voice 1: Oh dear.
Voice 2: Indeed, oh dear.
Voice 1: You see it's all just so difficult.
Voice 2: So tricky to know where to start.
Voice 1: What if people don't want to listen?
Voice 2: Don't like what I'm saying.
Voice 1: It's all just a bit embarrassing isn't it?
Voice 2: And certainly not very British.
Voice 1: To go around talking about what really matters.
Voice 2: Emotions.
Voice 1: Love.
Voice 2: Life.
Voice 1: Meaning.
Voice 2: Most people would rather talk about the weather.
Voice 1: Or dishwashers.
Voice 2: Or twin-headed camshafts.
Voice 1: Anything rather than God.
Voice 2: And if I'm to be quite honest.
Voice 1: Honesty is always good.
Voice 2: Then I'd have to say I'm frightened.
Voice 1: About what other people will think of me.
Voice 2: Particularly my friends.
Voice 1: Yes, particularly them.
Voice 2: And yet all the time there's this nagging feeling.
Voice 1: That talking about Jesus.
Voice 2: And how vital he is to me.
Voice 1: Is the most important thing in the world.
Voice 2: So I come to God.
Voice 1: And ask for the strength.
Voice 2: And the grace.
Voice 1: To talk of the things that matter to me most.
Voice 2: The love that I have found in Jesus.

SUNDAY BETWEEN 10 AND 16 JULY INCLUSIVE

Luke 10.25–37

DEVILS 2

(Two devils are standing centrally.)

Brimstone: Come in Treacle. Do sit down. You know why you're here don't you?

Treacle: Well I'm not entirely sure sir, no.

Brimstone: I'm very disappointed in you . . . very disappointed indeed. You know what happens to devils whose performance is less than satisfactory, don't you?

Treacle: Reassignment sir.

Brimstone: Exactly – I'll have you inside the head of a politician before you know it. Not very pretty, not very pretty at all.

Treacle: I don't quite understand sir. What, exactly, is the problem with my work?

Brimstone: Do I really have to mention Melton Mowbray to you Treacle?

Treacle: *(Shamefaced)* Oh, yes.

Brimstone: Exactly. What did you think you were doing? You had done so well. You had sown so many worthless, trivial unpleasant little thoughts in your patient's head. How could you have let him do something so generous?

Treacle: I was caught off guard sir.

Brimstone: Off guard? Off guard is when some sudden impulse takes you by surprise. This man asked a seller of *The Big Issue* to go with him to have a cup of tea and told him he'd been thinking about taking that action for some weeks.

Treacle: Yes sir, but I didn't think he'd do it.

Brimstone: 'Think', Treacle, 'think'? We don't expect you to think, we expect you to destroy people's lives and condemn them to everlasting hell. The last time I looked that wasn't too difficult – humans have a natural tendency in that direction anyway!

Treacle: I think the situation can be retrieved sir.

Brimstone: Oh yes, Treacle, and just how would you imagine we can do that?

Treacle: I . . . I'm not quite sure sir.

Brimstone: That's the most intelligent thing you've said so far. Now listen carefully – we are in a very dangerous situation. One of the strongest weapons that we have is prejudice. Humans love to think less of each other because of colour, gender, religion – it doesn't really matter, they just love to hate.

Treacle: So my patient is going against the trend.

Brimstone: And that's what makes this so difficult. Once he realizes that his ideas against the homeless have no foundation in fact he'll begin to wonder about his other prejudices as well. He'll begin to see everybody as the Creator does – infinitely precious, incredibly loved – just as they are. With no need to change to be more like him.

Treacle: He'll see everybody as a neighbour. Nobody as disliked or feared.

Brimstone: Our only chance is to get inside his head, make him start questioning what he's doing. Make him realize that he wants to fear and despise people because loving everybody would be too costly on his time and efforts.

Treacle: I'll get right on it Brimstone sir.

Brimstone: You better had Treacle. I'll expect a progress report by the end of the week. *(Exit.)*

SUNDAY BETWEEN 17 AND 23 JULY INCLUSIVE

Luke 10.38–42

DEVILS 3

(Brimstone is sitting at a desk. Treacle enters.)

Brimstone: Ah yes, come in Treacle. Come in. Now where is your progress report?

Treacle: I have it right here sir *(Hands over sheet of paper)*.

Brimstone: Good, good.

Treacle: Well I'm not sure it is good sir.

Brimstone: Oh, and why do you say that?

Treacle: Well the patient seems to be further away from hellfire and damnation than ever sir.

Brimstone: And just how do you figure that one out?

Treacle: Well he's doing so many good works. First it was cups of tea for homeless people, then it was campaigning for third world issues, now it's offering himself as a counsellor for the Samaritans. Every time I turn round he's got some other good work he's embarking on.

Brimstone: Good, excellent. This is wonderful! Are you sure you didn't plan this?

Treacle: Are you quite sure you heard what I said sir? The situation is disastrous. He's like Mother Teresa without the nuns.

Brimstone: On the contrary my dear Treacle. He is nicely on the way to hell and damnation.

Treacle: Well I'm glad you're pleased sir, but I don't quite see why.

Brimstone: Treacle, my dear tempter, whatever do they teach you junior devils at Grimbreath's Academy of the Foul Arts these days? It's certainly not the basics of the damnation of a human soul. You have made the most fundamental error of just looking at your patient's main works.

Treacle: Which are all saint-like sir.

Brimstone: Oh indeed, indeed. But you have failed to look around at what else is happening with the rest of his life. What took place last night?

Treacle: He had an argument with his wife sir.

Brimstone: Based on the fact that she hasn't seen him for three days because of this rash of good works he's up to his neck in. What happened on Tuesday?

Treacle: He couldn't find time to go to his church house group.

Brimstone: Because of yet more good deeds. You seem to forget Treacle that while the Almighty is very impressed with acts of love and kindness he also demands that they get their priorities right. Your patient is very close to believing in salvation by works.

Treacle: *(Seeing the point)* Oh yes.

Brimstone: And we all know what a nice little troublemaker that's been over the years. Treacle, this situation is very promising indeed. All you need to do is encourage him in his thinking that everybody is being incredibly unreasonable in wanting him to stop his acts of goodness.

Treacle: And not let him realize he's neglecting his relationship with the Almighty.

Brimstone: Exactly. With a bit of luck he won't realize what he's done until it's too late.

Treacle: And then he'll be ours.

Brimstone: Wonderful isn't it? You know Treacle we might just make a tempter of you yet. *(Exits laughing.)*

162

SUNDAY BETWEEN 24 AND 30 JULY INCLUSIVE

Luke 11.1–13

BEING PERSISTENT

(A schoolteacher is standing centrally.)

Baxter: Good morning everybody. My name is Baxter, Greg Baxter, and I am a teacher. Perhaps you could tell from the hunted, nervous expression on my face or the slightly depressed droop of the shoulders? You know people are never quite sure what to say to me. They start by going on about the wonderfully long holidays but then they usually end up by saying, 'You wouldn't catch me doing your job, I wouldn't have the patience.' Well that may be true but sometimes there are some magical moments; take Billy Cockburn for example. *Please* take Billy Cockburn! Since last September he's done nothing but hound my every waking moment. It tends to go something like this: *(Enter Billy)*

Billy: Sir, sir please sir. Please let me try out for the team, I'd be brilliant sir. I won't let you down sir please!

Baxter: It was like that every day. In lessons it was:

Billy: Sir, sir please sir! Please let me try out for the team.

Baxter: I'd be eating my lunch and I'd suddenly be aware of a presence looming over my shoulder, and again:

Billy: Oh go on sir please. You won't be sorry, honest!

Baxter: I'd be getting into my car to go home and suddenly leaping out from behind some bushes:

Billy: Hi sir, I just wonder whether you'd had any more time to think about letting me try out for the team?

Baxter: And so on. Week in and week out. Now you might be saying, 'Why on earth don't you just let him try out for the team?' Well, I had my reasons for being cautious. Billy Cockburn had come up to senior school with a reputation problem. Letting people down. Never being at the right place at the right time. Generally a bit of a mess. But I have to admit that by the half-term holiday in October he was beginning to wear me down. I said to him *(To Billy)*: Billy don't you ever stop? *(To audience)* And he said to me:

Billy: No sir – and it's just that kind of never-say-die spirit that you need on the team.

Baxter: He had an answer for everything. So in November I gave in. I said, 'Billy, I'm going to let you try out for the team. Don't let me down.'

Billy: *(Tremendously excited)* Oh thanks sir, thanks a lot! That's brilliant. You won't regret this sir. Honest you won't. I'm going to be the best player this team ever had. I'd kiss you sir, but that's not a very manly thing to do is it?

Baxter: Just be there on Thursday Billy. *(To audience)* And you know, he was, and he was good. Actually, he was very good. He's been on the team now for a couple of months and he's been at every practice and match on time, giving it 100 per cent. So I guess his persistence paid off. It certainly wore me down.

Billy: *(To audience)* And just think, Mr Baxter needed persuading. I wonder how much easier this would have been with someone who actually likes me?

SUNDAY BETWEEN 31 JULY AND 6 AUGUST INCLUSIVE

Luke 12.13–21

PLANNING PERMISSION

(A man and woman are sitting on chairs. The woman is reading a newspaper.)

Hilda: Harry. Oi, Harry. I don't believe it.

Harry: What's that then?

Hilda: He's doing it again.

Harry: He? Who's he? Prince Charles? Robert Redford? A tall dark handsome stranger?

Hilda: No you twit. Him next door. He's doing it again.

Harry: Oh he isn't is he?

Hilda: He is – look it's all here on page 9 – just underneath the beautiful baby photo contest winners. *(She shows him the paper.)*

Harry: Urgghh.

Hilda: See I told you.

Harry: No it's not that. It's this baby. Isn't that the ugliest child you've ever seen? It looks like Winston Churchill.

Hilda: Harry, this is important. Look. *(She points at the page.)*

Harry: Oh, I don't believe this. 'Trevor Thacker has applied for planning permission to tear down the barn currently situated at 23 Acacia Fields and build one double the size on the same plot of land.' How many does that make now?

Hilda: Four isn't it?

Harry: I thought it was five.

Hilda: Four, five . . . who cares? All I know is that we're in for it again. Diggers.

Harry: Pile drivers.

Hilda: Earth movers morning, noon and night.

Harry: This is getting beyond a joke. Every year it's the same thing. He decides he hasn't got enough room for all that veg he grows.

Hilda: It's like the first million wasn't enough for him.

Harry: He must have more money than he could ever spend in his entire lifetime.

Hilda: But still he has to have to have more.

Harry: And yet another eyesore of a barn.

Hilda: And we get all the inconvenience – the mice that infested us last year, the swarms of bees the year before that. *(Harry is looking out of the window.)* And then there'll be all that traffic to ship the goods in and out. Oh Harry, it's turning into a nightmare. Isn't there anything we can do about it?

Harry: Well Hilda – I think something might have happened already.

Hilda: What do you mean?

Harry: Look. That's a hearse isn't it?

Hilda: Oh my goodness it is. You don't think . . .

Harry: Who else could it be? He's the only person who lives there. 'Too busy making money for a real relationship' – isn't that what he told us last Christmas?

Hilda: Oh dear, now I feel terrible.

Harry: I just feel empty.

Hilda: Empty?

Harry: Well he was always so busy acquiring things we never really got to know him did we? All of that stuff and no enjoyment of life – it makes you think doesn't it?

SUNDAY BETWEEN 7 AND 13 AUGUST INCLUSIVE

Luke 12.32–40

BEING READY

(Two officers are on the bridge of a starship.)

Lester: Captain Thaddeus T. Lester of the starship *Quirky* – Captain's log stardate 34 point 46 point 336 and a half. We have been cruising round and around this galactic sector for days now cataloguing spatial anomalies and the strain is beginning to show on my crew.

Potty: Captain, help me! I just canna take the stress.

Lester: Easy Potty, easy. As First Engineering Officer on this ship it's your duty to remain calm at all times, tell me things cannot be done and then, just before the end of the episode, do them – thus saving the lives of everybody on the ship.

Potty: I know Captain. But I can't help it – I don't have the power!

Lester: Get a grip man! I know this mission has been hard on all of us.

Potty: It's not that Captain. It's your acting. If I have to listen to one more over-acted monologue I think I'm going to have to do something desperate!

Lester: I can't help it Potty. It's this mission – day after day the same thing. Little red lights on panels blipping and flashing, flashing and blipping. I wouldn't mind if I had any idea of what they meant.

Potty: Ah, you're right Captain. I canna even tell if it's day or not. Always the blackness of space and the twinkling of the stars.

Lester: And yet we're always up here on the bridge looking grim.

Potty: Aye, it's almost as if we never get any sleep.

Lester: Perhaps that's why I'm always tired.

Potty: It would be better if we could get off the ship.

Lester: Ah, yes indeed. Beam down to a planet surface with an away team. Then I, as Captain of the ship, could take needless risks as always. Find myself on a planet that looks a lot like Californian scrubland. Then find some nasty alien that I could wrestle around with on the ground for a bit.

Potty: Aye, that would be good. But we must be patient and wait for our new orders.

Lester: We're not very good at that, are we Potty?

Potty: Not very good at what sir?

Lester: Being patient. Waiting with concentration levels high.

Potty: I think, being human, sir, we're a bit impatient. We canna wait. An' we're no good at concentrating for long periods o' time.

Lester: Unlike Mr Splot, my trusty second-in-command. He seems to be ready for anything.

Potty: With those ears you'd have to be.

Lester: Indeed. But being ready for anything is part of our job.

Potty: It's part o' what they taught us at Federation Academy. Because as they always used to say – you canna tell when something really important is going to happen.

Lester: So we must always be at the ready Potty.

Potty: Aye Captain, with concentration levels high.

Lester: Ready to go where no one has gone before.

Potty: To infinity and beyond Captain.

Lester: Set a course Mr Potty.

Potty: Alert and ready to serve as ever Captain.

Lester: *(Pointing to the front)* Engage!

SUNDAY BETWEEN 14 AND 20 AUGUST INCLUSIVE

Luke 12.49–56

SIGN SEEING

(Two people are standing centrally.)

Voice 1: Perhaps it's too frightening.
Voice 2: Too upsetting.
Voice 1: Challenging.
Voice 2: Perhaps if we were to open our eyes we would see.
Voice 1: But then again, perhaps we do see.
Voice 2: And the sight of it is so terrifying that we ignore it.
Voice 1: Push it to the back of our minds.
Voice 2: Bury it under a mountain of trivia . . .
Voice 1: Paperwork . . .
Voice 2: Committee minutes.
Voice 1: Anything to avoid looking at the world around us . . .
Voice 2: And taking the issues seriously.
Voice 1: How is it that we see so much . . .
Voice 2: And yet see nothing at all?
Voice 1: We can get all the information we need.
Voice 2: And more besides.
Voice 1: Send documents around the world in seconds.
Voice 2: Find out what is going on anywhere at the touch of a mouse.
Voice 1: We're wired up.
Voice 2: Digitized.
Voice 1: Downloaded.
Voice 2: We know so much.
Voice 1: And understand so little.
Voice 2: Surrounded by all this truth we cannot cope.
Voice 1: And so we obsess about the latest gadget.
Voice 2: The newest technological breakthrough.
Voice 1: Anything to avoid looking at the world around us properly.
Voice 2: And asking the questions that really matter.
Voice 1: Or we look at our church.
Voice 2: And decide to reorganize it one more time.
Voice 1: After all that is the important stuff isn't it?
Voice 2: Actually it's the answers to the big questions that we do not like.
Voice 1: Because the answers are difficult.
Voice 2: They would require change.
Voice 1: A completely new way of seeing and doing things.
Voice 2: That would take a lot of hard work.
Voice 1: And effort.
Voice 2: And pain.
Voice 1: We're not sure that we're ready for all of that change quite yet.
Voice 2: And so we go out to the shops and spend some more money.
Voice 1: On things we do not need.
Voice 2: And Jesus longs that we would open our eyes and see the times.
Voice 1: But we don't. And he weeps out of love.

SUNDAY BETWEEN 21 AND 27 AUGUST INCLUSIVE

Luke 13.10–17

FREE

(One actor stands centrally.)

Narrator: Hello everybody. I am a narrator. Narrators tell stories don't they? So let's get on with it then. This is Jenny *(Jenny – aged seven, enters.)*, she is seven years old.

Jenny: No I don't want to play with dollies. Eurghh! I want to play football with the boys but they won't let me and Mum says it's too rough as well. I'm so miserable. Nobody ever lets me do what I want to. Rules for this, rules for that. I feel so trapped. I wish I was older. Then I'd be free.

Narrator: Be careful what you wish for Jenny, you might just get it. Oh dear. It's a story we've heard before I guess. Frustration, anger, wanting what you cannot have. Let's call back on Jenny at the age of eighteen and see whether things have changed.

Jenny: *(Now eighteen years old)* I cannot stand my life! It's awful. Nothing but work, work, work. I hate school. All the petty rules and restrictions – even for sixth formers. We're adults, why can't they understand that and treat us like people who can make our own decisions? And boys – don't talk to me about boys! They're so immature. One thing on the brain all the time. I wish I was at university – or better still at work earning some money. Then I'd really be free!

Narrator: Well you might be Jenny. But then again . . . We seem to be getting some recurring themes here. Let's revisit Jenny at the age of twenty-four.

Jenny: *(Now twenty-four years old)* I can't believe what a mess my life is! I've got a flat and I've got to work all hours just to afford it. I don't mind the job I'm doing but I can't see myself doing it for the rest of my life. Every morning brings another bill: mobile phone, gas, electric, council tax, TV licence, credit card – I feel like a little hamster in one of those exercise wheels, running round and round but never getting anywhere. If this is freedom it actually feels like a cage.

Narrator: Now I suppose you could tell Jenny to stop complaining, to look on the bright side of life, to be more positive. After all there must be good things happening in her life mustn't there? I'm afraid Jenny feels trapped, just like many other people feel trapped. Hemmed in by rules and restrictions, caught in a system that she can't get out of.

Jenny: *(Still at twenty-four)* Is this all there is to life? People telling me what I can and cannot do? Racing from one job to another, never really feeling like I've got any time to be myself?

Narrator: And Jesus sets people free. Free to be themselves. Free to be the people God has always wanted them to be. But freedom is not always easy – there are people who find it difficult – who would rather have the rules and the restrictions – after all at least then you know where you are. Jesus was faced constantly with people who preferred the cage.

Jenny: After all if there is a cage then somebody has the key to that cage, and that person has power. And the last thing they would want you knowing is that they don't have the power at all . . .

Narrator: Jesus does. *(Exit.)*

SUNDAY BETWEEN 28 AUGUST AND 3 SEPTEMBER INCLUSIVE

Luke 14.1, 7–14

CLIFTON AND A. J.

(Clifton – a big movie star – is pacing. A. J. is following him.)

Clifton: Are you getting all of this down A. J.?

A.J.: Oh absolutely Mr Moore, every word.

Clifton: Good, because I don't want there to be any misunderstanding.

A.J.: Oh don't you worry Mr Moore sir, the film studio will know that you are not a happy star, not happy at all.

Clifton: Good. Just who do they think they're dealing with here? I am Clifton Moore – star of *Game of Life and Death 2*. How much did my last picture make A. J.?

A.J.: Worldwide, 200 million sir.

Clifton: Exactly. Well they're not going to get away with this. Okay A. J., list my demands for me.

A.J.: Okay Mr Moore. You want three personal trainers paid for by the studio.

Clifton: Excellent, I must keep up my manly physique.

A.J.: Absolutely. You also want a hair stylist, a personal dresser, two personal assistants, and your dog Terry allowed on set at all times.

Clifton: *(Becoming a little tearful)* Where would I be without faithful Terry?

A.J.: I don't know Mr Moore sir.

Clifton: Carry on A. J.

A.J.: Oh, yes of course. You want your own gourmet chef to cook all your meals on set paid for by the studio and you want a guarantee that no member of the film crew will speak to you or make eye contact during filming.

Clifton: Quite right. What are the crew A. J.?

A.J.: Nothings Mr Moore.

Clifton: Worthless nothings A. J., carry on.

A.J.: You want a trailer that is guaranteed to be half as large again as any other member of the cast. You want access to your own personal gym. You want an assurance that your name will be first on the credits of the film and that your name will at the top of the poster and in larger print than any other name.

Clifton: What about my leading lady A. J.?

A.J.: Oh yes sir. You demand casting approval of your female co-star and an assurance that nobody ugly will be allowed within 100 metres of you at any point during filming. You also want to be seated at the head of any banquet or party table that may be held to publicize the movie.

Clifton: Excellent A.J. You know there are some people in this world that would say my demands are a trifle unreasonable.

A.J.: Surely not Mr Moore.

Clifton: Yes, yes. They think I am arrogant, thoughtless, uncaring about the little people. But you know what I say to that A. J.?

A.J.: No Mr Moore, what do you say?

Clifton: I say to them nobody ever became as great a star as I am today by being humble. Humility, my boy, is for losers. Come along.

A.J.: Following behind you as always Mr Moore. *(Exit.)*

SUNDAY BETWEEN 4 AND 10 SEPTEMBER INCLUSIVE

Luke 14.25–33

THE COST

(A TV presenter is standing centrally.)

Presenter: Good morning everybody, good morning and a warm welcome to *Crazy but True*. We're here in Bognor Regis to talk to shoppers at this local supermarket and our topic this week is that old chestnut, religion. Ah here comes a likely-looking victim. Good morning madam, how are you this morning? *(A shopper enters.)*

Shopper: Oh all right thank you very much, yes I'm fine, fine.

Presenter: Could you tell us your name?

Shopper: Hey, you're that one off the telly aren't you?

Presenter: Yes I am.

Shopper: Now don't tell me, I never forget a face . . . Bland, Tony Bland.

Presenter: Ha, ha, yes, and your name would be?

Shopper: Oh yes, I'm sorry. Just a little flustered there for a moment. Enid Snerd.

Presenter: Excellent, well good morning Enid, welcome to *Crazy but True*.

Shopper: Oh I love that show, I never miss it.

Presenter: Well now you're on it!

Shopper: Ooooer!

Presenter: Ooooer indeed! Well then Enid I've got one or two questions to ask you this morning. Is that all right?

Shopper: Oh yes, fire away.

Presenter: Right Enid, our show this week is all about religion.

Shopper: Oooh now there's a difficult topic.

Presenter: Indeed it is Enid, indeed it is. Here's the question. Christians tell us that following Jesus can be costly – what do you think?

Shopper: What, like going to church and that kind of stuff?

Presenter: Could well be Enid.

Shopper: Well, last time I was in church it was for me niece Doreen's christening and ooh it was lovely, the vicar did say some nice words and we sang some of the old hymns.

Presenter: So what do you think being a Christian should cost you then?

Shopper: Well everything's fine in its place isn't it? I mean if I had to go shopping or take one of the children to a football practice or get the lunch started or it was raining, or I slept in late, or I had something else that I had to be at, or it was a nice day and I just thought I might go out and enjoy meself then I probably wouldn't go to church would I?

Presenter: Well er . . . no you probably wouldn't.

Shopper: That's what I mean. Christians get so fanatical about it don't they? I mean you go one week and they expect you to turn up the next.

Presenter: That is annoying isn't it?

Shopper: You're telling me. Don't get me wrong, I like church and I'm a good Christian but I live my own life – I've got no need for any of this religious nonsense. It could end up taking over your life couldn't it?

Presenter: Well it certainly appears that following Jesus is costing you nothing at all.

Shopper: Oooh but I always put a little bit in the collection.

Presenter: *(Witheringly)* Yes, quite. This has been *Crazy but True* with Tony Bland.

SUNDAY BETWEEN 11 AND 17 SEPTEMBER INCLUSIVE

Luke 15.1–10

WE LOST ONE

(Two sheep are standing centrally – both wearing sunglasses.)

Sheep 1:   Greetings. How are you doing this morning?

Sheep 2:   Feeling mellow and laid back?

Sheep 1:   We certainly hope so.

Sheep 2:   Now you've heard of cool cats?

Sheep 1:   Well we are cool sheep.

Sheep 2:   Stop that laughing at the back, I saw you.

Sheep 1:   We enjoy nothing better than lazing around all day in the sunshine.

Sheep 2:   Warming our woollens.

Sheep 1:   We nibble a bit of grass now and then.

Sheep 2:   Of the green, in the field variety.

Sheep 1:   And we hang out with the other sheep in our flock.

Sheep 2:   Passing the time in style.

Sheep 1:   It is sooo relaxing.

Sheep 2:   We don't even notice when one of our colleagues in wool wanders off.

Sheep 1:   No we don't notice.

Sheep 2:   But the shepherd does.

Sheep 1:   And he is off like a shot.

Sheep 2:   He looks high and low.

Sheep 1:   In streams, behind hedges.

Sheep 2:   Down ravines, between rocks.

Sheep 1:   Man, he is out there in all weather.

Sheep 2:   Until that sheep is found.

Sheep 1:   He just hates it when one of us gets lost.

Sheep 2:   Like last week with Clive.

Sheep 1:   Ah yes, Clive. Now he's always been a bit of a wanderer.

Sheep 2:   Wool between the ears as well as on his back.

Sheep 1:   I mean – it is dangerous out there.

Sheep 2:   Anything could happen to a sheep that is lost.

Sheep 1:   And we're not exactly packing much in terms of defence you know?

Sheep 2:   Well as soon as the shepherd spotted Clive was missing . . .

Sheep 1:   He was gone, y'know? Out there looking.

Sheep 2:   It was night, there was a wind blowing and it was raining.

Sheep 1:   Boy was it raining.

Sheep 2:   But the shepherd, he goes out there anyway.

Sheep 1:   Just as dangerous for him as it was for Clive.

Sheep 2:   Absolutely, but he will not rest until Clive is found.

Sheep 1:   It must have been three in the morning when the shepherd returned.

Sheep 2:   With Clive in tow.

Sheep 1:   The shepherd must have been tired, but instead of going to bed . . .

Sheep 2:   He threw us a party.

Sheep 1:   He was so pleased that Clive was found.

Sheep 2:   That is why, although we are cool sheep . . .

Sheep 1:   The shepherd of the sheep is way more cool.

Sheep 2:   Respect to the shepherd. You all have a good day now. *(Exit.)*

SUNDAY BETWEEN 18 AND 24 SEPTEMBER INCLUSIVE

Luke 16.1–13

MONEY!

(Two characters enter from opposite directions.)

Reggie: Hi there, welcome.

Regina: Listen carefully.

Reggie: Because the next three minutes could change your life.

Regina: Absolutely. This is my colleague Reggie, and I am Regina.

Reggie: We're something big in the City.

Regina: Huge in fact. And this morning we've come down to your level.

Reggie: To tell you all about money.

Regina: Let's hear that lovely word again . . .

Reggie: Money.

Regina: We love money.

Reggie: We worship it.

Regina: Everything about it is exciting to us.

Reggie: The crisp sound of new bank-notes folded together.

Regina: The lovely chink of loose change in the pocket.

Reggie: The thought of interest accumulating.

Regina: Stocks and bonds.

Reggie: Assets and liquidated funds.

Regina: Investment portfolios and pension funds.

Reggie: We live for money.

Regina: We love money.

Reggie: We worship money.

Regina: And we know you do too.

Reggie: Now we are aware that this is a church.

Regina: And we also know that Jesus had some pretty tough things to say about money.

Reggie: Like you can't worship God and money at the same time.

Regina: Well that's okay because we didn't want to worship God anyway.

Reggie: No – that would tear us away from the money and business sections of the *Sunday Times*.

Regina: And have you ever wondered why most new shopping malls look like cathedrals?

Reggie: It's because we designed them! And we wanted everybody to be able to worship money just like us.

Regina: I think we've been pretty successful, don't you?

Reggie: After all people worry a lot more about money than they do about God don't they?

Regina: You know you like money too.

Reggie: You think about it.

Regina: You dream about what it would be like to be rich.

Reggie: And as soon as you do that . . .

Regina: We've got you.

Reggie: Of course there is one thing that's got us slightly worried.

Regina: Indeed – what is going to happen to all this lovely money when we die?

Reggie: More importantly – what is going to happen to us?

SUNDAY BETWEEN 25 SEPTEMBER AND 1 OCTOBER INCLUSIVE

Luke 16.19–31

THE CONVERSATION

(An actor sits centrally. Another actor enters.)

Lazarus: I'm glad we could have this conversation. *(Sits down.)*

Rich man: *(Bitterly)* Are you? Are you indeed? How very nice that you're glad!

Lazarus: Look, I'm sorry if this is difficult for you.

Rich man: Well then perhaps you should have thought about that before insisting that we have this little chat in the first place.

Lazarus: I can understand how bitter you must feel.

Rich man: Oh can you? How very condescending of you. After all it *is* you who is in the heavenly places isn't it Lazarus? You who have God's pleasure? You who, no doubt, sits around on a cloud all day strumming on a harp.

Lazarus: It isn't quite like that.

Rich man: Isn't it? Well don't feel you've got to tell me exactly how it is Lazarus. I don't think I need that kind of detail.

Lazarus: I can see I'm wasting my time here. *(Moves to leave.)*

Rich man: Oh going so soon? After all it is your name that will go down in history isn't it Lazarus? I mean let's be honest – Luke didn't even bother to mention my name when he wrote the parable down. It wouldn't do to have people having a rich man with an actual name to feel sorry for would it?

Lazarus: I've got one question to ask.

Rich man: Oh yes, and what's that?

Lazarus: If we could go back – do things differently – would you change anything?

Rich man: What, is this some kind of sop to ease your conscience?

Lazarus: Not at all, I really want to know.

Rich man: Okay then. Yes of course I would change things. I would change everything. I wouldn't be the greedy, self-centred idiot that I was. I'd give you food, clothing, a decent roof over your head. Not only you but the dozen other beggars that were sitting next to you by that gate. I would have noticed. Noticed the hunger, the running sores, the desperate need. I would have noticed and acted. *(Now tired but not bitter)* I would have done something. But it's not that easy is it?

Lazarus: Isn't it?

Rich man: No. Because knowing what I know now anybody would have changed. But at the time I was so busy with my own life, my own troubles, getting to where I had to go. To be honest, most of the time I didn't even see you lying there.

Lazarus: I am so sorry that this happened.

Rich man: Not half as sorry as I am.

Lazarus: Do you think people will change?

Rich man: To be honest, no. Look at my five brothers. They're even worse than I was. More grasping, more obsessed with their own luxury than the needs of others. It's pitiful.

Lazarus: It is indeed.

Rich man: *(Pause)* I'm sorry Lazarus.

Lazarus: So am I Joshua, so am I. *(He gets up to leave.)*

SUNDAY BETWEEN 2 AND 8 OCTOBER INCLUSIVE

Luke 17.5–10

SERVANT

(A Roman master is sitting centrally.)

Marcus: Lucius? Lucius?

Lucius: *(Entering)* Coming master.

Marcus: Now then Lucius – I need you to go down to the market this morning and buy me some fresh olives.

Lucius: Absolutely master, it would be my pleasure.

Marcus: Would it?

Lucius: I beg your pardon sir.

Marcus: Would it be your pleasure? I mean, do you like being a servant Lucius?

Lucius: Oh yes sir I like it very much.

Marcus: You don't wish for anything else?

Lucius: Like what sir?

Marcus: Like your freedom. The ability to go where you want when you want.

Lucius: Why should I want that sir?

Marcus: I don't know – it would seem attractive to some people.

Lucius: I'm sure it would sir, to some people. But I think they would be wrong.

Marcus: How do you figure that one out?

Lucius: Well sir, if you think about it I owe you everything. You brought me out of poverty, I live with you and your family in this fine house, you treat me extremely well. You even give me money to send home to my mother and family. I enjoy serving you. I am treated with respect. That feels a good deal like freedom to me.

Marcus: I suppose if you put it like that.

Lucius: I do put it like that. Sir I respect you. You are a great man – it is my pleasure to serve you.

Marcus: Well, thank you.

Lucius: You need not thank me sir. After what you have done for me all I need to know is that I am doing what you want.

Marcus: But *I* have to serve no one.

Lucius: Is that true sir? You serve the Senate surely, and the wishes and needs of your wife and family. Surely you are servant to a great many people.

Marcus: I suppose I am.

Lucius: And does that service feel difficult or binding to you?

Marcus: Not at all.

Lucius: Then why should mine? Sir, all that I want to do is to serve you. It is my job, it is also my joy. It is my way of repaying the love and the kindness that you have shown to me. I do not expect thanks but I do want to know that I have done what you want. To me, sir, knowing that is complete freedom.

Marcus: I believe the Christians have started talking about this kind of relationship between themselves and their God.

Lucius: I believe they have sir.

Marcus: That would put me in the place of God – not a very comfortable place to be Lucius.

Lucius: Not very comfortable at all sir. Let me go and get those olives. *(Exit.)*

SUNDAY BETWEEN 9 AND 15 OCTOBER INCLUSIVE

Luke 17.11–19

SHARON AND MICHELLE ON SAYING 'THANK YOU'

(Michelle is sitting at a bar.)

Sharon: *(Entering)* Ooh Michelle buy me a half of shandy quick before I hit someone.

Michelle: Oh dear Sharon, what's got you so flummoxed then eh? Your cat not been using his litter tray again?

Sharon: No.

Michelle: Your Damian forgotten to compliment you on your beautiful new haircut?

Sharon: No, it's not that either.

Michelle: You been savaged by man-eating spiders?

Sharon: Have you been watching *Tarantulas of Death Part 3* again on the telly? Anyway, no, it's none of those things, it's Cynthia Scoggins from accounts.

Michelle: Oh not the horrible Cynthia.

Sharon: The very same. You know she applied to go on *Blind Date* but she failed the audition.

Michelle: No, why was that then?

Sharon: They reckoned that no man, after hearing her whiney voice, would choose her.

Michelle: Makes sense. So what's she done to upset you then?

Sharon: Well you know all that running around I've been doing for her on the shop floor over the past three weeks?

Michelle: What, delivering all those redundancy slips?

Sharon: Oh, is that what they were? No wonder people have been ignoring me recently. Anyway, she told me yesterday that we'd finished so there wasn't any need for me to go up there again.

Michelle: Well that's good isn't it?

Sharon: As usual 'Chelle you're missing the point. That's because I'm the one with the brains in this outfit. I'm the one with qualifications see. I'm the one with a GCSE in Media Studies ain't I? The point is that not a word of thanks passed the horrible Cynthia's lips did it? No expression of gratitude, no small word saying she was grateful for all what I'd done.

Michelle: Oh that's awful. Everybody ought to say thank you. It's only right innit? That's what Sister Eugenia used to tell us at school.

Sharon: Ah, St Olave's Institute of Chronic Neglect – happy days. She used to say in her suspiciously deep voice, 'Girls, if in doubt, say thank you.'

Michelle: Yeah, an' Rodney Simpkins, the Christian down in Packing, he was saying the other day that we don't say thank you nearly enough.

Sharon: Well, I don't usually agree with Rodney, but this time I think he might be right.

Michelle: Yeah, 'cos like we've got a load to be thankful for ain't we? Even your Damian.

Sharon: Steady on a bit girl. So who do say thank you to?

Michelle: Rodney says we should give thanks to God.

Sharon: God? What kind of a stupid idea is that? Anybody would think God was responsible for something. You've got to stop listening to Rodney an' start buying me halves of shandy Sharon. Thank you to God . . . rubbish!

SUNDAY BETWEEN 16 AND 22 OCTOBER INCLUSIVE

Luke 18.1–8

ACTION TIME

(Two children's TV presenters are sitting centrally – hugely enthusiastic.)

Chris: Hello everybody and welcome to *Action Time*! I'm Chris.

Jane: And I'm Jane.

Chris and Jane: Hello!

Chris: Now I think you'll remember everybody that last week Jane had a jolly exciting time in a very poor country miles away from here. Where is it on the map Jane?

Jane: I don't think the children need to know that now Chris.

Chris: *(Producing globe)* Oh I think they do Jane. Just point to it.

Jane: *(Pointing vaguely)* It's somewhere over there. And the really important thing is that it's very hot and the people are very poor.

Chris: I gather you met lots of nice folk while you were there Jane.

Jane: That's right Chris I did. But they didn't seem to be very impressed when I showed them how to make a lovely ski resort for their dollies using only three cereal boxes, sixteen hair clips and lots of sticky-backed plastic.

Chris: I can't think why.

Jane: No, neither can I. Anyway they were ever so excited when I told them that all of you lovely viewers at home had saved a total of sixteen million milk bottle tops to help them dig a well to get clean water.

Chris: That's excellent news Jane.

Jane: It certainly is Chris.

Chris: And we needn't worry our pretty little heads about the economic situation that helps to keep them in this mess.

Jane: Absolutely not. After all, this is children's television and the last thing we need to think about are issues of justice.

Chris: Quite right Jane. We'll just keep on coming back to you viewers every other year and ask you to collect more milk bottle tops.

Jane: Or aluminium cans.

Chris: Or postage stamps.

Jane: But we'll certainly never encourage you to ask why the situation in these countries has not improved.

Chris: Or inspire you to ask questions about why it is that world trade is so unfair.

Jane: Heavens, if we got you asking questions like those you'd want to go out campaigning or something.

Chris: Sending postcards, organizing petitions.

Jane: Hounding world leaders every minute of the day and night.

Chris: And after all they're very busy people.

Jane: And the last thing they need is annoying young people asking them awkward questions about justice and fairness.

Chris: Questions which they'd really rather not answer.

Jane: And anyway, pestering people like that never did any good.

Chris: Certainly not.

Jane: So instead, what we're going to do here on *Action Time* . . .

Chris: Is to encourage all of you to go out and collect as many used car tyres as you can and that way we'll buy a bath tub for a man in Africa somewhere.

Jane: But first on *Action Time*, here's a man who can play tunes through his nose.

175

SUNDAY BETWEEN 23 AND 29 OCTOBER INCLUSIVE

Luke 18.9–14

SOUR GRAPES

(Two actors stand centrally.)

Grape 1:   Oh the indignity of it all.

Grape 2:   I couldn't agree more. I didn't attend RADA to do this kind of work.

Grape 1:   I was a member of the Royal Shakespeare Company and, oh that it should come to this!

Grape 2:   Ladies and gentlemen we should apologize for this sudden outburst of emotion but we have been asked this morning to play the parts of two . . .

Grape 1:   Grapes.

Grape 2:   Yes, not to put too fine a point on it . . . grapes.

Grape 1:   I mean how do I emote? What is my motivation for this scene?

Grape 2:   Are we freshly plucked from the vine, or wizened old has-beens?

Grape 1:   Anyway, let's just read the script.

Grape 2:   I'll have words with my agent about this.

Grape 1:   *(Reading from script)* Hello, hello! Take a seat.

Grape 2:   We are the most important grapes you will ever meet.

Grape 1:   On a Communion table we sit and gaze.

Grape 2:   Down at the congregation as the minister says . . .

Grape 1:   'This Holy Communion is for all . . .

Grape 2:   Whoever you are great or small.'

Grape 1:   I am afraid with that comment we must take exception.

Grape 2:   Because many of your lives could do with correction.

Grape 1:   Take for example the man over there.

Grape 2:   That's right, the one with the thinning hair.

Grape 1:   We know for a fact that before this worship.

Grape 2:   He was leaning over a fence having a good old gossip.

Grape 1:   And the lady at the back in the stunning hat.

Grape 2:   Outside of this place is a bit of a rat.

Grape 1:   She lies and cheats and sometimes steals.

Grape 2:   At least, she cooks the books of the WI meals.

Grape 1:   We know that Jesus died for all.

Grape 2:   But that just leaves us a little galled.

Grape 1:   Because to be quite frank your lives are a mess.

Grape 2:   And how God can forgive we can but guess.

Grape 1:   There *are* two here today whose lives are like light.

Grape 2:   Whose actions and works are righteous in God's sight.

Grape 1:   Who of bread and wine are deserving.

Grape 2:   Who with dignity and honour have been serving.

Grape 1:   It's *us* of course who are better than you.

Grape 2:   Whose wonderful lives have been lovely and true.

Grape 1:   So we'll have bread and wine and you can go home.

Grape 2:   You'll never be worthy so please don't moan.

Grape 1:   You know some folk may say we're a little cruel.

Grape 2:   When we say we deserve Communion and you deserve gruel.

Grape 1:   But we're not being unkind, just stating the case.

Grape 2:   That our lives are excellent and yours are quite base.

SUNDAY BETWEEN 30 OCTOBER AND 5 NOVEMBER INCLUSIVE

Luke 19.1–10

SUCH A DISAPPOINTMENT!

(The characters are talking over a fence.)

Rebekkah: So tell me Rachel, is the news true?

Rachel: What, you mean about yesterday?

Rebekkah: Of course yesterday – there is something else that is on everybody's minds?

Rachel: Well . . . yes it is true.

Rebekkah: NO!

Rachel: Yes I'm afraid so.

Rebekkah: Tell me everything Rachel – you must be so disappointed.

Rachel: That is the understatement of the year. I mean it started off as such an ordinary day.

Rebekkah: I know, I saw Zacchaeus going off to work just like normal.

Rachel: Quite, just like normal. He did say he might try and go and see Jesus.

Rebekkah: Not the preacher!

Rachel: The very same. He has fascinated Zacchaeus, and he knew Jesus was visiting town today.

Rebekkah: That spells nothing but trouble.

Rachel: When you're right, you're right. The next thing I know Zacchaeus is standing on the doorstep out of breath looking more excited than I've ever seen him before and behind him is a huge crowd of people.

Rebekkah: It must have been a terrible shock.

Rachel: It was, but worse was still to come. He looks at me rather sheepishly and says, 'I've bought some people round for tea, dear.' And without another word he ushers a dozen people into our front room, which I've just cleaned, and invites them to sit down.

Rebekkah: Who were they?

Rachel: The biggest bunch of dropouts you've ever met. Jesus and his followers. And there's all the smart people of the town, all of the people we've been trying to impress for the last six years standing outside our house looking in the windows, tut-tutting at what's going on.

Rebekkah: Oh the shame of it.

Rachel: Exactly. But there's worse.

Rebekkah: NO!

Rachel: Yes! In the middle of all of this Zacchaeus stands up, in front of everybody and says, 'I'm going to give away half of everything I own to the poor and pay back anybody I've cheated four times what I owe them.' And I'm standing there saying, 'Oh no you're not!'

Rebekkah: You poor thing.

Rachel: Look Rebekkah I know we're not the most popular people in the town, you wouldn't expect it with the job Zacchaeus does, but at least we were wealthy. Now we're not even that.

Rebekkah: It sounds awful.

Rachel: It is. But if he thinks I'm giving up my hard-earned lifestyle just because of the words of some no-account travelling preacher he's got another think coming. That Jesus has got a lot to answer for. *(Exit.)*

SUNDAY BETWEEN 6 AND 12 NOVEMBER INCLUSIVE

Luke 20.27–38

ISSUES PLEASE!

(A shopkeeper stands to one side. A customer enters.)

Shopkeeper: Ah, good morning, good morning. What can I do for you on this fine day? Some gift-wrap perhaps? Or maybe a good book? What about a nice piece of haddock?

Customer: No thank you. I'd like some issues please.

Shopkeeper: Issues madam?

Customer: Yes, nice current issues. News headlines, medical debates, perhaps something a little bit controversial? Anything so long as it's good and up to date.

Shopkeeper: Now madam, are you sure I can't interest you in a cream bun and a cup of tea instead?

Customer: No, issues, current issues. Haven't you got any?

Shopkeeper: Oh yes I've got loads of them. Starving children on city streets, the latest in medical ethics, all kinds of questions about crime and punishment. You name the area and I've got a current issue to cover it.

Customer: Good. I think I might have something on the arms trade.

Shopkeeper: Look madam, I don't want to be rude or anything. After all, the customer is always right.

Customer: Yes, we are, aren't we?

Shopkeeper: It's just that I can't understand why a nice person like you would want to buy some nasty old current issue which will only cause hours of pain and suffering, arguments and heartache. Why not buy a toaster instead?

Customer: You don't seem to understand . . . I'm a Christian.

Shopkeeper: Yes, so?

Customer: Well Jesus in the Bible was always taking on the issues of the day, addressing current debates and I wanted to do the same.

Shopkeeper: But Christians have successfully been ignoring what's been going on around them for hundreds of years. Why break a tradition that's taken that long to build up?

Customer: Now that's just being cynical, lots of Christians have involved themselves in the affairs of the world.

Shopkeeper: And always ended up getting hurt doing it.

Customer: Well that's the risk you take isn't it? I mean the world is not exactly a safe place – that's no reason not to get involved.

Shopkeeper: Well madam I can see that you are determined.

Customer: I certainly am.

Shopkeeper: You're sure I can't sell you a packet of lettuce seeds instead?

Customer: No. You know why it was that ordinary people heard Jesus gladly?

Shopkeeper: I'm not sure that I do.

Customer: I think it's because Jesus answered the questions the people were asking. He met them where they were with the issues they were facing. That just leaves me with two questions. The first is – why should we feel that we are any different?

Shopkeeper: And the second?

Customer: Are you going to sell me my current issue or not?

178

SUNDAY BETWEEN 13 AND 19 NOVEMBER INCLUSIVE

Luke 21.5–19

SAY WHAT THEY WANT

(A politician and adviser are standing centrally.)

Politician: Okay Jean. The election is in two weeks. What does our research tell us?

Jean: Well Bob – the message from the voters is clear. They like you.

Politician: That's good isn't it?

Jean: Absolutely. All the polling we've done with our key target group of twenty- to thirty-five-year-old female voters tells us that they like what we've done with your hair. They also like the alterations we've made to your speech patterns – emphasizing key words with hand gestures has really helped.

Politician: Good, I've been working very hard on getting just the right degree of spontaneity.

Jean: And it's really working for you – it really is. They also like the new wardrobe we picked out for you. Soothing yet manly colours reflecting strength and old-fashioned values – it's working a treat.

Politician: I can't help feeling you're working your way round to a 'but'.

Jean: There's no fooling you is there? I'm afraid there is a 'but'.

Politician: What is it?

Jean: They think your message is too strong.

Politician: What?

Jean: They think on some key issues you're too outspoken, too ready to speak out with your own views.

Politician: But I thought that's what they wanted. Somebody who wasn't afraid to say what he thought.

Jean: They do. Then they find they disagree with what you say.

Politician: But I can't compromise what I believe.

Jean: I'm not asking you to compromise what you believe, just don't speak about it quite so often.

Politician: Whatever happened to having the courage of your own convictions?

Jean: It's still there Bob, it just doesn't get politicians elected.

Politician: But what about having the strength to say uncomfortable things? Things that some people are going to find difficult to hear?

Jean: That's all very well Bob but 75 per cent of a focus group of key voters said that you came over as having opinions that were too strong.

Politician: Well excuse me for feeling passionately about things!

Jean: See, that's exactly what they're talking about. People don't want to be told uncomfortable things, unpleasant facts about the way they live their lives – it makes them feel bad. They want a politician who's going to say lots of positive upbeat things and then not ask them to do anything that's going to be difficult or costly.

Politician: What about rising to a challenge? Struggling for what you know is right? Facing up to tremendous odds?

Jean: All wonderful and laudable, but they won't get you elected.

Politician: Maybe you're underestimating what people will accept. I happen to think that if you tell people the facts of how things are, no matter how difficult or dangerous, then they'll be more likely to follow you simply because at last they have somebody who is prepared to tell them the truth.

SUNDAY BETWEEN 20 AND 26 NOVEMBER INCLUSIVE

Luke 23.33–43

KING OF THE JEWS

(Two characters are busying themselves centre stage.)

Ben: Come on, come on! If we don't hurry up we're going to miss it.

Shim: It's not a matter of missing it, it's a matter of getting a good place where we can see everything.

Ben: Exactly, so will you hurry up! Last time we were right at the back and I couldn't see anything. I even had trouble hearing the screams.

Shim: All right, all right.

Ben: It's been weeks since we had a good crucifixion.

Shim: Absolutely. So what's the story behind the ones today?

Ben: Well, according to Gideon there's two thieves being done.

Shim: I thought there were three on the list for today?

Ben: There are. The third one's Jesus of Nazareth.

Shim: Not the preacher guy?

Ben: The very same.

Shim: The one who rode into town last week on a donkey?

Ben: How many preachers called Jesus are there? Yes, that Jesus.

Shim: So what did they get him on then?

Ben: Word has it that they were so eager to crucify him, in the end it didn't really matter much what he'd done or hadn't done, they just made something up.

Shim: I don't get it.

Ben: Now there's a shocker. What don't you get?

Shim: Well I saw Jesus ride into the city, I even heard him speak later on in the week. He seemed pretty harmless to me.

Ben: Well he must have done something or they wouldn't be crucifying him would they? Gideon reckoned that they've got him on political charges.

Shim: Oh yes, and what are they?

Ben: Claiming to be the King of the Jews or something.

Shim: What!?

Ben: You heard me, they reckon he claimed to be our king.

Shim: Well I'm sorry, that sounds pretty far-fetched to me.

Ben: Apparently not that far-fetched because it's actually happening and if you don't hurry up we're going to miss all the fun.

Shim: I'm not sure I want to go now.

Ben: You are kidding me aren't you?

Shim: No. What if Jesus has done nothing wrong, then we'll be watching an innocent man die – that'll take all the fun out of it. I'll feel all guilty.

Ben: Look, he's been tried, he's been found guilty, what more do you want?

Shim: I just don't like the sound of it.

Ben: But just think of it, there's two others being done as well. Two thieves who are guilty as anything. You just watch them.

Shim: I suppose so.

Ben: Of course, of course. Two nasty thieves getting the just punishment for their crime, excellent. There's no way either of them is on their way to Paradise today. Come on. *(Exit.)*